FAMILIES IN SOCIETY

Boundaries and relationships

Edited by Linda McKie and
Sarah Cunningham-Burley

Consultant Editor: Jo Campling

First published in Great Britain in September 2005 by

The Policy Press
University of Bristol
Fourth Floor
Beacon House
Queen's Road
Bristol BS8 1QU
UK

Tel +44 (0)117 331 4054
Fax +44 (0)117 331 4093
e-mail tpp-info@bristol.ac.uk
www.policypress.org.uk

British Library Cataloguing in Publication Data
A catalogue record for this book is available from the British Library.

Library of Congress Cataloging-in-Publication Data
A catalog record for this book has been requested.

ISBN 1 86134 643 3 paperback

A hardcover version of this book is also available

Linda McKie is Research Professor in Sociology at Glasgow Caledonian University. **Sarah Cunningham-Burley** is Professor of Medical and Family Sociology at the University of Edinburgh.

Cover design by Qube Design Associates, Bristol.
Front cover: photograph kindly supplied by www.third-avenue.co.uk
Printed and bound in Great Britain by Hobbs the Printers, Southampton.

This book is dedicated to the memory of Sue Innes, feminist historian, journalist, mother and researcher.

Sue was appointed Research Fellow at the inception of the Centre for Research on Families and Relationships. Sue was a warm colleague and committed social researcher. We hope the contents of this book will help to promote some of the issues she worked on and felt passionately about.

Contents

List of tables vii
Acknowledgements viii
Notes on contributors ix

Introduction **1**

one Families and relationships: boundaries and bridges 3
Linda McKie, Sarah Cunningham-Burley and John H. McKendrick

Part One: Families in society **19**

two Balancing work and family life: mothers' views 23
Sarah Cunningham-Burley, Kathryn Backett-Milburn and Debbie Kemmer

three Gender, care, poverty and transitions 39
Gill Scott and Sue Innes

four Families, education and the 'participatory imperative' 57
Janet Shucksmith, Lorna McKee and Helen Willmot

Part Two: Children, families and relationships **73**

five Children's boundaries: within and beyond families 77
Malcolm Hill

six Family within and beyond the household boundary: children's constructions of who they live with 95
Helen Sweeting and Peter Seaman

seven Children managing parental drug and alcohol misuse: challenging parent–child boundaries 111
Angus Bancroft, Sarah Wilson, Sarah Cunningham-Burley, Hugh Masters and Kathryn Backett-Milburn

Part Three: Health, illness and well-being **127**

eight Intersections of health and well-being in women's lives and relationships at mid-life 131
Kathryn Backett-Milburn, Laura Airey and Linda McKie

nine Families, relationships and the impact of dementia – insights into the 'ties that bind' 149
Dot Weaks, Heather Wilkinson and Shirley Davidson

ten Violence and families: boundaries, memories and identities 169
Linda McKie and Nancy Lombard

Part Four: Relationships and friendships **185**

eleven Boundaries of intimacy 189
Lynn Jamieson

twelve Solo living, individual and family boundaries: findings from secondary analysis 207
Fran Wasoff and Lynn Jamieson with Adam Smith

thirteen Boundaries of friendship 227
Graham Allan

fourteen Living and loving beyond the boundaries of the heteronorm: personal relationships in the 21st century 241
Sasha Roseneil

Conclusion **259**

fifteen Perspectives on social policies and families 261
Fran Wasoff and Sarah Cunningham-Burley

Index 271

List of tables

6.1	Children for whom the balance of data suggested they were not living with a birth father	101
12.1	Solo living in Great Britain, 2001	211
12.2	Trends in solo living in Great Britain: one person households as a % of all households, 1971-2002	211
12.3	Trends in solo living in Great Britain: people living alone as a % of all people aged 16+, 1971-2002	212
12.4	Proportion of people aged 30-74 in all sweeps who ever lived solo, by gender as a % of their age cohort, UK, 1991-2001	213
12.5	Men and women living alone by age as a % of all people aged 16+, Great Britain, 2002	214
12.6a	Marital status by gender and age of people living alone aged 30-74, 2001, Great Britain, 2001 (%)	215
12.6b	Women expecting no children by ageband, Great Britain (%)	215
12.7a	Housing tenure of solo person households by age group and gender, Great Britain, 2001 (%)	216
12.7b	Housing tenure of multi-person households by age group and gender, Great Britain, 2001 (%)	216
12.7c	Economic status: 'permanently sick or disabled'	217
12.8	Solo and multi-person household links to family, friends and community (%)	218
12.9	Solo person household links to family, friends and community, by age group and gender (%)	220
12.10	Transitions to or from solo living of people aged 30-74 in all sweeps who ever lived solo by gender, UK, 1991-2001	221

Acknowledgements

We would like to thank all the contributors to this book for the timely production of their chapters. Comments from the anonymous referees helped to reshape the book and we are grateful to them. We have also been greatly supported by our editors at The Policy Press, Dawn Rushen and Emily Watt, and our project manager, Penelope Allport and copy editor, Helen Baxter. Our consultant editor, Jo Campling, has been a champion of the Centre for Research on Families and Relationships and provided us with much helpful advice. Lastly, we also thank Anne-Margaret Campbell, Kathryn Dunne, Greg Cole and Mary Anne Kochenderfer for helping us get the typescript into shape. All research participants should also be thanked. Any names have been changed to protect anonymity.

Notes on contributors

Laura Airey is currently based at the Centre for Research on Families and Relationships (CRFR), working as a research fellow on a European Social Fund study of work–life balance in Scottish food retail companies. Laura's PhD, completed in 2002, was a qualitative study of the geography of health inequalities. Her research interests include lay experiences of health, illness and well-being across the lifecourse; spatial and social inequalities in health; women's experiences of mid-life; and women's experiences of combining paid employment and unpaid caring work.

Graham Allan is Professor of Social Relations at Keele University. He was previously Reader in Sociology at the University of Southampton. He is particularly interested in the sociology of friendship and has published a number of books on this topic, the most recent being *Placing friendship in context* (Cambridge University Press, 1998), co-edited with Rebecca Adams. He has also researched and written on various aspects of family life. His publications in this area include *Families, households and society* (Palgrave, 2001), co-authored with Graham Crow, and *The sociology of the family: A reader* (Blackwell, 1999). His other publications include *Social relations and the life course* (Palgrave, 2003), co-edited with Gill Jones; *Social networks and social exclusion* (Ashgate, 2004), co-edited with Chris Phillipson and David Morgan, and *The state of affairs* (Lawrence Erlbaum, 2004) co-edited with Jean Duncombe, Kaeren Harrison and Dennis Marsden. His current research includes a study of stepfamily kinship.

Kathryn Backett-Milburn graduated in sociology from the University of Edinburgh, where she also did her PhD. Since then she has worked as a contract researcher at the University, for much of the past 20 years in the Research Unit in Health, Behaviour and Change (RUHBC). She was also a research commissioner at the Health Education Board for Scotland. In 2001 she co-founded and became a co-director of the CRFR. Kathryn has published widely and her research interests have focused on the sociology of the family and of health and illness, with a special interest in health promotion/public health. She has specialised in qualitative research methods, conducting studies that have regularly brought together these three main research interests. Her current research interests include: researching with children and young people; work–life balance; women's health; health inequalities and low income households; food choice and eating behaviour; fertility; researching family groups and qualitative research methodology.

Angus Bancroft is a lecturer in sociology at the University of Edinburgh, teaching on the sociology of intoxication; intimacy; and health and illness. He started his academic career working with Gypsy-Travellers, and his book *Roma and Gypsy-Travellers in Europe* was published by Ashgate in 2005. He has published on HIV/AIDS, globalisation, smoking, and social theory. He has, with colleagues, been researching the experiences of children of substance misusers for the past three years. He is currently preparing a book entitled *Drugs, intoxication and society*.

Sarah Cunningham-Burley has many years of research experience in the fields of family and medical sociology. She graduated with a BSocSc in sociology and social policy from the University of Birmingham, and did her PhD entitled 'The meaning and significance of grandparenthood' at the MRC Medical Sociology Unit, University of Aberdeen. She has been working at the University of Edinburgh since 1990 where she is now Professor of Medical and Family Sociology. Her current research projects include a range of work on early years' policies, public engagement in genetic and stem cell research; she also has an interest in issues relating to work–life balance as well as research with children and young people. She has published several edited books, the most recent being *Families and the state* (Palgrave, 2003) as well as numerous articles. She is also involved in many dissemination activities, in line with CRFR's aim to link research, policy and practice. She is a co-director of the CRFR.

Shirley Davidson completed a Masters degree by research in social policy at the University of Edinburgh in 2004. She works as a research assistant and in 2003 carried out a research project commissioned by the Scottish Executive on the early implementation of Part 5 of the 2000 Adults with Incapacity (Scotland) Act, which deals with consent to medical treatment. Prior to her return to university, Shirley was a partner in a large legal firm in Edinburgh.

Malcolm Hill is Professor and Director, Centre for the Child & Society, University of Glasgow. He has carried out research and teaching in Scotland on children and families for over 20 years, with particular attention to looked-after children. A considerable proportion of his research and writings has involved evaluations of services for young people and their families. He is an associate director of the CRFR.

Sue Innes (1948–2005) returned to study in 1993, following a career in journalism. She graduated with a PhD in politics from the University of Edinburgh in 1998. She was a founder member of Engender in Scotland and continued to be committed to bringing about positive change in women's lives until her untimely death at the age of 57 in 2005. She was Research Fellow with the CRFR, Universities of Edinburgh and Glasgow Caledonian 2001-02. The study reported in Chapter Three was carried out with Gill Scott as part of the first year of that Fellowship.

Lynn Jamieson is a professor in sociology and co-director of the CRFR. She has a long-standing interest in families and relationships and social change. Publications include a collection edited with Sarah Cunningham-Burley on *Families and the state: Changing relationships* (Palgrave, 2003), the book *Intimacy: Personal relationships in modern societies* (Polity, 1998), and jointly authored books *Country bairns: Scottish rural childhood 1900-1930* (Birlinn, 2000) and *Sex crimes on trial: The uses of sexual evidence in Scottish Courts* (Edinburgh University Press, 1993). Current work includes a study of 11- to 14-year-olds' experiences of family change within Scotland's families with Gill Highet. She recently coordinated a comparative project in six European countries concerning young adults' orientations to citizenship and European identity. Although other pressures have reduced her involvement in campaigns, she remains committed to campaigning against nuclear weapons and militarism.

Debbie Kemmer studied social history and sociology before gaining her PhD at the University of Edinburgh. She was an academic researcher for over 15 years, working in fields as diverse as historical demography, the sociology of food choice and the relationships between family, household structure and paid and unpaid work. Although one of the founder members of CRFR, and a senior research fellow there, she left academia to carry out research into the provision of activities and programmes encouraging wider participation in higher education. This was a topic about which she had always been interested, having contributed to a wider access programme in Edinburgh as researcher, administrator and summer school teacher. She is now a freelance consultant/researcher specialising in wider access and related areas in education.

Nancy Lombard is undertaking doctoral studies in the School of Law and Social Sciences at Glasgow Caledonian University. She is investigating the attitudes of primary school children towards violence against women. She has both practical and theoretical experience in this field having worked as a caseworker at a women's aid refuge in London and she was also part of the research team commissioned by the Scottish Executive to investigate male domestic abuse in Scotland. Her research interests include violence against women, feminist methodology, childhood and gender. Nancy lives in Glasgow with her son Dylan.

Lorna McKee is Professor of Management at the University of Aberdeen and an associate director at the CRFR. Lorna studied social sciences at Trinity College, Dublin, and undertook her PhD work at the University of York. She has held research posts at the Universities of York, Aston, Warwick and Aberdeen and also spent time as a NHS departmental manager. Lorna is Co-Vice Chair and a member of the Board of the National Co-ordinating Centre for NHS Service Delivery and Organisation R&D. She has also served as an expert panel and advisory committee member for the Canadian Foundation for Innovation (CFI) and the CFI Regional Hospital Fund Advisory Committee. Current research interests include healthcare management, the management of change and innovation and the sociology of work and family life.

John H. McKendrick is Lecturer in Geography at the School of Law and Social Sciences, Glasgow Caledonian University. During 2002 and 2003 he was seconded to the CRFR as Senior Research Fellow. He is Viewpoints Editor of *Children's Geographies* (Taylor and Francis) and on the editorial board of *Children, Youth and Environments* (University of Colorado/National Science Foundation). He edited 'Children's playgrounds in the built environment', a special edition of the *Built Environment* (Alexandrine Press, 1999) and *First Steps*, a collection of 21 'retrospective' autobiographical short notes written by geographers on one their favourite readings from the geographies of children and youths (Royal Geographical Society and Institute of British Geographers, 2004) and has recently completed a book entitled *Geographies of children* for the Geographical Association. He also recently completed a survey of all state sector preschool and school playgrounds for children in Scotland (for **sport**scotland, Play Scotland and Grounds for Learning).

Linda McKie is Research Professor in Sociology at Glasgow Caledonian University and an associate director at the CRFR. She is a trustee for the British Sociological Association, Evaluation Support Scotland and the Institute for Rural Health. Current research interests include work–life and family–life issues, concepts of care, and gender and violence. Recent publications include *Families, violence and social change* (Open University Press, 2005).

Hugh Masters, RMN, MPhil, PG Cert T&L HE is a senior lecturer (Mental Health) in the School of Community Health, Napier University, Edinburgh. He has extensive experience of working in the mental health field both as a researcher and as a mental health nurse. Research interests include acute mental healthcare and, in particular, observational studies; teaching evidence-based mental health practice; HIV and substance misuse; and service user involvement in healthcare research, practice and education. Recent research projects include: a service user-focused evaluation of psychosocial interventions training; the impact of parental substance misuse; the use of reflection in the nursing curriculum; and involving service users in curriculum design and delivery.

Sasha Roseneil is Professor of Sociology and Gender Studies at the University of Leeds. She is the author of *Disarming patriarchy* (Open University Press, 1995) and *Common women, uncommon practices: The queer feminisms of Greenham* (Cassell, 2000). She is also co-editor of *Stirring it: Challenges for feminism* (Taylor and Francis, 1994), *Practising identities* (Macmillan, 1999), *Consuming cultures* (Macmillan, 1999), *Globalization and social movements* (Palgrave, 2000) and special issues of *Citizenship Studies* (2000), *Feminist Theory* (2001, 2003), *Current Sociology* (2004) and *Social Politics* (2004).

Gill Scott is Professor in Social Inclusion and Equality at Glasgow Caledonian University and was an associate director of the CRFR until April 2005. She is Director of the Scottish Poverty Information Unit. Gill's research interests include poverty, childcare and social inclusion. She is co-editor with Gerry Mooney of *Social policy in Scotland* (2005, The Policy Press). Gill is an adviser to the Scottish Cabinet Group on Closing the Opportunity Gap and is part of the editorial collective for the journal *Critical Social Policy*. She is also a member of the advisory group for Child Poverty Action Group for Scotland.

Peter Seaman is Research Fellow at the Glasgow Centre for the Child & Society, University of Glasgow. Peter has an MA in sociology and studied for his PhD at the Medical Research Council's Social and Public Health Sciences Unit. His doctoral thesis explored the role of parents in young people's transitions to adulthood with particular reference to the structural diversity of contemporary families. Since then he has worked on an evaluation of an emergency contraception health intervention at the University of Edinburgh and a Joseph Rowntree Foundation-funded project exploring parenting in disadvantaged communities while at the Glasgow Centre for the Child & Society. His research interests include understandings and enactments of contemporary families and family resilience, particularly in relation to socioeconomic disadvantage.

Janet Shucksmith is Professor of Public Health, School of Health and Social Care, University of Teesside. Until recently she was Senior Lecturer in Sociology at the University of Aberdeen and a founder member of the Rowan Group, a focus for policy-related research on young people's education and general well-being. She is also an associate director of the CRFR. Her work centres on issues concerning children's and young people's education, health and social development. Longitudinal studies in the 1980s gave rise to a book, *Young people's leisure and lifestyles* (Routledge, 1993), and a series of articles examining the variations in young people's health behaviours and the relationship of these to family patterns and parenting styles. Subsequent qualitative studies have sought to explore children's and young people's welfare in relation to a variety of contemporary policy debates that affect the family. Themes of participation and empowerment have been explored in the context of young people's education and health needs. Janet's current work centres on issues concerning the negotiation of responsibility for children's well-being between families and the state.

Adam Smith was the research associate working on the ESRC-funded project 'Solo Living Across the Adult Life Course' from January 2004 to January 2005, conducting secondary analysis of the Scottish Household Survey, the General Household Survey and the British Household Panel Survey. He previously completed an MSc and MA in the Department of Sociology at the University of Edinburgh, focusing his research interests on young people, education, socialisation and peer group interaction.

Helen Sweeting has worked at the Medical Research Council (MRC) Social and Public Health Sciences (formerly Medical Sociology) Unit, based at the University of Glasgow, since 1990. The aim of the unit is to promote human health via the study of its social and environmental determinants. Prior to that she was employed as a clinical psychologist. She studied psychology and clinical psychology at the University of Edinburgh and her PhD thesis (University of Glasgow) focused on the anticipatory grief reactions of those caring for a relative with dementia. Her work at the Social and Public Health Sciences Unit focuses on young people's health and health-related behaviours, largely based on quantitative analyses of data from two large, ongoing cohort studies.

Fran Wasoff is a reader in social policy in the School of Social and Political Studies and a co-director of the CRFR at the University of Edinburgh. Her research interests are in the areas of family policy, gender and social policy, family law and social policy and socio-legal studies. She teaches research methods, gender and social policy, and family research and policy. With Lynn Jamieson and Adam Smith, she carried out the ESRC-funded study of solo living on which Chapter Twelve is based. With colleagues at CRFR she has also done research on early years policies, older women and domestic violence and the implementation of legislation regarding adults with incapacity in Scotland. Her socio-legal research has focused on civil and family law in Scotland, the financial consequences of divorce and child support and the socio-legal study of legal professionals and informal legal processes.

Dot Weaks is a qualified community psychiatric nurse with a Masters degree in counselling. She has been working in the field of dementia care, in a variety of settings, for over 25 years, and has been advocating early diagnosis of dementia since around 1990. She is co-author of *The right to know* ([with Kate Fearnley and Jane McLennan] Alzheimer's Scotland, 1997). She is currently seconded from, and funded by, NHS Tayside to complete a PhD entitled 'The psycho-social impact on patients, their families and medical practitioners of early diagnosis of dementia'. She was awarded an OBE in 1998 for her services to nursing.

Heather Wilkinson is a reader at the University of Northumbria, Newcastle, and is also an associate researcher based at the CRFR. She directs a programme of research on aging and social relationships with a particular focus on the experiences of people with dementia and people growing older with an intellectual disability. Current work includes projects funded by the Community Fund, Joseph Rowntree Foundation, and the University of Albany, USA.

Helen Willmot completed a sociology PhD in 2001 at the University of Leeds. Her thesis explored the interplay between young women's intimate relationships with men and their education and employment experiences. In 2002 she took up a CRFR research fellowship at the University of Aberdeen and carried out research that looked at how parents in low income neighbourhoods balance involvement in their children's education alongside paid employment while also maintaining time for their families. After working briefly as a research interviewer for the ESRC Families and Social Capital Group at South Bank University, Helen joined the Centre for Analysis of Social Exclusion (CASE) at the London School of Economics and Political Science in 2003. As research officer for the northern strand of the Neighbourhood Study, Helen is currently researching and writing on parenting in socially excluded neighbourhoods.

Sarah Wilson is currently an ESRC postdoctoral fellow based at the CRFR. A qualified solicitor, with an LLM in comparative law and bioethics, she was awarded her PhD in social policy at the University of Edinburgh in 2003. Her thesis examined HIV-positive mothers' use of statutory and voluntary social services. Her subsequent research fellow positions have also reflected this interest in the sociology of health and illness. She worked on an appraisal of Scottish Executive mental health policy in the light of mental health improvement and the examination of young people's experience of parental substance use problems. She was also the grantholder for an ESRC seminar series entitled 'The impact of parental substance misuse: research, practice and policy' which brought together interested academics, practitioners and policymakers from across the UK.

Introduction

ONE

Families and relationships: boundaries and bridges

Linda McKie, Sarah Cunningham-Burley and John H. McKendrick

Introduction

The family remains a complex and dynamic concept, variably defined and experienced. Families take many different forms and these, together with changing expectations and anticipations of family life, provide crucial frames through which we engage in society (Carling et al, 2002). Experiences of families and relationships are critical to the development of personal and group identities as well as providing material and emotional resources as we proceed through the lifecourse (Beck and Beck-Gernsheim, 1995; Cheal, 2002). The topic of families in society has spurred a range of research and policy projects, with 'the family' becoming one of the building blocks of social scientific enquiry and one of the welfare 'pillars' of society (Esping-Andersen et al, 2002).

This book offers a unique contribution to critical studies of families and relationships through the engagement with, and development of, the concept of boundaries. The book has three aims. First, through a critical application of the concept of boundaries, contributions offer an enhanced understanding of families and relationships. Familial and relationship practices and processes are explored through contemporary empirical data and related theoretical developments. Contributors have addressed the concept of boundaries in a variety of ways; in some chapters conceptual analysis is underpinned by the notion of boundary and boundary practices; in others the authors relate their work to the concept of boundary in order to assess its usefulness for analytical purposes and theory building. Second, chapters all move beyond the notion of a clearly 'bounded' family by examining diversity, particularly in family forms, including non-familial relationships and networks. However, chapters also recognise that traditional values and approaches still form part of daily experience and expectations and therefore still need to be integrated into current social scientific thinking, but perhaps in more reflexive and cautious ways than hitherto. Third, the contributions work towards a reconfiguration of family and personal life through the use of the boundary metaphor. The emphasis is on the processes that underlie boundary construction, deconstruction and reconstruction, particularly with respect to relationship formation, choices and diverse meanings of families and relationships. Chapters cover dimensions of family life, relationships and friendships that span the lifecourse and different contexts.

A range of research work is brought together in this book in order to take forward a theoretical and conceptual agenda that challenges the way we think about families and relationships. This book is organised into four parts and these reflect the breadth of work on, and issues pertaining to, critical studies of families and relationships. Part One, 'Families in society', brings together chapters that examine the boundaries between families and paid work or training and families and schools. Part Two, 'Children, families and relationships', examines the different ways in which children and adults may construct and perceive boundaries between families and the outside world, and also within families, between different generations. Part Three, 'Health, illness and well-being', takes as its focus issues of well-being, illness and violence and draws out how boundaries are challenged and reconstructed in different circumstances. Part Four, 'Relationships and friendships', reaches towards an understanding of personal relationships and the boundaries that may exist, be constructed or challenged as people move in and out of different ways of living and different types of relationship. There is an introduction to each section linking the chapters' themes to the overall conceptual focus of this book: boundaries and boundary processes.

At the same time as the individual chapters provide an opportunity to reconsider how we understand and conceptualise families and relationships, we link these efforts to current policy concerns: the book concludes with a contribution to policy debates that draws on the empirical and theoretical developments offered in earlier chapters (Berridge and Thom, 1996). This bridge from theoretical and empirical work to policy analysis and recommendations emerges from the ongoing collaborations and links among authors through the Centre for Research on Families and Relationships (CRFR). This research centre brings together a range of empirical and conceptual projects to explore the concept of 'the family' within a broader understanding of relationships, including friendships, and in the context of the wider institutions of society to which families and individuals relate. The CRFR, through its own programme of research and research dissemination, investigates key social issues as they relate to families and relationships. It also seeks to broaden our understanding of the relationships that shape our lives, whether within families, with wider kin or with friends. Further, the work of the CRFR explores the interface between families and a range of government and non-governmental agencies (see www.crfr.ac.uk).

In this introductory chapter we provide a critical engagement with some key ideas and theories about families and relationships. Our aim is twofold: first, to explore the potential for the concept of boundaries to help deconstruct and reconstruct families, relationships and family practices in ways that promote critical scholarship relevant to the development of policy, practice and further research; second, to reprise and question presumptions about 'the family' through a critical review of 'traditional' family values and the changing and complex nature of families and personal life.

Boundaries and boundary practices

Social scientific accounts of families and family life have themselves reflected and constructed the changing realities of families. Work has also illuminated the interweaving of various forms of family life, societal and global trends. Family research and policy work reflect a range of political, moral and academic positions and, as such, are often hotly contested. Thus the potential to debate and develop evidence-informed policies could be difficult, as no resolute position can or should be obtained. Here we offer an approach to understanding families in society based around the concept of boundary. This, we argue, enhances the potential to mesh analysis and understandings across spatial and temporal frameworks, between families and society, within families and other personal relationships. Through adopting and adapting the boundary metaphor, across different substantive issues, from work–life balance to solo living, we might attend to the challenge to both appreciate the traditional and contemporary perspectives and experiences of families.

How might we conceive of boundaries? Luhmann (1982, p 245) offers the following definition:

> Boundaries delimit society's internal environment and establish selective relations between internal and external

> environments. They do not forestall and they may even encourage traffic, cooperation, and conflict across the borders.

In this definition the notion of space and location is drawn upon, as is the idea of movement – of traffic – that can enhance cooperation or potentially promote conflict. In summary, Luhmann (1982) asserts that boundaries are seldom fixed and are more usually permeable and malleable.

Boundaries have been considered further in terms of the potential to encourage the analysis of the nation state, social and religious movements and socioeconomic change. Newman and Paasi (1998, p 187) offer the following comment on the notion of boundaries:

> Even if they [boundaries] are always more or less arbitrary lines between territorial entities, they may also have deep symbolic cultural, historical and religious, often contested meanings for social communities. They [boundaries] manifest themselves in numerous social, political and cultural practices.

More recently, what might be termed 'boundary studies' have explored the primacy of entities and the dynamic ways in which the social, cultural and material interweave. Here again we cite ideas from Newman and Paasi (1998, p 194) on the workings of boundaries: 'Boundaries create practices and forms which, for their part, are the basis of meaning and interpretation'.

In relation to professional practices, boundary work has been identified as actively constructing the relationship between, for example, experts and the wider public, relationships that need to reinforce expert authority at the same time as building bridges between experts and publics. Boundaries (and bridges) thus serve to create and sustain dynamic sets of relationships. So how might the concept of 'boundary' aid an analysis of and critical reflections on families, relationships and society? At this point we offer some suggestions. Boundaries may be used to define an entity or to challenge a priori definitions. Subject matter that is defined through boundaries, such as families, may be viewed as both internally coherent and externally unique, yet because boundaries are permeable and malleable, also as dynamic and changing.

Boundaries may be constructed in different ways. For example, there is the demarcation between states – that is, the physical marking of boundaries through both relationships and physical entities such as the family home. Or, boundaries may offer a 'metaphorical' sense of the farthest limit in terms of familial relationships, networks and goals. The notions of the frontier zone, border and margins offer analytical concepts that may help with understanding the nature of families and relationships and shifting certainties regarding 'us' and 'other', and the bridges and gaps between. They, boundaries, may be drawn and redrawn to constantly define and redefine the entity. What constitutes a family, my family, and personal relationships and friendships is not fixed by predetermined boundaries but constructed through boundary maintenance, whether through controlling knowledge, defining spaces, negotiating roles, practices of inclusion and exclusion and negotiating relationships between families and wider social institutions. In summary, the boundary metaphor offers the potential to develop theoretical and empirical work in a hybrid fashion. This includes the transgression of boundaries and the reconstruction of entities across boundaries, namely the formation, re-formation and dissolution of families and relationships and the changing relationships between families and the state (Cunningham-Burley and Jamieson, 2003).

One boundary that has been the focus of much theoretical and empirical work is that of the public and the private (Morgan, 1996). The notions of the public and the private are both material social arenas and heavily ideological constructions that can have quite different forms, meanings and significances for different social categories, not least men and women (Hearn, 1992). Families constitute a dominant private sphere, a haven from the pressures of 'the outside world'. Friendships and other intimate relationships may challenge the notion of family as 'home', but retain a clear 'public/private' boundary. Relationships and friendships located in, and around, the space of the home and family, offer a particular contrast to experiences of paid work. Certainly families and friendships can be stressful and for a surprising number of people they can be infused with violence (McKie, 2005). Yet a commonly held expectation, and actual experience, is of boundaries between home and the outside world that offer respite from the pressure of paid work and the opportunity to be intimate with others (Parsons, 1943; Bourdieu, 1996; Jamieson, 1998; Bailey, 2000).

Contemporary politics has crept into a range of arenas, not least of which is aspects of the private, with the growth in concerns about risk (environmental, health, personal, property) and personal conduct. Governments are increasingly concerned to encourage individuals and families to take additional responsibility for myriad aspects of socioeconomic and health matters (Rose, 2001). As Bourdieu (1996, p 25) notes:

> The public vision ... is deeply involved in our vision of domestic things, and our most private behaviours themselves depend on public actions, such as housing policy or, more directly, family policy.

The public/private boundary, then, does not suggest two isolated spheres, but a permeable interface, which shapes and is shaped by our personal lives. Government policies and services can and do impact on the private sphere and more often than not, draw upon presumptions about gendered roles and responsibilities. One obvious example is the presumption in many health and education policies of the unpaid work of relatives, generally mothers and women, to provide informal care and support, and indeed support for health and education. However, ongoing, and sometimes heated, debates on interventions in private relationships and related locales, have led to a neoliberal approach to gender relations in which inequities in the private sphere are noted and rarely challenged. For example, women continue to experience lower incomes and earning potential across the lifecourse and yet undertake much of the informal and unpaid domestic and care work (Cabinet Office, 2000). Governments, the state, agencies, families and individuals actually presume and draw upon these very inequities in the development and organisation of policies and services (Sevenhuijsen, 1998). Parallel to these shifts in governmentality, social practices have opened up to choice, prudence and experimentation, albeit that inequities in gender, income and power ensure the exclusion of many.

Interpreting families and relationships

Regardless of socio-demographic data that illuminate the diversity of family forms, some features of families, and family life, are more generally accepted in wider society as normative positions. For example, many politicians and commentators, both on the left and right of political ideologies, will, in some ways, espouse the notion of 'traditional' family values (Morgan, 1995). These values are predicated on a range of assumptions, not least of which is the notion of the heterosexual, nuclear family based around members' active engagement with education, training, employment and childrearing, even though the balance between these may alter. Currently, it is both more common and more acceptable for mothers to be in paid work. Such normative positioning has led to a range of tensions and debates, as the everyday experiences of many people do not match traditional values or assumed trends towards equality within relationships (Jamieson, 1998; Leira, 2002; Hansen, 2005).

Academics and policymakers alike are not immune from making assumptions and unreflectively reinforcing rather than exploring family boundaries and practices. For example, uncritical acceptance of age- and gender-specific roles in families as a basis for the provision of informal care work, and engagement in the labour market influences research as well as policy agendas (Sevenhuijsen, 1998). In many ways, there remains a presumption that mothers, rather than fathers, will take on the majority of caring responsibilities for children, such as taking time out of paid employment if a child becomes ill (Hochschild, 1989; Backett-Milburn et al, 2001; Cheal, 2002). Thus while many speak of family-friendly policies and work–life balance, debates on such matters quickly shift from discourses about the role of parents to that of mothers (Leira, 2002; McKie et al, 2004). The role of fathers is marginalised and presumed to be of less relevance in both practical and policy terms, and remains under-researched (Lupton and Barclay, 1997). Academics, too, may reinforce such assumptions through choice of empirical work (there is much more work on familial relationships than on friendships, on mothers rather than fathers, for example). It may be that the plurality of experience can no longer be captured through reconceptualising 'the family' as 'families' or by focusing on 'family practices', but requires some further blurring of conceptual boundaries between families and relationships.

In the remaining sections of this introduction we explore tensions and contradictions that help to illuminate myriad ways in which boundaries frame ideas and values about families. First, we explore some commonly held presumptions about families and subsequently how the recognition of changing families has resulted in what might be termed fuzzy boundaries in both physical and metaphorical terms.

Firm boundaries: families as we knew and know them

An orthodox story emerged in the decades after the Second World War when welfare support for families expanded across Europe and industrial societies more generally. In this orthodoxy, families were moulded around the emergence of the companionate heterosexual partnership legally recognised through marriage (Bott, 1971). Families were seen to form a private domain and a haven from the pressures of the world of work. They operated in ways that enabled active participation in employment (at least for men), education and training. In this so-called nuclear family a division of labour was promoted, not solely on the grounds of gender – the wage-earning husband and the homemaking wife – but also age, with, for example, the teenage years becoming a recognised stage in growing up. This type of family household was perceived to offer intimacy and emotional support with women encouraged to prioritise the physical and psychological well-being of others. Thus, this idea of the family came to dominate the ideas of many sociologists, policymakers and politicians as the conventional and preferred mode of household with its clear roles and boundaries (Parsons, 1943; Bernardes, 1987). Those not conforming to this norm were often pathologised, leading to a deficit model of the family in these cases. Boundaries thus became normative constructions and breaches suggestive of the need for intervention.

Although there is, today, greater acceptance and recognition of the diversity of family forms, it is also the case that strongly held ideas of families and family life continue to shape our expectations and experiences. Here we provide a brief resume of a number of key features of such expectations of families and family life that assist in any explanation of the particular place 'the family' continues to play in our social experiences.

The family remains a strong institution that forms one of the foundations of the world in which we live. Governments, charities, religious groups, employers and a range of organisations support an array of bodies and agencies that reinforce the status of families as an institution, either implicitly or explicitly (Bourdieu, 1996; Ermisch and Franceconi, 2000). For example, social work services and benefits agencies operate with particular boundaries around family life and the needs of different family members. Political parties generally develop and publicise family-related policies, as do international organisations such as the World Health Organisation, International Monetary Fund and United Nations. The work of families in informal care is fundamental to the welfare of dependants and support for those growing up is crucial to economic development. Most of these presumptions often institutionalise gendered notions of 'doing family' with public policies premised on the availability of family members (frequently women) to undertake informal domestic and care work (McKie et al, 2001). Despite considerable changes in patterns of paid employment for both men and women, there does not seem to have been much lessening of responsibilities regarding informal care, domestic labour and socialising children (Sullivan, 2000).

Alongside such variables as social class, education, gender and ethnicity, family status and composition are the conceptual tools we use to document and understand the world in which we live. The family continues to be an important social category. Increasingly, this social category includes a range of family forms (for example, lone parent families and families in multipart households), but not all forms of households are embraced in social commentary and policies: for example, same-sex couples. There remains a tendency to think of 'the family' as a unit comprising two adults, who while perhaps not married are cohabiting in a heterosexual relationship with dependent children (Bourdieu, 1996).

The institution of the family is also perceived to be a durable and an enduring feature of individuals' lives. While diverse forms of families may be recognised, the contemporary version of the nuclear family – heterosexual partners both in employment, bringing up children with limited recourse to state support – continues to be perceived by many as the most stable and, therefore, favoured unit. Furthermore, even within those family forms that are considered to be less stable, family members are still considered to provide support, care and affection for the duration of one's life (Morgan, 1996; Miller and Rowlingson, 2001).

There is a presumption that families have shared objectives or orientations. These may include broad ones such as the economic survival of the family unit and emotional support for family members, as well as the everyday, for example, getting the children to school on time, ensuring that food choices are catered for and homework is done. Working towards goals gives a shared sense of purpose and creates family 'ties' and 'bonds', through collective experiences and narratives (Cheal, 2002). Families are often associated with their own material space, set apart from the wider world. The family home strengthens the sense that families are somehow set apart from this wider world, although again there is increasing recognition of ties beyond the home. This is also expressed in the rhetoric of 'domestic matters' and the tensions around the state intervening in 'private' family matters (Thomas, 1995; Standing, 1999).

In the orthodox framing, families imply rather predetermined roles. Individuals within the family have expectations placed on them, according to age, gender and family position. In previous decades the male breadwinner and women carer model was promoted as the 'natural' family, and in the minds of some remains an aspirational or preferred model. However, tensions around work and family are now very much to the fore as increasing numbers of mothers participate in paid employment. Families remain the main arena for the nurturing and socialisation of children and, in particular, for their preparation as future workers. They are also arenas and networks in which interdependency and care needs for young, old, sick and infirm are largely addressed (Hochschild, 1989). Although evidence suggests a plurality of roles and expectations, change in the gendered domestic division of labour is slow; and roles may be additive, especially for women who are increasingly both carers and earners.

Traditionally, families are perceived to be a dominant feature of social life across time and space. For example, history is dominated by the progress of elite families, and increasingly the documentation of the everyday experiences of the less powerful through oral histories and the rise of genealogy can be noted (Hagerstrand, 1984). Further, in contemporary terms, our engagement with other individuals, groups and organisations is often framed by the exchange of information on living and family arrangements. Such boundary work, with the revelation of some and the withholding of other knowledge, constructs who we are in the context of where we come from and with whom we are or were related (Holloway, 1999). The boundaries of our families may or may not reflect legal or administrative categories but are given meaning through our day-to-day interactions with others.

Challenging boundaries: changing families

Traditional understandings of the family are constantly challenged by experiences and expectations of many, whatever their family circumstances. Although the mismatch between everyday experience and normative framing has no doubt always been present, the situation today puts this into sharper focus with rapid social change bringing about explicit recognition of family diversity. These shifting patterns of family lives have been documented and analysed by a range of social scientists, who themselves have pioneered new ways of thinking about, understanding and conceptualising families. Changes in the formation and dissolution of households have received particular attention. The increasing involvement of women in the labour market, and trends in divorce and fertility, have been of particular interest (Hochschild, 1983; McKie et al, 2001). While these changes might be interpreted as contemporary in nature, many have their origins in earlier social and public policies, for example, the educational and economic policies that enhanced the potential for women to enter the labour market or scientific and medical advances, such as the control of female fertility. Thus a diverse range of policies ensures that the potential for families to operate as 'islands' immune to the practices and policies of other institutions and organisations is challenged (Ermisch and Franceconi, 2000). Although families and family life may appear to offer a range of certainties, they are, in fact, complex and confounding terrain. Here we draw attention to a number of critiques.

While the family remains a central institution in the building bricks of social, economic and political life, it is one without clear boundaries, and one that is likely to be in a constant process of construction and negotiation at both macro and micro levels. The significance of the family in, and on, the lives of individuals is thought to be less overarching than it was several decades ago; the shape and working of families cannot be deterministically mapped from institution to individual (Bourdieu, 1996). These shifts are components of broader changes in thinking and behaviours that are likely to pose challenges to the primacy of institutions more generally. The prominence afforded individuals and their agency is evident in the evolution of patterns of consumption and the formation of identities, although families and relationships are important sites of consumption and identity formation (Rose, 2001).

The family is a flexible social category. At its simplest this becomes evident in debates on defining families (Carling et al, 2002). Given that it is now accepted that there is a multiplicity of ways in which families are constructed, how might the 'the family' be operationalised in social statistics? Further, while the prevalence of lone parent families has, it could be argued, led to a more inclusive definition of 'the family', other family forms are still not as widely recognised as, or perceived to be, 'families'; for example, stepfamilies, non-resident families, families of same-sex couples, families with adult children who are 'dependants' and the family and personal ties of those living alone. There are also different ways in which its members construct the family. One example is the way in which children define their families; it is not unusual for their definitions to include many close family friends with whom they are not linked by birth ties or marriage (Jamieson, 1998). The boundaries of families are thus flexible and permeable.

There are dynamic processes that re/create families and the social category of family (Cheal, 2002). This may be expressed through the biographies of individual family units (for example, using lifecourse perspectives to unravel the complexities of family change) and the changing nature of families in society through time (for example, lone parenthood was largely a function of the death of one adult in the 19th century, whereas today divorce/separation is the primary route into lone parenthood). Some new family forms are constructed through choice; living on one's own is a particularly recent trend that challenges notions of families and home.

Families shape identities and this is a multifaceted and interweaving process. The significance rests not in the ways in which roles determine life experiences, but rather with the way in which different members use family experiences to construct identities (Morgan, 1996; Cheal, 2002). Family responsibilities are one element of the process of identity formation. This also opens up the 'theoretical space' for conceiving of the family as a means of reinforcing or challenging 'normative' constructions of the world in which we live, as boundaries are constructed, broken or transcended (Finch and Mason, 1993).

Thus family objectives and orientations can be both regressive and progressive. While these can work to the mutual benefit of all family members, for example, economic survival, others work to constrain some family members. The most notable example of this is the continued gendered division of labour within families. This affects women's and employers' constructions and expectations of the labour market and the work/family interface. As a consequence this leads to a gendered labour market that constrains women's capacity to achieve equal pay. As a result, and in the longer term, women are more likely to be in poverty generally and in later life, in particular (Cabinet Office, 2000). They may well bear the brunt of work/family tensions. At another level, challenges to the notion of a pure relationship – a bond between couples rather devoid of structural context – demonstrates the persistence of inequalities between couples and within families.

Families are increasingly associated with a multiplicity of spaces (Hagerstrand, 1984; Holloway, 1999). To some extent this assertion follows from the practical implications of the changing nature of families. For example, stepparenting may imply more than one family home for children. There is a growing importance of grandparents as carers. Yet, the increasing spread of extended networks of families across communities and continents (a move away from the co-presence of multiple generations and siblings within particular communities) may mean that fewer domestic family spaces assume an importance in children's everyday lives. In a more mobile society where barriers of distance can be transcended, by the same token, relationships may be maintained across geographical boundaries. More generally, institutions such as schools are attempting to open up to families, perhaps promoting greater involvement of families in their domain; commercial leisure spaces (one example is family pubs) would be a further example of the opening up of wider society to families, breaking the boundary between the public and private sphere. Friendships and non-familial intimate relationships are also increasingly recognised as important to many individuals in ways that challenge the assumptions of the centrality of the family as the site of support, care and intimacy across the lifecourse.

Conclusions

There is now greater recognition that any conceptualisation of the family will be porous but also limited, as families contribute to, and are influenced by the wider world (Bourdieu, 1996). One contemporary example is the interplay of family-friendly employment practices, and family values and the work ethic. The former policies impact on the way in which the family organises and provides for care while attitudes to work are shaped, at least in part, by the values acquired through family life. Rather than conceiving the domains of work and family life as separate, it should be recognised that work can enhance/impair the quality of family life; and the boundaries and spaces between the two need to be constantly managed.

Traditional views of 'the family', associated concepts, and the more recent empirical and theoretical challenges, could be said to reflect the somewhat arbitrary boundaries between modernity and postmodernity in accounts of societies and social change (Eagleton, 2003). Postmodern accounts of social change may seek to replace others, through, for example, offering discursive approaches to the analysis of families as a social category. However, there is a need to reconcile, theoretically, the persistence of traditional structures and practices with contemporary reform, change and challenge. We should progress to new ground in our understandings of, and work on, families and relationships and reflexively address the persistence of traditional and sometimes repressive boundaries, with new demarcations and analytical flexibility. This book offers an attempt to address these challenges through the presentation of empirical and theoretical work that draws and critically reflects on the concept of boundaries, exploring families and relationships in societies across different contexts.

References

Backett-Milburn, K., Cunningham-Burley, S. and Kemmer, D. (2001) *Caring and providing: Lone and partnered mothers in Scotland*, Bristol: The Policy Press.

Bailey, J. (2000) 'Some meanings of "the private" in sociological thought', *Sociology*, vol 34, no 3, pp 381-401.

Beck, U. and Beck-Gernsheim, E. (1995) *The normal chaos of love*, Cambridge: Polity Press.

Beck, U. and Beck-Gernsheim, E. (2001) *Individualization: Institutionalized individualism and its social and political consequences*, London: Sage Publications.

Bernardes, J. (1987) *Family studies: An introduction*, London: Routledge.

Berridge, V. and Thom, B. (1996) 'Research and policy: what determines the relationship?', *Policy Studies*, vol 17, no 1, 23-34.

Bott, E. (1971) *Family and social network*, London: Tavistock.

Bourdieu, P. (1996) 'On the family as a realised category', *Theory, Culture and Society*, vol 13, no 3, pp 19-26.

Cabinet Office (2000) *The female forfeit – the cost of being a woman*, London: Cabinet Office (Women's Unit).

Carling, A., Duncan, S. and Edwards, R. (2002) *Analysing families: Morality and rationality in policy and practice*, London: Routledge.

Cheal, D. (2002) *Sociology of family life*, Basingstoke: Palgrave.

Cunningham-Burley, S. and Jamieson, L. (eds) (2003) *Families and the state*, Basingstoke: Palgrave Macmillan.

Eagleton, T. (2003) *After theory*, New York, NY: Basic Books.

Ermisch, J. and Franceconi, M. (2000) 'Patterns of household and family formation', in R. Berthoud and J. Gershuny (eds) *Seven years in the lives of British families: Evidence on the dynamics of social change from the British Household Panel Survey*, Bristol: The Policy Press.

Esping-Andersen, G., Gallie, D., Hemerijk, A. and Mykes, J. (2002) *Why we need a new welfare state*, Oxford: Oxford University Press.

Finch, J. and Mason, J. (1993) *Negotiating family responsibilities*, London: Routledge.

Hagerstrand, T. (1984) 'Presence and absence: a look at conceptual choices and bodily necessities', *Regional Studies*, vol 18, pp 373-80.

Hansen, K. (2005) *Not-so-nuclear families: Class, gender and networks of care*, New Jersey, NJ: Rutgers University Press.

Hearn, J. (1992) *Men in the public eye: The construction and deconstruction of public men and public patriarchies*, London: Routledge.

Hochschild, A. (1983) *The managed heart: Commercialization of human feeling*, Berkeley, CA: University of California Press.

Hochschild, A. (1989) *The second shift: Working parents and the revolution at home*, Berkeley, CA: University of California Press.

Holloway, S. (1999) 'Reproducing motherhood', in N. Laurie, C. Dwyer, S. Holloway and F. Smith (eds) *Geographies of new femininities*, London: Longman.

Jamieson, L. (1998) *Intimacy: Personal relationships in modern societies*, Cambridge: Polity Press.

Leira, A. (2002) *Working parents and the welfare state: Family change and policy reform in Scandinavia*, Cambridge: Cambridge University Press.

Luhmann, N. (1982) *The differentiation of society*, New York, NY: Columbia University Press.

Lupton, D. and Barclay, L. (1997) *Constructing fatherhood: Discourses and experiences*, London: Sage Publications.

McKie, L. (2005) *Families, violence and social change*, Maidenhead: Open University Press.

McKie, L., Bowlby, S. and Gregory, S. (2001) 'Gender, caring and employment in Britain', *Journal of Social Policy*, vol 30, pp 233-58.

McKie, L., Gregory, S. and Bowlby, S. (2004) 'Starting well: gender, care and health in family context', *Sociology*, vol 38, no 3, pp 593-611.

Miller, J. and Rowlingson, K. (eds) (2001) *Lone parents, employment and social policy: Cross-national comparisons*, Bristol: The Policy Press.

Morgan, D. (1996) *Family connections: An introduction to family studies*, Cambridge: Polity Press.

Morgan, P. (1995) *Farewell to families*, London: Institute of Economic Affairs.

Newman, D. and Paasi, A. (1998) 'Fences and neighbours in the postmodern world: boundary narratives in political geography', *Progress in Human Geography*, vol 22, pp 186-207.

Parsons, T. (1943) 'The kinship system of the contemporary United States', *American Anthropologist*, vol 45, pp 22-38.

Rose, N. (2001) 'The politics of life itself', *Theory, Culture and Society*, vol 18, no 6, pp 1-30.

Sevenhuijsen, S. (1998) *Citizenship and the ethics of care*, London: Routledge.

Standing, K. (1999) 'Negotiating the home and school: low income, lone mothering and unpaid schoolwork', in L. McKie, S. Bowlby and S. Gregory (eds) *Gender, power and the household*, Basingstoke: Macmillan.

Sullivan, O. (2000) 'The division of domestic labour: twenty years of change?', *Sociology*, vol 34, pp 437-56.

Thomas, C. (1995) 'Domestic labour and health: bringing it all back home', *Sociology of Health and Illness*, vol 17, pp 323-52.

Part One: Families in society

The first part of this book is concerned with how families engage with organisations and services as they seek to combine caring, working, training and education. Issues relating to the broad themes of family life and working life have received much attention in recent decades. Governments, employers' organisations, trades unions and professional associations, along with a range of voluntary sector agencies and groups, have considered a range of policy and practice ideas to support families with children and other caring responsibilities. The changing patterns of fertility, childbearing and childrearing, combined with presumptions about engagement in the labour market, regardless of parenting status, have led to tensions for many as they seek to combine caring work and paid employment. Further, government policies in most post-industrial societies now consider paid employment as the main means of alleviating poverty and deprivation. The gendered nature of much caring work, as well as engagement with services such as education, is taken for granted. Thus women and mothers are seeking to combine care and employment responsibilities and to organise and deliver care in ways that minimise distributions to paid work. Men and fathers are more involved in care work than previously but there remains much to be changed if they are to be enabled to take on further responsibilities in caring and domestic work, and be willing to do so.

The three chapters in this part of the book present an analysis of recent empirical work on these issues. The first chapter by Cunningham-Burley, Backett-Milburn and Kemmer (Chapter Two) presents data drawn from interviews with lone and partnered mothers in non-professional, non-managerial occupations. This project was funded by the Joseph Rowntree Foundation as part of a programme of research on work and family life. Findings reported in the chapter illuminate the range of negotiations and tensions that mothers in paid work outside the home report. Family responsibilities were a top priority for these women as they sought to keep the spheres of home and work separate. This boundary could be maintained as long as a crisis situation or important activities did not suddenly emerge and become imperative. Nevertheless women were keen to be seen as reliable workers who did not need time off. However, as in line with other research there was a clear conclusion, namely that work should not take precedence over mothering.

In the following chapter, Scott and Innes (Chapter Three) present data from a study on women who are seeking to move into training, education and employment after a period of parenting or unemployment. The women in this study kept care diaries over a three-week period and participated in a focus group at the start and end of data collection. Women lived in a deprived locality in Glasgow and at times had struggles with benefit, education and employment services that appeared to pose hurdles rather than opportunities for them. Scott and Innes note the existence of a 'gender culture' in which women are perceived as (and want to be) primary carers, and a 'worker culture' in which engagement in employment or training is seen as paramount to active and useful notions of the citizen. Familial, friendship and social networks were crucial to managing the needs of balancing care responsibilities, training, education and employment. Support in transitions for women in low income households must recognise care roles and responsibilities and fully consider the range of social and familial resources that low income families depend on.

The last chapter in this part of the book (Chapter Four) takes up the boundary metaphor through an exploration of the relationships between families and education services. Through an analysis of data from a recent study undertaken in Aberdeen, Shucksmith, McKee and Willmot explore elements of what they term the 'push and pull' around the boundaries between families and professional educators. The study involved 19 adult members of working-class families. From these data the authors considered how boundaries between school and home have shifted seemingly in respect of the school's power to dictate aspects of childrearing, domestic timetables and parenting practices. However, parents still reserved a space around the boundary where they felt free to demand appropriate standards of care and concern for their child; for example, on issues of bullying or healthcare. Boundaries between families and school have often been identified as crucial elements in educational and related social policies. A combination of macro social trends and policy responses to perceived social problems in the last few years appears to have alerted the boundary conditions between state and family over schooling.

In all these chapters the changing nature of families, family life and policy context is considered. Families continue to offer the major location for nurturing, care and intimacy and yet, as data across all chapters illuminate, the relationships between families, organisations and institutions are always in a state of flux.

TWO

Balancing work and family life: mothers' views

Sarah Cunningham-Burley, Kathryn Backett-Milburn and Debbie Kemmer

Introduction

This chapter explores the range of negotiations and tensions that mothers in paid work outside the home report as characterising their lives. Drawing on interview data with 30 lone and partnered mothers in non-professional, non-managerial occupations, the notion of boundary is explored as an analytical device to conceptualise the tensions, both ideological and practical, that these women report as experiencing. The chapter explores how the respondents seemed to construct boundaries between work and home, while recognising and dealing with their permeable and flexible features. The chapter examines how boundaries between family and work are constructed through the type of paid work undertaken as well as through the value attached to paid work in terms of identity as both woman and mother. It then goes on to consider how these boundaries are permeated and breached as work life spills into home life and home life spills into work life (Daly, 2000). Although the construction of boundaries implies the separation of distinct spheres of experience, thus serving as a way of balancing work and family life, in practice, the meanings and daily reality of both are played out in relation to each other. Temporal and spatial boundaries are therefore continuously challenged, requiring negotiation of both practical management strategies as well as the development of discourses that can transcend time and space.

In the UK there are increasing numbers of mothers in the labour market (65% of women with dependent children in 2001 [Labour Market Trends, 2000]), many of whom work part time (Dex, 2003). The UK government is also emphasising paid work as a route out of poverty and as part of active citizenship, especially for lone parents, the vast majority of whom are mothers (Millar, 2000). Paid work is highly valued by government and a range of policies is in place to promote and support work for those outside the labour market, including those currently caring for children. Tax credits have been introduced to help make work 'pay' and the extension of nursery education and a range of childcare options have been initiated to help work to 'work' for families. The potential for conflicting demands on parents' time and energy can be recognised as an issue in the policy context, with work–life balance a key concern in several documents, legislation and policies (Dex, 1999, 2003). Negotiation and balance must be achieved between work, home, caring, family and other activities and responsibilities, and responsibility for this balance is seen to lie with governments and employers as well as with families themselves. However, although there is rhetoric of equality in policy and legislation, gendered assumptions and traditional divisions of labour remain present (McKie et al, 2001), making the exploration and understanding of women's experiences a particularly relevant area of research. These conflicting ideologies of work and home are played out in the accounts that mothers give of their experiences of earning and caring.

It has long been noted that the study of work and the family, often treated as separate spheres, need to be examined together (Kanter, 1977; Pleck, 1977; Rapoport and Rapoport, 1978; Beaujot, 2000). More recently, sociologists have begun to develop conceptual tools for examining the specific ways in which the experiences of home and work are interwoven in everyday life. Hochschild's work on the double shift provides a clear exposition of the time squeeze affecting so many families (1997) and Daly has provided work on the conceptual use of time as a way of understanding work–life balance (1996, 2000). Managing time, then, is one way in which parents may deal with the work/family interface; spatial boundaries are also important both within the home and between home and work (England, 1996).

Armstrong and Armstrong (1990) note that an adequate explanation of women's work must connect the labour processes in domestic and wage labour. Motherhood itself also needs to be understood as now operating at the interface of domestic and wage labour (Brannen and Moss, 1990). Duffy et al (1989) also observe that women's decisions about paid work and family are intermingled and that they reflect the interpenetration of domestic and wage labour. Uttal (1996) notes how women's understandings of their situation not only resolve the work and family conflicts but also transform our ideological assumptions about what mothering is supposed to be. Daly suggests that those who have little control over their time at work are more likely to have "very strong boundaries between work time and family time", whereas those of higher rank are likely to have blurred boundaries (1996, p 128). As this chapter explores, for some respondents, the decision to choose work that is more likely to be low paid (and therefore for time at work less flexible in itself), actually enables a strong boundary between home and work. While traditional roles may be lessening across all social classes, the experience of managing work and family life is likely to vary by socio-cultural circumstances, for example by whether one's work is well paid and whether it is spatially segregated from home. Moreover, while studies of work and family life must, as noted above, connect domestic and wage labour, maintaining different roles and identities between the two may be important for women, as Christine, a lone parent from the study reported here said: "I'm not a mother in work, I'm an individual if you like".

However, it may be possible to extend such analyses to consider other ways in which parents, or in the case of the current focus, mothers, may negotiate the work–family balance. Descriptions of the practices of everyday life alongside the moral accounts that mothers provide show how boundaries between the private and public spheres of home and paid work are constructed, permeated and breached.

Concepts of boundary and the process of boundary construction and maintenance may be useful ways of exploring the interface between home and family without reifying the separation of the two spheres, which are, of course, deeply intertwined. Boundaries between the two spheres are maintained at the same time as they are crossed, by bridges or breaches. Temporal and spatial dimensions can be incorporated into the analytical frame, thus extending the conceptual work that has been so influential in family studies in recent years, both in terms of the work/home interface as well as in research and theorising on care and caring as noted earlier.

The study

The analysis developed here is based on interview data generated from a study 'Caring and providing: the experiences of lone and partnered working mothers in Scotland' (Backett-Milburn et al, 2001).[1] The study aimed to investigate mothers' experiences of their domestic lives and paid work and to examine the day-to-day challenges and practical decision making involved in combining parenting and paid work. This involved exploring the social contexts and cultural values around parenting and paid employment and investigating the experiences of lone and partnered mothers as they combined the parenting of primary school-aged children with paid work outside the home. The study involved two in-depth interviews, approximately six months apart, with 15 lone and 15 partnered women each with at least one child at primary school (and no children of preschool or secondary school age).

The study adopted a range of recruitment methods to encourage participation from women in diverse circumstances with different work, family contexts and childcare arrangements. All the women, and their partners as appropriate, were in non-professional and non-managerial occupations: most were in low income households. In total, 58 interviews were conducted (two women were lost to follow up). The first interviews explored the women's experiences and perceptions of work, family and domestic life, childrearing and their own feelings about these areas; the second interviews identified and explored changes in work, domestic and childcare arrangements, health-related issues and views about government policy and its impact on them. Analysis was inductive, involving repeated interpretive readings of transcripts, analytical discussion within the research team and subsequent indexing within Nud*ist. Themes and codes were then examined in further depth and interaction between text segments and the whole transcript maintained for each focus of analytical writing. The respondents' accounts were reflective, providing insight not only into what they actually did, their 'family practices' (Morgan, 1996), but also the explanations they gave for their behaviours and views.

Respondents were aged 24-44 years (median 33.5 years); the children were aged 4-12 years. Half the women were in secretarial or administrative occupations, the remainder were cleaners, shop, bar or catering assistants, care workers or workers in call centres. Most worked more than 20 hours per week and many worked evening and weekend shifts. Although the study involved both lone and partnered mothers, similarity of experience in both the daily negotiation of caring and providing and underlying values was the overriding feature of the interview accounts. The main differences between lone and partnered women can be summarised as follows: lone mothers could not rely on a partner or ex-partner for childcare cover when they were at work and the children were not at school, so often had more fragile arrangements; however, all of the partnered mothers also had other childcare arrangements. Lone mothers were also acutely aware of a stigma attached to lone parenthood and thus were particularly strong in their assertions about the value of work. In this way, they seemed to be distancing themselves from 'other' lone parents 'on welfare benefits'. Lone mothers were more likely to be working fewer hours and were, on the whole, on lower incomes than women in partnerships, whose household income included that of their partners (Kemmer et al, 2001).

All the women in the study seemed to adopt a strong work ethic (they were, of course, all in paid work themselves). They considered that they were in paid jobs 'for themselves' and, as the analysis that follows will go on to show, also 'for their children'. Respondents also seemed to be grappling with a 'new motherhood' that retained traditional values associated with care for and socialisation of children, while embracing newer values associated with paid work, forming an independent and individual identity. All mothers were experiencing and reporting on the tensions that conflicting values and demands meant for them and their family life, in particular the challenges of managing work and home. As Tizard has noted, dominant ideologies at work are those of not allowing family commitments to impinge: "Cultural directives prescribe that women should become mothers and subsequently reduce their involvement in paid work or, more recently, that women can fulfil all the demands of full-time exclusive mothers and full-time paid work without modifying the demands of either" (1991, p 195). Practical and ideological negotiation of these tensions, we argue, can be understood through the use of the concept of a 'boundary' at a number of different conceptual levels.

Boundaries and balances

Analysis of respondents' accounts of their experiences of work and home suggested, in many ways, a clear demarcation between work and home. This did not seem to be just a feature of the interview setting or the difficulties of talking about interwoven experiences, but rather is suggestive of a particular practical and rhetorical strategy. Such a traditional distinction reinforced values that meant that self-esteem and status were derived from work (now for mothers as well as fathers), yet, at the same time, traditional motherhood, where family comes first, maintained its place. However, the boundaries created by the dominant discourse of separation (public/private, work/home) are simultaneously sustained and challenged in and by daily life. Effecting a separation between home and work was one strategy that respondents described in relation to balancing their caring and providing roles. Constructing such a boundary seemed to involve a range of practices and invoked diverse discourses about work, family and identity, as the respondents talked about balancing the two spheres.

The women in our study seemed to try to prevent work demands impinging on family and family impinging on work; ensuring that the former did not happen meant particular decisions about the nature of work done had to be made. Putting family first was frequently cast as an ideological priority. To prevent family impinging on work, a range of practices had to be developed, for as Tizard (1991) has explained, the dominant ideology at work means that family commitments should not impinge. Later in the chapter we explore the construction of a reliable worker. The respondents expressed a high value of being at work within a discourse of putting family first. Balancing the distinct, yet intertwined, spheres meant careful management of a separation between work and family, to enable reliable working and effective mothering. Any balance achieved was fragile and constantly threatened; the boundary is permeable and flexible. In examining these processes and features, we look first at how the women constructed boundaries between work and home and what decisions followed from such a strategy of boundary construction.

Constructing boundaries

One of the ways in which the women in this study constructed a distinct boundary between work and family was in the type of job they said they had chosen. As has been noted elsewhere (Desai and Waite, 1991), women sometimes choose occupations that are easier to combine with parenting. The women in our caring and providing study tried to circumscribe their work in terms of the type of work conducted and the hours that they worked, in order to create and maintain a boundary between home and work and not let work impinge on home life; the following quote was typical:

> *Doreen*: "The ideal? The ideal would be for me to have a part-time job, say mornings, so that I only had part-time childcare, I was here for children coming out of school and after school activities and things like that ... that would be the ideal." (partnered)

However, as this quotation suggests, many said that they could seldom achieve their ideal, so had to compromise and negotiate a less than ideal boundary. None of the respondents had work that fitted neatly into school hours.

For many, especially for the lone parents, seeking part-time work was a way of maintaining a boundary between work and family, allowing time for both and ensuring one did not impinge on the other. While this seldom meant the ideal hours of 9am to 3pm during school term-time only, part-time work was described as being less demanding, not only in terms of time but also emotional energy, leaving respondents with more time and emotional space to deal with family life before and after work. However, this positioning of oneself in the labour market as a part-time (and often therefore a low paid) worker was very much seen as a compromise as many respondents also described losing out on work-related benefits, not being able to find suitable hours and working at a lower level than they had in the past or felt capable of doing now. Opting for part-time work also reinforced the mothers' felt responsibility for family and home, where boundary maintenance seemed to be of prime importance and one's needs as a paid worker given secondary importance, as the following respondent explained:

> *Susan*: "I, sometimes, I feel resentful because I feel that I could have a better job than I have, you know, when – when I worked for [big company] before my son was born I had a, a quite a high-powered secretarial job. I had people under me and I earned a lot more than I do now. And sometimes I resent the fact that I'm back, I cannae get back to that level without having to work full time. You know?" (partnered)

Taking part-time, less demanding work was a strategy for maintaining a boundary between home and work, but it did not guarantee such a separation. Respondents also talked about their strategies for keeping the two worlds apart, sustaining the boundary, so that if it did have to be breached, this would not bring down the whole edifice. The respondents knew that family life could always 'leak' into work in ways over which they did not always have control. This knowledge required daily management of work and home in order to shore up the boundary, making it able to withstand being broken from time to time. For these mothers this meant constructing themselves as extra reliable workers who could be seen to be managing the work/family interface well, particularly in not allowing family and domestic commitments to interfere with work, as is illustrated here:

> *Janet*: "I've been more reliable to my employer because I've been more determined to make it in there, hail, rain or shine sort of thing, you know, 'cause I would never have anybody casting it up, to say to me, 'Oh, your kids are always, you know, you're always not at work because your kids are not well'." (partnered)

Boundary maintenance was an ongoing process, imbued with moral imperatives. Managing well meant separating the spheres of home and work, making them seem as if they were not intertwined while acknowledging by daily practices that they were irrevocably so.

The interviews also showed how children were involved in the process of demonstrating extra reliability and therefore in boundary maintenance. The mothers described encouraging their children to carry on and go into school if mildly unwell, which also enabled the work/family boundary not to be breached. The following extract shows how one respondent explained this to her children:

> *Jane*: "Yeah, yeah, 'cause I mean, you know, I say, 'When you go to work, you stay off work, you lose money. You know, you stay off school, you lose anything, you know, you lose your learning. You must go'. So I mean they do go. They obviously enjoy school because they don't sort of play on it if, you know, they just go off, off they go. Toddle off." (partnered)

In addition to decisions about the kind of jobs they took on and the construction of reliability, the mothers in this study also seemed to be constructing a boundary between work and family by separating roles and identities, although a new identity of 'working mother' perhaps helped to build a bridge across the two worlds. Work was constructed as good for oneself in the moral accounting of everyday life as a working mother. That a work identity was something separate from family seemed to be highly valued in its own right, as the following typical extract shows:

> *DK*: "What are the best things about being a working mum?"
> *Jean*: "The money, the talking to adults bit, that's good, that's nice. Getting out, having a bit of a social life." (partnered)

So, having a life apart from home, even if limited by choice of employment, was highly valued as providing an identity beyond the family. However, pushing that identity too far would perhaps compromise their other identity as a mother and carer, able to manage the sphere of home well. Interestingly, the interviews suggested that respondents were aware of that possible interpretation and they seemed actively to build a feedback loop between their needs to be in work, to have a 'worker identity', and their family life. A bridge between the two was constructed by respondents maintaining that a working mother was considered to be a better mother, thus bringing into the sphere of home the benefits, but not the disadvantages, of work. Again, children were brought into the frame: work was also constructed as something good for children, suggesting that there was an interplay between family and work, which meant that the latter was beneficial to the former. A similar argument was also constructed by some respondents that formal childcare, itself often necessitated by work, was also good for children. Being children of working mothers meant that the children learnt to socialise, play with others and learnt the value of work, as the following respondents explained:

> *Louise*: "I like to get out and sometimes, even, I know people think that's daft and like, but, that's my time away from Heather. It's like I'm doing something different. And I, and then I come home in a better mood for Heather 'cause being away and I – I've got out and I've done, like okay it's only behind a bar doing, but it's – it's different. You know, it's different scenery for me." (lone)

Kim refers here to the benefits she feels that an after school club provides for her daughter:

> *Kim*: "Karen is an only child and none of my sisters have children, do you know, therefore it's, like, she's at the Club and she's mixing with kids of her age. 'Cause, I mean, when she's outside the Club, I mean, it's mostly adults anyway, therefore I think that's like, em, a really important factor." (partnered)

The ways in which the mothers in this study talked about and managed work and home, suggest that they tried to maintain a separation between the two spheres so that they did not impinge on one another in negative ways. However, it is also clear that the boundaries were not fixed and solid, but permeable, meaning that there could be both positive and negative 'traffic' between the two spheres.

Permeable boundaries

As noted earlier in this chapter, much research suggests the intertwining of the spheres of home and work. Therefore, the boundaries that the women in the caring and providing study seemed to construct so carefully could only work if they could withstand possible breaches but also bend to meet the everyday contingencies of family and work life. Such boundary work, as a practice, tells us something about how mothers deal with work–family balance. Analysis reveals underlying values in how respondents' account for their behaviour and decisions. It also suggests what is within their control and what is not. Boundaries, it seems, can only work as discursive and practical devices if they can be both flexible and permeable. No matter how much a mother in paid work outside the home might wish to prevent work intruding on family or family on work, this will happen at some time, no matter how carefully she has tried to separate the two through careful boundary construction and maintenance. Flexibility may be necessary within each sphere in order to maintain a separation and permeability may help maintain some sense of a boundary despite transgression.

Boundaries can be transgressed or threatened by a range of factors – work demands, childcare changes, changing children's preferences. The two spheres of work and family are not static but themselves change, requiring flexible boundary work before they can be reinstated and stasis recovered.

As noted in the previous section, a clear boundary between work and home based around temporal separation through suitable work hours was an ideal, but this was seldom realised. All the respondents could maintain some sort of spatial separation as their paid work took them outside the home, although as we examine later, this too could be breached. The boundary between work and home could be threatened by work-related demands, particularly if these involved 'taking work home', either literally or metaphorically, or, as the following quote illustrates, by a request to extend working hours. The respondent had sought to maintain a balance between work and home by 'keeping Fridays free' to spend time at home and with her daughter after school (which finished early on Fridays). However, she found that this strategy was being jeopardised by work demands:

> *Helen*: "I am still trying to keep Fridays free as much as I can, I can protect Fridays. But recently there's been quite a lot of pressure on me to work Friday mornings. So at the moment I'm kind of pushing back. But I've ended up having to work a few Friday mornings recently … I'm not happy with that." (partnered)

By the second interview a few respondents had changed their work situations because of these kinds of breach of established boundaries. One woman, for example, stopped work, as she said that her work-related stress was impinging on her family life. However, for most, carrying on despite such challenges to carefully established boundaries was the only option because they could not or did not wish to stop paid work.

The need to preserve particular times for children seemed to be particularly important, especially 'being there' after school. The following quotations show that, if work prevented this, the mothers felt particularly bad or guilty:

> *Jean*: "The worst thing's having to leave your children. I feel bad working in the evenings, having to leave them when the evenings is the kind of busiest time really." (partnered)

She went on to say:

> *Jean*: "I hope they [the children] understand that I'm doing it for their benefit.…
>
> I have tried to get something else during the day while they're at school. Nothing's come through with that yet, eh, and sort of give up working in the evenings."

The boundaries are also crossed when work creeps into home life in less obvious ways, through stress or bad temper, meaning that the quality of time left for children is jeopardised:

> *Jackie*: "I prefer my family life to my work life, my family life puts no pressure on my work life, but my work life puts

> pressure on my family life … I can get so unreasonable you know, and especially if I don't have a good day at work you know, I bring it home, you know, I find it difficult to leave." (partnered)

Maintaining a boundary between work and home is also dependent on solid childcare arrangements, which again was something few respondents said that they could achieve easily and reliably. Most relied on a combination of formal and informal childcare and valued different aspects of both. However, working hours were such that formal childcare was not always available and, of course, it was not always affordable. Informal arrangements were often described as fragile and could break down, causing problems with work time, as the following respondent describes:

> *Lucy*: "I've got myself a bit of a scenario going on at the moment that I'm kind of getting myself ill about a Saturday now. I'm starting to think about looking for another job and whatnot and on a Saturday when Sheena has him, she usually takes her mother.... And her mother and I really don't get on and we had a bit of a run in a couple of weeks about and I'm now in the, I'm not at the stage where I would rather she wasnae anywhere near him. So it's causing me grief every time I've got to go away and leave him with her, 'cause I know that he's going to be in their company and I'm just not happy." (lone)

The mothers in this study also talked about children's needs and preferences in relation to childcare as also changing, so an arrangement that had worked well hitherto might need to be changed, causing stress to the boundary between work and home life and another round of negotiations as new arrangements were put in place. School time often does not mesh well with work time and school holidays certainly do not. In these respects the need for greater flexibility with the boundary between work and home was not always achieved, as was shown in many interviews, including the following:

> *Sheila*: "Well, there's the Easter holidays coming up and the childcare centre, I've no' got worked out what I need him in. Like if I was putting him in all day every day I

> mean it wouldnae be worth my while working. While he's at school it's fine, because it's only before and after school, but em, my neighbour says she would take him for a couple of days during the holidays and my sister-in-law says she would take him. So I maybe put him in for a couple of days which suits me." (lone)

Respondents also described strategies for dealing with the spillover, or the breaching of boundaries, both in practical ways and in terms of how they accounted for or talked about their actions. Although the mothers wanted to construct a secure boundary between work and home as far as their employer was concerned, it seemed that informal relations within the workplace could allow a more permeable interface. Here, workmates could support each other if time off work was needed because of family matters. Outside work, having flexible informal childcare arrangements might sometimes help deal with contingencies, but few had reliable resources and most felt that they should be there, themselves, for children if they were sick (Cunningham-Burley et al, forthcoming) or in other ways needing specific attention, for example for a school meeting.

At a different level, many respondents described a breaching of the boundaries of the temporal and spatial separation of home and work, roles of mother and worker, in terms of 'being there' for their children even while not being there, so that they could maintain a sense of always putting their family first, even while at work. The practical outcome of such discursive strategies was to put something extra into time at home or with one's children, in a sense shoring up the 'home' sphere just as the preceding discussion suggested a shoring up of the 'work' sphere. Kathleen describes 'making up for lost time' by providing extras when she is physically present:

> *Kathleen*: "He's not deprived of anything. I mean, if I've got extra money and I feel I haven't seen him a lot then I try to treat him to the pictures or something, you know, just to say, well, I know I've been working a lot but I will treat you, ken, just so that we can, like spend time together or something ... I do try to treat him when I've got the money." (lone)

Although some breaches in boundaries could be managed or remedied, both in a practical and ideological sense, others had much greater effect and upset the precarious balance between home and work. The strategy of separating the two spheres could be seriously undermined by major changes at work, stress on self or family or child sickness (Cunningham-Burley et al, forthcoming).

Conclusion

Researchers working in the area of work–life balance remind us that the two spheres are interrelated and have helped develop conceptual tools for understanding that interrelatedness. This has helped fields traditionally separated into those interested in work and those interested in families, to move towards a more integrated appreciation of their connectedness. However, the research reported in this chapter suggests that maintaining a symbolic and practical distinction between work and family serves important purposes for mothers combining work and family. Constructing a boundary between work and home seems to help preserve the integrity of both spheres and a mother's role and identity within them. It enables the responsibilities of both to be met and seems to prevent one impinging on another. It seems to be one way of managing the inherent and inevitable tensions of a work–family balance.

However, the breaching of boundaries was also considered inevitable, suggesting that the boundary between work and family was neither strong nor fixed. This was managed in both practical and ideological ways. The permeable nature of the boundary between work and home was not always considered to be negative, as paid work for a mother was also viewed as something good for her children. But frequently, the breaching of the boundary was more problematic, requiring changes in childcare arrangements, working hours or, indeed, work itself. While the permeation of boundaries seemed to be inevitable and contingent, flexible boundaries were harder to construct, other than through informal support mechanisms inside and outside work. Working hours and school hours seldom coincide and, even with the best of efforts, work life and home life are always likely to impinge on each other.

The potential for or, indeed, the actual deconstruction of carefully maintained boundaries brought into sharp focus a hierarchy between the two spheres. As Tizard (1991) has noted, the good mother role never allows paid work to take precendence over mothering. Putting family first, despite clear boundaries separating the two spheres, was the 'bottom line', put to the test when the two spheres of work and home impinged unmanageably on one another, such as when a child's needs required immediate, maternal attention during work time. The needs of the workplace also asserted themselves through boundary breaches, such as in the demand to work extra hours or to be extra reliable, holding to ransom the 'bottom line' so carefully cherished and maintained through boundary building.

Note

[1] The study was funded by the Joseph Rowntree Foundation 1998-2000 under the Work and Family Life Programme.

References

Armstrong, P. and Armstrong, H. (1990) *Theorizing women's work*, Toronto: Garamond Press.

Backett-Milburn, K., Cunningham-Burley, S. and Kemmer, D. (2001) *Caring and providing: Lone and partnered working mothers in Scotland*, London: Joseph Rowntree Foundation/Family Policy Studies Centre.

Beaujot, R. (2000) *Earning and caring in Canadian families*, Ontario: Broadview Press.

Brannen, J. and Moss, P. (1990) *Managing mothers: Dual earner households after maternity leave*, London: Unwin Hyman.

Cunningham-Burley, S., Backett-Milburn, K. and Kemmer, D. (forthcoming) 'Constructing health and sickness in the context of motherhood and paid work, *Sociology of Health and Illness.*

Daly, K. (1996) *Families and Time: Keeping pace in a hurried culture*, Thousand Oaks, CA: Sage Publications.

Daly, K. (2000) *Keeps getting faster: Changing patterns of time in families*, Ottawa: The Vanier Institute of the Family.

Desai, S. and Waite, L.J. (1991) 'Women's employment during pregnancies and after the first birth: occupational characteristics and work commitment', *American Sociological Review*, vol 56, pp 551-66.

Dex, S. (ed) (1999) *Families and the labour market: Trends, pressure and policies*, London, York: Family Policy Studies Centre/Joseph Rowntree Foundation.

Dex, S. (2003) *Families and work in the twenty-first century*, Bristol, York: The Policy Press/Joseph Rowntree Foundation.

Duffy, A., Mandell, N. and Pupo, N. (1989) *Few choices: Women, work and family*, Toronto: Garamond Press.

England, K. (ed) (1996) *Who will mind the baby? Geographies of child care and working mothers*, London: Routledge.

Hochschild, A.R. (1997) *The time-bind: When work becomes home and home becomes work*, New York, NY: Metropolitan Books, Henry Hold and Co Ltd.

Kanter, R.M. (1977) *Work and family in the United States: A critical review and agenda for research and policy*, New York, NY: Russell Sage Foundation.

Kemmer, D., Cunningham-Burley, S. and Backett-Milburn, K. (2001) 'How does working work for lone mothers on low incomes?', *Benefits, A Journal of Social Security Research, Policy and Practice*, vol 32, pp 10-14.

Labour Market Trends (2000) London: The Stationery Office.

McKie, L., Bowlby, S. and Gregory, S. (2001) 'Gender, caring and employment in Britain', *Journal of Social Policy*, vol 30, no 2, pp 233-58.

Millar, J. (2000) *Keeping track of welfare reform: The New Deal programmes*, York: Joseph Rowntree Foundation.

Morgan, D. (1996) *Family connections: An introduction to family studies*, Cambridge: Polity Press.

Pleck, J.H. (1977) 'The work-family role system', *Social Problems*, vol 24, pp 417-27.

Rapoport, R. and Rapoport, R. (eds) (1978) *Working couples*, London: Routledge and Kegan Paul.

Tizard, B. (1991) 'Employed mothers and the care of young children', in A. Phoenix, E. Woollett and E. Lloyd (eds) *Motherhood: Meanings, practices and ideologies*, London: Sage Publications.

Uttal, L. (1996) 'Custodial care, surrogate care and coordinated care: employed mothers and the meaning of child care', *Gender and Society*, vol 10, no 3, pp 291-311.

THREE

Gender, care, poverty and transitions

Gill Scott and Sue Innes

Introduction

Encouraging and supporting mothers to cross the boundary between family and work to become workers is increasingly seen as a way to reduce poverty and address gender inequality (Folbre, 1994; Lister, 1999). In this chapter we explore the issues currently facing parents in low income households in the UK, where the state plays a significant role in the resources that parents have for managing the transitions between the worlds of work and family (Sainsbury, 1994; Gardiner, 1997; Bang et al, 2000; Scott and McKay, 2001; Williams, 2001; McKie et al, 2002). In doing so we draw upon data from a case study on gender, care, poverty and transitions conducted in a community-based lifelong learning centre and a project that is largely resourced by the European Social Fund (Innes and Scott, 2002). We draw upon the notion of boundary maintenance and management so as to highlight the need to conceptualise care as involving the act of provisioning for care as well as its delivery. We also examine how these are negotiated by those most affected by state intervention. The range of active labour market policies currently being used in the UK as a way of reducing poverty is based on a limited view of a transition across home and work boundaries, that is, from 'mother' to 'worker/breadwinner'. It is a view that oversimplifies the boundaries that have to be negotiated. Thus we explore the transitions that low income mothers manage, and examine evidence of active negotiation of caring roles. In doing so we explore the issues of demarcation and boundaries – of the limits in familial relationships, the goals that individuals are prepared to accept and the material limits on change.

Care: the changing policy context

Care, when considered at both the micro and macro levels of economic and social organisation, and at the boundaries between them, is a highly controversial topic. Its conceptualisation is historic, subject to norms and culture, places and time. Mary Daly (2001, p 36) comments that "care began life as a woman specific concept" but that the "relationship between public policy on care and the wider societal settlements around family and 'private' relations remains unexplored". Commenting on the welfare and care implications of the move from unpaid care work to paid work involves exploring the whole range of changed relationships and associated costs and benefits (Brannen and Moss, 2003). Care roles and associated relationships are not set, but subject to time, place and cultural contexts (Folbre and Nelson, 2000; McKie et al, 2004). Research has identified a wide variety of personal and domestic resources used and exchanged in order to support or extend levels of resources for care among low income households (Kempson et al, 1994; Morris and Ritchie, 1994; Ritchie et al, 1998; McKay and Scott, 1999).

Nevertheless little has been done to identify the shift in caring patterns consequent on a move into the paid labour market. By caring patterns we mean not only direct care but also the planning and management of care – what a number of writers have called 'provisioning functions within the family'. These include the transfer of skills and knowledge, negotiating care with other professionals and providing an environment where safety and emotional needs are met (McKay, 2001). The research reported here highlights that when such activities are considered in more detail it becomes clearer that complex and time-consuming activities supporting family members make up a significant part of domestic life and do not disappear when mothers enter employment and use formal childcare.

Motherhood is no longer seen as a lifetime status of choice that precludes active and long-term involvement in the labour market (Hantrais, 1996; Gardiner, 1997). The UK now has something closer to a childcare policy that addresses the needs of children, mothers and the economy – what Daly calls a 'coherent care policy' and which is evident in other European states. However, this is not at the level of public provision for working mothers long enjoyed by countries such as France and Sweden (Daly, 2001, p 38). Early education has become a universal service for children over three but it remains part time and purely child focused.

When it comes to childcare, rather than education, resources have not been directed to developing universal services for children and working mothers but on developing targeted services for the poor. Easing the work–family balance for all has been taken up at national level in the UK, by the Department for Work and Pensions, as well as through new legislation and policies on parental leave, but childcare policy is generally more focused. Ending family poverty has become by far the main aim of family policies of government at UK, regional and devolved levels (Wasoff and Dey, 2000; Brever et al, 2003; Scottish Executive, 2003; SEU, 2004; Williams, 2004; Scott et al, 2005). The idea that paid work is the only permanent way out of poverty for families is now a powerful logic driving family policies. At national level these include policies such as the New Deals for Lone Parents and Partners of the Unemployed, new tax credits, minimum wage legislation as well as large elements of the National Childcare Strategy.

There can be little doubt that the strategy has had some positive effects. However, it should be remembered that labour market entry may not be positive for every family. Bennett (2002) argues that there are tensions between the trend towards 'individualisation' inherent in tax credits and the growing emphasis on the couple/household as a policy focus. Policies are aimed at reducing the number of workless households rather than expanding individuals' opportunities; and while, for example, joint claims for jobseeker's allowance and work-focused interviews involve increased responsibilities for partners, there is no right of access to individual income.

The potential contradiction between encouraging parents, particularly lone parents, into the workforce and emphasising parenting responsibilities continues to be largely fudged (Hogarth et al, 2001). To some extent this is because the role of citizen as worker rather than citizen as carer drives the thinking of welfare reform and the value of caring work done by parents is simply not recognised. The National Childcare Strategy is seen as facilitating the access of mothers to paid employment, but the continuing need for informal care and the resources involved in provisioning for care within the family is less recognised. This is worrying when access to formal care remains restricted but also when knowledge about the meaning and nature of care during times of change in low income households is limited.

Gender, care and transitions: a case study

The focus on care in low income households in this chapter occurs for a particular reason. Choice is far more constrained by the state in such families and has long been so. Current changes in the UK system of benefits, tax credits and childcare, moreover, suggest that women in low income households, particularly lone parents, are firmly located at the fissure of change in class, gender and state boundaries. They are not an inconsiderable group. Between 1979 and 1997 the number of children living in households in the UK with incomes below 60% of the median increased from 1 in 10 to 1 in 3, in marked contrast to countries like Denmark, Norway and Finland where child poverty showed a marked decrease (UNICEF, 2000; Bradbury and Jantti, 2001; Bradshaw, 2001; Kenway et al, 2002). At the same time the proportion of lone parents in the UK living in households below half average income increased from 19% in 1979 to 63% in 2001 (Brown et al, 2002). Policies since 1997 have focused on reducing this child poverty, with some very positive results (Duncan, 2004; Palmer et al, 2004). However, there is growing concern that the needs of families who find it most difficult to use work as a route out of poverty have scarcely been addressed (Adelman et al, 2003).

The importance of understanding how established patterns of care can affect the transition to work or education of family members and how worries about the resourcing of new patterns of care can affect change is highlighted by studies that suggest that work does not automatically pay, particularly in areas of deprivation and particularly when there are children to be cared for (Jenkins and Rigg, 2001; Kemp, 2002; McKendrick et al, 2003). Studies of poverty dynamics have found that changing the source of income to work or a student loan may not produce greater stability and adequacy of income (Kempson et al, 1994; Jenkins and Rigg 2001; Scott et al, 2003). Recent changes to financial support and in-work benefits delivered through a new tax regime mean that the financial decisions necessary to make the transition from welfare benefits to education and employment are becoming ever more complex, but we know little about how they are experienced by households making the move or how community-based, individually focused services can support individuals crossing the boundaries between family, employment and education.

Locality is important. There is often, but by no means always, a spatial dimension to the poverty experienced by low income households. In Scotland, for example, areas within Glasgow are ranked among the poorest in the UK: 22 out of the 25 most deprived postcode areas of Scotland are in Glasgow (Brown et al, 2002). Further, Duncan and Smith (2002) comment that there are marked regional and local variations in patterns of parenting. They argue that these patterns emerge, in part, from the specific nature of local cultural, economic and social contexts. Locally dominant ideas are built up and reinforced by social networks and everyday interactions. A significant element that they do not consider, however, is the effect of anti-poverty and urban regeneration policy on families in low income areas. Local or community intermediaries are often used to encourage women with dependent children to move into paid employment or local training. Often funded by urban regeneration funding or the European Social Fund, they represent interventions that lie at the interface of community ideas and wider national or European policy. The role of community-based interventions and of informal and family care may be highly significant in poor communities, where women commonly have multiple caring roles and sustain important family and social relationships.

The research reported in this chapter is drawn from a small-scale, multi-method case study involving women from low income households actively engaged with a community-based lifelong learning centre. The centre is based in an area of regeneration and provides a community-based programme of vocational training, family support and childcare. Here we examine the care that the women involved in the study saw themselves as providing and the shift they report in their views of caring as they negotiated new boundaries between family, work and education. In particular, we report on the changes that occurred as they took up educational and employment opportunities that they were offered as part of the community-based 'transition to employment' programme.

The centre caters predominantly for women and members of minority ethnic groups, offering vocational training with associated early years and after-school care. It is funded by the European Social Fund as a demonstration project with a remit to reduce poverty by increasing life chances through lifelong learning and helping women from low income households attain adequately paid, sustainable employment. The area that the centre serves has high and persistent levels of multiple deprivation and one of the highest rates of unemployment in the country.

The study comprised: 'care diaries' that the women filled in for three weeks, on their daily activities and those of their youngest child; two focus groups with the women, the first at the beginning of the study to draw up a 'care index' and the second at the conclusion of the data gathering focusing on issues at transition; a semi-structured interview with each woman of approximately one hour, including biographical inquiry; short follow-up interviews six months later to find out about changes and outcomes since the end of the course. This intensive methodology generated very rich data and enabled specific themes to be returned to and enlarged on (Elliott, 1991; Ribbens and Edwards, 1998; Innes and Scott, 2002). Because of that, and the personal development work as part of the courses at the centre encourages reflection on aims and possibilities, the interviewees' thoughtfulness about the issues raised and willingness to explore them meant that considerable depth and detail was possible for such a short study.

The women who took part can be described as a purposive sample: people whose experience was located at a significant juncture of policy development and of social change. The major transitions being negotiated by the participants was a potential move from the arena of the home, where the main financial resources were income support, to that of the world of employment supported by in-work benefits. Their involvement in the one-year course at the centre was seen by all as part of this transition.

Caring

The initial focus groups discussed the meaning of care and drew up a 'care index' of tasks and aspects. The classic analysis of the time costs of care by Piachaud (1984) makes a division between basic tasks/life-support activities, subdivided into activities directly involving the child and servicing activities that can be done without the child (mainly housework and shopping); educational and entertaining tasks; and indirect supervisory/on-call responsibilities. All of Piachaud's categories were included by the group but other aspects were added. These were 'emotional work' (the consideration of feelings of children and other family members); moral/behavioural guidance (understood separately from education and as a particularly family responsibility); overall organising and planning. This was characterised in discussion by the phrase 'making sure that …'. The concept of provisioning is discussed later and acknowledges that all of the types of tasks listed by Piachaud require a dimension of managing or 'scripting' that is of considerable, and sometimes onerous, importance in the daily experience of care-giving. This emphasis may arise particularly when care is managed alongside other activities of training and employment. It is an aspect of caregiving that has proved harder to describe or measure than are the tasks of cooking, washing clothes or reading stories, but that women in all circumstances commonly name as a major aspect of their unpaid work in families.

The variety of aspects of care raised in the study emphasises that care is not simple, is not easily defined and is not static. Caring for children was seen as taking time, thought and understanding, as well as involving a strong will and willingness to put your own feelings aside. Hilary Graham defines care as "an unspecific and unspecifiable kind of labour, the contours of which constantly shift" (1993, p 79). This study suggests that care diaries and focus group discussion supplemented by individual interviews can do much to specify the work of care in a useful way, but confirms the changing contours over time and according to circumstance. In particular, it highlights that expectations of mothers and the care needed by children depend on the changing needs of children and aspirations of mothers.

A number of specific aspects of caring for children were discussed: the invisibility of care, time and location and provisioning for care.

A sense of the *invisibility of care*, even to those who do it, was a common response to filling in the diaries, a process that made participants realise how much they did that usually they did not even notice:

> "I would sort of think, you know, when I was writing things down, oh God, I didn't realise that I done so much, you know, in a day. It was trying to fit everything in ... just sort of makes you look a lot differently at your life, I mean because when you're just going from day to day, you just take it for granted, you know, you do one day and the next day and you don't really think about it."

Time and location issues in relation to care and to combining care with other activities were also very important and raised in a number of ways. Time was presented as a pressure, with life as a daily race to make everything fit together. It was also a resource to be managed through routine and structure, with some self-criticism for not managing time better commonly voiced. The importance of routine, in general and as a coping strategy, and problems that occur when routines are disrupted, was raised by several women. Also at issue was that the need for routine in order to manage employment plus care could make life dull and unvarying.

Elson's definition of care as *provisioning* resonated with many of the women's accounts. "'Provisioning' is the activity of supplying people with what they need to thrive, including care and concern as well as material goods. At the heart of provisioning is looking ahead and making preparations" (Elson, 1998, p 207). It is about, as one of the women put it, 'thinking forward':

> "I think – in the morning, soon as the children have finished their breakfast and the plates are in the sink, that's history, you need to start thinking forward. As soon as the dishes have hit the sink, that's it, you need to start thinking right, dinnertime, what are we gonna make for their dinner the night? You're always thinking forward."

The organising role of women in families included managing time, locations, transport, food, other caregivers and adults in need of care as well as managing the different needs of older less dependent children. Women commented on how important it was to be well organised but how difficult that was with young children around and that arrangements were routinely disrupted by 'common emergencies' such as childhood illnesses and school closures or when informal caregivers changed their plans.

Some participants said they were not good at planning and spent little time in 'looking ahead and making preparations', which implies a conscious organisational focus. Even so, it was usually apparent that their lives were increasingly organised around provisioning activities as they crossed the boundaries between work, training and family.

Crossing the boundary

A key question for the women in this study was how they managed the transition across the boundaries of home and work and whether the transition disturbed existing boundaries. All the women saw boundary crossing as normal, they took for granted that they would return to paid work, although two of the women decided, following the course and a problematic move to full-time further education, to postpone doing so until their children were older (for further discussion see Innes and Scott, 2002; Scott et al, 2003). Although they were critical of government benefit policies and of pressures on lone mothers to return to paid work, the aims of most of the women were congruent with policies to encourage mothers in low income families to take up employment. Participants hoped both to better their family's material circumstances and, if also possible, to continue their own educational progress. Returning to paid work was financially necessary for both lone and partnered participants, although those on benefit worried about being caught in the 'poverty trap'.

Negotiating change and boundary limits

Participants' understanding of motherhood as requiring of them both paid work and care reinforces the findings of the previous chapter, namely that for low and medium income women in employment both paid work and parenting are important and the dilemma that mothers face is how to manage that, rather than whether or not to work outside the home at all (Backett-Milburn et al, 2001). In our study, returning to education and the labour market did not represent any lack of value accorded to caring for their children; rather, there were benefits for the children and the family as well as for the woman herself, although these could be outweighed by long hours and stress. Women were seen as having multiple roles with caring for children having an impact on most of them. Childcare, moreover, was not presented as a problem so much as a value and a fact of life.

Problems in moving between and negotiating boundaries occurred, not because the women resisted change but for two reasons. First, because they sought to manage changes so that there were no detrimental consequences for their children and, second, because the external resources that could assist the transition were not easily available. Asked what she wanted to do, one woman (two of whose children have special needs) described what would be ideal but she knew was unrealistic:

> "To be able to get a job and a job that isn't gonna give any [pause] added pressure.... A job that could be flexible. A job that would be quite understanding because you have to have quite a lot of appointments. But there aren't many jobs like that out there."

Historically, paid work and care have been positioned dichotomously and that opposition still structures thinking (Lister, 1999). It was not an opposition that the women's accounts supported. The women articulated a view of 'responsible mothering' that included, as well as financial imperatives, recognition of the mother's needs as an individual, although the nature of children's demands meant that the mother's and child's needs were not weighted equally. Their discussion of desires and options reflected not only a practical assessment of possibilities and constraints but also the social and personal value of care. Paid work and care were both needed if children's needs were to be met. The difficulties lay not in an inherent incompatibility but in difficulties in finding good, affordable childcare and the lack of acknowledgment of caring responsibilities by employers and by institutions, such as colleges and schools. Their pragmatic approach proposes an integrated model of work and care, giving each due weight, that recognises paid work as necessary to support care as well as vice versa.

Marginalising care?

Nevertheless the women's accounts expressed a growing marginalisation of care in the negotation of work and family boundaries, even by those who bear the responsibility and practice of caring. They recognised the necessity and value of their caregiving yet described it in ways that minimised it. The women's accounts were threaded through with both individualisation (Beck and Beck-Gernsheim, 2001), with its message 'do something with your life', and the experience of caring roles with their equally strong messages about maternal identity and family creation. When work is defined as paid work and given primary value, identities that are other than employment based become less stable and the experience of care can be of loss of identity. Attending the course was contrasted to the experience of caring for young children at home and seen as important in regaining a sense of individual identity, as the following example illustrates:

> "I used to feel as though I should have been out doing something, you know, before I started on the course. You know, this bit of pressure – oh, single mum, she's just a drain on society."

The political and moral discourse of lone motherhood has been identified by writers as significant and contested (Duncan and Edwards, 1999; Backett-Milburn et al, 2001). Although that pressure was felt most strongly by lone mothers, it was experienced, in this study, as about low income families and 'benefit dependency' rather than family form. Pressure to return to work was also felt by partnered mothers irrespective of whether their partners were employed or not.

Such pressures are an expression of an adult worker norm. The promise of economic independence implicit in welfare-to-work policy, however, remains to be demonstrated for many women, who make up the majority of low paid workers and those on the minimum wage. In the UK, women with children experience a 'mother gap' in income, over and above the gender gap in lifetime incomes between all women and men. That gap is widest for low skilled women and those who have their children in their teens (Women's Unit, 2000). As well as appropriate support to enable the transition to be the sustainable and the better paid employment that many women in such circumstances want, it is important to acknowledge that paid work may not be the best route out of poverty for all women with caring responsibilities and to ensure viable alternatives (McKay and Van Every, 2000; Gray, 2001; Dean and Shah, 2002).

Competing or complementary discourses in a local setting

Rather than seeing the value given to both parenting and to participating in education and paid work as contradictory, it is more useful to see the women's understandings of care and work as expressing competing discourses of gender, care and biography. The discourse utilised by the women in the study did not readily accord with many aspects of their experience of daily caregiving. What was apparent in the study was that maternity itself remains an important element of the women's identity but the circumstances created by maternity also offered an opportunity to rethink aims and possibilities and acted as a catalyst to learning and new opportunities (McKendrick at al, 2001). The need for a change of direction, for example, was frequently given as a reason for applying to the community facility:

> "I felt as though I needed a change in my life and I had to turn it – see if I didn't turn it now, I was never going to turn it, so I would've went back tae what I was always kind of doing, so … I don't know what made me change, I just thought, that looks great – I'm going to go for that."

Most of the women's accounts also suggested that maternity created a break in their lives that led to a change of direction and for some that was strengthened by a health or personal crisis, associated in some cases with abuse or other problems in relationships. Health and other problems created a need for support and new directions and, in disrupting previous routines and expectations, crisis could function to open up the possibility of doing something different. In particular, getting out of the house and having adult company was seen as important in combating depression. The lifelong learning centre, where the study took place, was described as a space where mothers could have a break from caregiving, could deal with difficult personal issues if need be and could think about their lives and explore choices. The women identified a number of benefits from attending the centre. Of particular interest for boundary analysis was the support they identified in identifying new horizons and overcoming problems that faced them as they tried to develop new roles and relationships, at the same time as maintaining existing relationships:

> "I left school early and thought, oh I couldn't do this, or I'm not clever enough to do that, but, when you come here, that all changes. You know they give you confidence to do things."

The study suggested that, whether or not individual women progress to the labour market, learning opportunities can deliver resources for change that are of personal worth. Those resources were not simply income but were also associated with the opportunity to explore the boundaries between family, community and economy. They included developing options for roles outside and inside families in a supportive setting and without compulsion (Innes and Scott, 2002). It also highlights the role of trusted intermediaries in managing the boundaries between home and work and in the development of employability. Very few of the women trusted government bodies, such as the Job Centre Plus, to provide them with advice and support for managing the transitions in care and relationships they were going to be faced with. However, activities or organisations not directly related to formal learning or labour market entry can be important sources of information and guidance when uncharted boundaries are being negotiated by the socially excluded (McGivney, 1999; Gillespie and Scott, 2004; Whittaker et al, 2004).

Conclusion

Returning to the boundary metaphor central to this book, it is worth asking whether the data given in this chapter provide any evidence about the way in which boundaries between home, community and work are asserted as well as reconstructed. Certainly the research points to changes and constraints in the choices available to mothers in low income households in a society where welfare support is coming to be increasingly dependent on the acceptance of responsibilities related to mothering and working. The study confirms the argument that there is a lack of coherence between models of managing new boundaries between work and care as constructed by policy and as experienced by mothers in low income households. A 'gender culture', which stressed the importance of mothering, was evident and might be seen to limit the extent and preference for roles beyond those of caring.

However, there was also a strong 'worker culture'. Despite sometimes long-term dependence on welfare benefits these were women who wanted to work and who, for personal or relationship reasons, saw both dependence on state welfare and on a male breadwinner model as a limited answer to the needs of themselves or their children. They saw themselves as adult workers and mothers, but had been forced to recognise that resolving the changes in a way that suited them and their children was not easy. Family relationships, wider kin and local economic conditions were key factors here, but in this particular study we also see the role that local, community-based facilities that address caring and work-related developments can play in resolving boundary management.

Examining the relationship between poverty, care and choices is essential to understanding the meaning of policy change for the families at whom it is directed. An integrated model of work/care arrangements would better meet the needs of low income families in the UK negotiating changing work and family boundaries: it could support parenthood and other care without allocating responsibility in such a way as to place it in opposition to meeting individual needs or to improving the material circumstances of the family. It suggests that more attention must be paid to specific issues for women in low income households, who have fewer material resources and possibly more vulnerable social resources with which to manage tensions between paid work and care. Too many analyses of the work/family boundary have ignored social class.

If mothers in low income households are to make the sustainable transitions to the labour market that they wish to, and that government anti-poverty policies require, the multitasked and demanding nature of care and its social role, particularly in excluded communities, must be acknowledged and supported. Provision to address child poverty and social exclusion must fully recognise care roles and responsibilities and must take into account the range of social and familial resources that low income families depend on. To do so would involve a range of policies, from gender-sensitive national, fiscal and employment policy through to support for locally based accessible intermediaries providing services that are responsive to the needs of parents at different stages of their work and care roles.

References

Adelman, L., Middleton, S. and Ashworth, K. (2003) *Britain's poorest children: Severe and persistent poverty and social exclusion*, London: Save the Children.

Backett-Milburn, K., Cunningham-Burley, S. and Kemmer, D. (2001) *Caring and providing: Lone and partnered working mothers in Scotland*, London: Family Policy Studies Centre.

Bang, H., Jensen, P. and Pfau-Effinger, B. (2000) 'Gender and European welfare states: context, structure and agency', in S. Duncan and B. Pfau-Effinger (eds) *Gender, economy and culture in the European Union*, London: Routledge.

Beck, U. and Beck-Gernsheim, E. (2001) *Individualization*, London: Sage Publications.

Bennett, F. (2002) 'Gender implications of current social security reforms', *Fiscal Studies*, vol 23, no 4, pp 559-84.

Bradbury, B. and Jantti, M. (2001) 'Child poverty across the industrialised world', in K. Vleminck and T. Smeeding (eds) *Child well being, child poverty and child policy in modern nations*, Bristol: The Policy Press.

Bradshaw, J. (2001) 'Child poverty under Labour', in G. Finister (ed) *An end in sight: Tackling child poverty in the UK*, London: Child Poverty Action Group.

Brannen, J. and Moss, P. (2003) 'Concepts, relationships and policies', in J. Brannen and P. Moss (eds) *Rethinking children's care*, Buckingham: Open University Press.

Brever, M., Clark, T. and Goodman, A. (2003) *The Government's child poverty target: How much progress has been made?*, London: Institute of Fiscal Studies.

Brown, U., Scott, G., Mooney, G. and Duncan, B. (eds) (2002) *Poverty in Scotland 2002: People, places and policies*, London: Child Poverty Action Group.

Crompton, R. and Harris F. (1999) 'Attitudes, women's employment and the changing domestic division of labour: a cross-national analysis', in R. Crompton (ed) *Restructuring gender relations and employment: The decline of the male breadwinner*, Oxford: Oxford University Press.

Daly, M. (2001) 'Care policies in Western Europe', in M. Daly (ed) *Care work: The quest for security*, Geneva: International Labour Office.

Dean, H. and Shah, A. (2002) 'Insecure families and low paying labour markets: comments on the British experience', *Journal of Social Policy* vol 31, no1, pp 61-80.

Duncan, P. (ed) (2004) *Ending child poverty by 2020: The first five years*, London: Child Poverty Action Group.

Duncan, S. and Edwards, R. (1999) *Lone mothers, paid work and gendered moral rationalities*, Basingstoke: Macmillan.

Duncan, S. and Smith, D. (2002) 'Geographies of family formations: spatial differences and gender cultures in Britain', *Transactions of the Institute of British Geographers*, vol 27, pp 471-93.

Elliott, J. (1991) *Action research for educational change*, Buckingham: Open University Press.

Elson, D. (1998) 'The economic, the political and the domestic: business, states and households in the organisation of production', *New Political Economy*, vol 3, no 2, pp 189-208.

Folbre, N. (1994) *Who pays for the kids: Gender and the structures of constraint*, London: Routledge.

Folbre, N. and Nelson, J. (2000) 'For love or money – or both?', *Journal of Economic Perspectives*, vol 14, no 4, 123-40.

Gardiner, J. (1997) *Gender, care and economic*, London: Macmillan.

Gillespie, M. and Scott, G. (2004) *Advice services and transitions to work for disadvantaged groups: A literature review*, Glasgow: EQUAL and Glasgow Caledonian University.

Graham, H. (1993) *Hardship and health in women's lives*, London: Harvester Wheatsheaf.

Gray, A. (2001) '"Making work pay" – devising the best strategy for lone parents in Britain', *Journal of Social Policy*, vol 30, no 2, pp 189-207.

Hantrais, L. (1996) *Families and family policies in Europe*, London: Longman.

Hogarth, T., Hasluck, C. and Pierre, G. (2001) *Work–life balance 2000: Results from the baseline study: DfEE Research Report RR249*, London: Department for Education and Employment.

Humphries, J. and Rubery, J. (eds) (1995) *The economics of equal opportunities*, Manchester: Equal Opportunities Commission.

Innes, S. and Scott, G. (2002) *Gender, care and transitions: Research report 1*, Glasgow: Centre for Research on Families and Relationships and Scottish Poverty Information Unit, Glasgow Caledonian University.

Jenkins, S.P. and Rigg, J. (2001) *The dynamics of poverty in Britain: Research Report No 157*, London: Department of Work and Pensions.

Kemp, P. (2002) *Child poverty in social inclusion areas*, Edinburgh: Scottish Executive Social Research.

Kempson, E., Bryson, A. and Rowlingson, K. (1994) *Hard times – how poor families make ends meet*, London: Policy Studies Institute.

Kenway, P., Fuller, S., Rahman, M., Street, C. and Palmer, G. (2002) *Monitoring poverty and social exclusion in Scotland*, York: New Policy Institute/Joseph Rowntree Foundation.

Lister, R. (1999) 'What welfare provision do women need to become full citizens?', in S. Walby (ed) *New agendas for women*, Basingstoke: Macmillan.

McGivney, V. (1999) *Returning women: Their training and employment choices and needs*, London: National Institute of Adult Continuing Education.

McKay, A. (2001) 'Rethinking work and income maintenance policy: promoting gender equality through a citizen's basic income', *Feminist Economics*, vol 7, no 1, pp 97-118.

McKay, A. and Van Every, J. (2000) 'Gender, family and income maintenance: a feminist case for citizens basic income', *Social Politics*, vol 7, no 2, pp 266-84.

McKay, A. and Scott, G. (1999) *What can we afford? A woman's role: Money management in low income households*, Glasgow: Scottish Poverty Information Unit.

McKendrick, J., Cunningham Burley, S., Backett-Milburn, K. and Scott, G. (2003) *Life in low income families in Scotland: A review of the literature*, Edinburgh: Scottish Executive Social Research.

McKendrick, J., Scott, G., Milligan, B. and Frondigoun, E. (2001) *Guidance learning and training in Drumchapel*, Glasgow: Scottish Poverty Information Unit.

McKie, L., Gregory, S. and Bowlby, S. (2002) 'Shadow times: the temporal and spatial frameworks and experiences of caring and working', *Sociology*, vol 36, no 4, pp 897-924.

McKie, L., Gregory, S. and Bowlby, S. (2004) 'Starting well: gender, care and health in family context', *Sociology*, vol 38, no 3, pp 593-611.

Morris, L. and Ritchie, J. (1994) *Income maintenance and living standard*, London: Social and Community Planning Research.

Palmer, G., North, J., Carr, J. and Kenway, P. (2004) *Monitoring poverty and social exclusion 2003*, York: Joseph Rowntree Foundation.
Piachaud, D. (1984) *Round about fifty hours a week: The time costs of children*, London: Child Poverty Action Group.
Ribbens, J. and Edwards, R. (eds) (1998) *Feminist dilemmas in qualitative research: Public knowledge and private lives*, London: Sage Publications.
Ritchie, J., Elam, G. and Hulusi, A. (1998) 'Eking out an income: low income households and their use of supplementary resources', paper presented at the Seebohm Rowntree Centenary Conference, York, 1997.
Sainsbury, D. (1994) *Gendering welfare states*, London: Sage Publications.
Scott, G. and McKay, A. (2001) 'The welfare function of emotional labour: the role of caring in the social economy', paper presented at the IAFFE Annual Conference, Oslo, 22-24 June.
Scott, G., Gillespie, M. and Innes, S. (2002) *Breaking barriers: Poverty, childcare and mothers' transitions to work*, Glasgow: Rosemount Lifelong Learning/Scottish Poverty Information Unit..
Scott, G., Mooney, G. and Brown, U. (2005) 'Managing poverty in a devolved Scotland', in G. Mooney and G. Scott (eds) *Exploring social policy in Scotland*, Bristol: The Policy Press.
Scott, G., Frondigoun, E., Gillespie, M. and White, A. (2003) *Making ends meet: An exploration of parent–student poverty*, London: Child Poverty Action Group.
Scottish Executive (2003) *Social justice report*, Edinburgh: Scottish Executive.
SEU (Social Exclusion Unit) (2004) *Tackling social exclusion: Taking stock and looking to the future – emerging findings*, London: SEU.
UNICEF (United Nations Children's Fund) (2000) *Innocenti Report Card No. 1 'A league table of child poverty in rich nations'*, Florence: UNICEF Innocenti Research Centre.
Wasoff, F. and Dey, I. (2000) *Family policy*, London: Gildredge Press.
Whittaker, S., Gallacher, J. and Crossan, B. (2004) *Learner perceptions of information, advice and guidance: A review of research*, Glasgow: Centre for Research into Lifelong Learning.
Williams, C. (ed) (2004) *Report of the child poverty task group*, Cardiff: Welsh Assembly Government.
Williams, F. (2001) 'In and beyond New Labour: towards a new political ethics of care', *Critical Social Policy*, vol 21, no 4, pp 467-93.

Women's Unit (2000) *Women's incomes over the lifetime – the mother gap*, London: Cabinet Office.

FOUR

Families, education and the 'participatory imperative'

Janet Shucksmith, Lorna McKee and Helen Willmot

Introduction

This chapter explores the interface between the family and one of our main public institutions. The introductory chapter pointed to the ways in which traditional notions of family life still tend to dominate public policy provision, being based, for example, on (gendered) understandings of the availability of family members to perform certain caring or socialisation functions. Families, as we have seen, are accepted as appropriate sites for the socialisation of children, but it is also clear that society, since the mid-19th century, has also taken the view that the family should not be left on its own to perform this function in so far as it is construed in terms of providing an appropriate education for children. Public institutions like schools have traditionally been seen as sites of hegemonic discourse, where public notions of appropriate childhood behaviour and good parenting, for example, are instilled through both the formal and the hidden curricula and through social relations between school and family members. The calculation of how far professionals could intrude on and determine the agenda of private family life, or how far families could retreat into the private territory of the family to evade professional demands and claims on their behaviour, makes fascinating reading over the last hundred and thirty odd years since the 1870 Education Act. Thus boundaries between families and school have often been identified as confusing, ambiguous and even dangerous. A combination of macro social trends and policy responses to perceived social problems in the last few years seems, however, to have altered the boundary conditions between state and family over schooling and makes this an area worth revisiting.

Perhaps most marked has been a shift whereby it is no longer appropriate for parents as proxy education service users to be merely passive recipients of service. Instead a normalising discourse now operates where active participation by parents is seen as key to children's success. The rhetoric of citizenship and the imperative to participate which had been evident in other policy areas (Peterson and Lupton, 1996) appeared in the UK Conservative government reforms of education in the 1980s and 1990s. These saw the 'rebadging' of education and other public service users (for example parents, not children, and patients) as consumers and signalled a growth in the marketisation of education (Ball, 1995; Dehli, 1996). This 'new' public management has been characterised as an attempt to replace old administration-based templates with more professionalised management, increased value-for-money imperatives and a heightened end-user focus (Ferlie et al, 1996). New Labour's agenda for public services and education, in particular since 1997, has not dispensed with this public management orientation or with the rhetoric of consumer involvement and voice and choice, but has grafted onto it an additional vocabulary about partnership. In the educational context, partnership emphasises enhanced engagement between parents and educational professionals and formalisation of such relationships through home–school contracts, school mission statements and other performance goals that parents are invited to endorse. At its heart the philosophy of parental involvement in education is promoted and for parental involvement in education to be seen as an integral tool in the raising of educational standards and levels of achievement. Policy goals of greater social inclusion and the eradication of poverty and inequality are seen to be closely tied up with efforts to persuade all sectors of the population of the value of education. Partnership approaches aim to enlist parents in a bigger project of social advancement. For example, recent debates about increased access to higher education and the role of higher, further and vocational education also suggest that education holds the key to economic prosperity and that this goal should be embraced by parents and educators alike.

'Partnership' might seem to have the dissolution of boundaries as an implicit part of the agenda, but a number of writers have cast doubts on whether the intention is really the achievement of the sort of partnership that makes a boundary permeable and almost irrelevant, or whether the New Labour agenda isn't actually one of pushing the school's/professional educator's territory well into the domain of the family and the home. Thus McNamara et al (2000) have referred to the Blairite project of Total Schooling, and Scanlon and Buckingham have pointed to the range of initiatives such as homework clubs, summer schools and so on, commenting that 'Education, it would seem, is the *work* of childhood, and it cannot be allowed to stop once children walk out of the classroom door' (Scanlon and Buckingham, 2004, p 287; original emphasis)

The rationale for such policy activity is clear, given the recognition of 'cycles of disadvantage' in children's home circumstances, and, in particular, as Scanlon and Buckingham (2004) point out, the clear dissonance between working-class children's home cultures and the culture of schools. Gewirtz (2001), in her article 'Cloning the Blairs', is but one author who has seen the raft of education reforms as an attempt to re-socialise working-class parents, by getting them to adopt the ways used by middle-class parents in transmitting cultural capital by educating their children at home. This involves not just homework and reading but is also about how to behave, for example encouraging observation and discussion. In Bourdieuian terms, these things are viewed as part of the habitus of the middle classes – the unspoken habits of mind and daily practices that are routine, assumed and performed almost unconsciously (Bourdieu, 1977).

A number of commentators have felt that such policy movements may be counterproductive (Lareau, 1989; Toomey, 1989). Working-class parents have different orientations to teachers and schooling, they argue, not because they are less committed to their children's welfare, but because schools position them so that they feel they lack the necessary competence and understanding to respond to school requests for involvement. Emphasis on partnership on the school's terms may further disadvantage them in comparison to middle-class families.

But if policy shunts the boundary in one direction, macro social forces might be seen to be pushing it in the other. Boundary disputes between professionals and the population groups with which they work have become a marker of postmodern society. The decline of deference and the end of unquestioning belief in expertise and rationality have led all professional groups into a new set of relations with the public. A clear example from a different policy area came in the form of the challenges made by families over the right of medical professionals to retain the organs of their dead children, a discursive space that was opened up by the separate cases involving the Bristol Royal Infirmary and the Alder Hey Children's Hospital in Liverpool (Bristol Royal Infirmary Inquiry, 2000; Royal Liverpool Children's Inquiry, 2001).

While there have (fortunately) been no correspondingly stark consumerist challenges in the field of education, the boundary between professionals and families in this area is also now subject to continuous negotiation and can at times be fragile. Examples of where professional–parent spaces and authority (and indeed government control) are contested include where parents withdraw children from school in favour of home schooling; in fierce disputes over religious schools; and in episodes of parent–teacher confrontations, even outbreaks of violence (as we discuss later) and increasing cases of litigation when parents feel schools and local authorities have failed in the duty of care.

It may indeed be more useful to construe the boundary between the family and the professional realm of the school and the educator not as a linear one, but rather as a piece of territory that separates two forces – a no man's land or a discursive space in which major issues about the care, nurture and education of children and young people are negotiated and constructed throughout the child's school lifetime. It may be that differing degrees of authority rest with different parties at different stages and ages and that boundaries are dynamic and continually being formed and reformed as the child matures and needs and expectations change.

In this chapter we explore some elements of the 'push and pull' around the boundaries between families and professional educators. We examine one side of the 'partnership' and ask how does it feel to be part of this bigger social project of parental involvement? We ask what does participation mean in reality? We do this through the voices of 19 adult members of working-class families involved in a pilot study in Aberdeen. This study is described briefly in the following section before we go on to explore the negotiation of the boundaries in more detail.

The study

The pilot study was carried out in two predominantly low income areas of Aberdeen. Access was gained to community centres through two contacts; and leaflets outlining what the study was about and what would be required of anyone who volunteered to take part were designed by the researchers and then distributed by the two contacts among parents at the community centres. The response rate was very good, although finding fathers to interview took greater perseverance. This was clearly linked to the characteristics of the families in the two areas. Broadly speaking, the parents who took part in the study were from families organised around traditional gender roles, that is, involving a mother who takes the bulk or all of the responsibility for domestic work and childcare, and may or may not also work in paid employment, and a father who is the breadwinner and may or may not take some responsibility for domestic work and childcare. The first set of interviews was with mothers, the aim being to pursue the issue of interviewing their male partners where possible. However, this worked out in only once instance (and there was a strong sense with this interview that the father had been volunteered by his wife). A further four fathers were eventually interviewed, via snowball sampling and with further help from a contact in one of the community centres who worked with a group of fathers.

The interview schedule had a semi-structured format. It began with basic questions concerning the numbers and ages of the respondents' children and any experiences of paid employment, before moving on to address four forms of involvement in children's education. These were: talking to children about their school day; helping children with their homework; talking to teachers; and getting involved in children's school lives, for example via participating in school trips, events, jobs and committees. To explore further parents' experiences of talking to teachers, parents were asked about a 'critical incident' concerning their child and their education or the school.

A total of 19 interviews were carried out and transcribed. With only a small amount of data, a non-cross-sectional form of data organisation and analysis was used. Each transcript was read and notes were taken on the key themes emerging. The 19 sets of notes on key themes were then looked at, to establish the overall key themes, as well as any smaller patterns within the data. This approach to data analysis enabled themes for analysis to emerge from the data (Bhopal, 2000) and enabled both the particular and the holistic to be explored (Mason, 1996).

Total schooling?

The boundary between the school and the family is clearly being tweaked when schools not only want parents to come to school and participate in traditional ways (for example, attending concerts, school open days, parent evenings), but when they adopt the rhetoric about parents as 'first educators' and push responsibility back into the home for literacy and numeracy development. Parents (and particularly mothers) are encouraged both within government schemes like Sure Start and through the commercial availability of materials (see Scanlon and Buckingham, 2004, for a discussion of this) to develop early or pre-reading skills in their infants, to socialise children in appropriate types of collective behaviour, to undertake various domestic activities in which children can learn to count and weigh, to identify colour, to use language. Ordinary, everyday parent–child interactions must be turned into object lessons, where each episode of contact becomes a learning opportunity (Walkerdine and Lucey, 1989). As a consequence family homes are being encouraged to become more 'school-like' (David et al, 1993).

Despite the fact that these have been characterised as middle-class ways of operating and transmitting cultural capital, there was also considerable acceptance of and adherence to this mode of interaction with children in our working-class sample. Colin, a father of three who had himself left school at 16, talked about ways in which he tried to make learning fun for his children:

> "I suppose little things like, you know, spelling. You know, play scrabble – you are still learning to spell, but he's not spelling, he's playing a game.... The middle one, he likes writing books, so you maybe go in to the computer and say, 'Right, write us a story, on the computer'. So you'll sit there and type out on the computer a story. Same again with the older one, you'll put the spell checker on, so when he's actually typing it'll bring up the mistake. We won't let them just click on the spell checker; we'll ask them to try to correct the word, you know, maybe, two or three attempts to correct it. If he doesn't correct it then OK, click the spell check, and see what the correct spelling is. So it's things like that."

However, some commentators have worried that such trends run the risk of establishing normalising discourses around family behaviour and of rendering other behaviours deviant (Lareau, 1989; Toomey, 1989). Middle-class hegemonic norms for parenting are clearly built into these new policy initiatives. Do they inevitably put other parents in deficit? Does the education engine push parents who have the time, resources and skills into intensifying their unpaid labour to supplement the work of schooling while dumping the children of those who do not into an educational underclass?

One clear way in which the school presses across the boundary and intrudes into home life is by the insistence on homework, now handed out in considerable quantities, even for the youngest children. Children, parents are told, must be encouraged or pressed into homework, tutored and helped (Ribbens, 1993). For some families, where children are bright, keen and eager, this presents few problems. Indeed the quantity of homework undertaken by the child may often be seen as a marker of the quality of the school and the seriousness with which it takes its duty towards the child.

Within the study reported here, some parents did indeed welcome the opportunity to see what their children were working on and enjoyed feeling involved. Most parents tried to encourage children to do their homework while they 'were still in school mode', as soon as they got home from school and before having supper or relaxing, and certainly before any evening leisure activities commenced. Home and family life was thus made to be more school-like while these tasks were accomplished.

Where children struggled with their work, however, this became an almost intolerable burden, with hours spent on homework throughout the evening, and resentment building up in both parent and child. Aileen, a married mother of four who had left school at 16 and now combined motherhood with two part-time cleaning and delivery jobs, spoke of the struggles with her son:

> "He's had the learning support since primary one and he's still got learning support, and that's, that's who he gets all his homework from as well. Some nights he does get a lot, and at the end of the day I know it's for his benefit, but I just think sometimes that he's getting too much homework and he should be doing more in school. Because when you've got four kids it isn't easy to sit and set aside an hour and a half at night with each one [laughs a little]."

She clearly felt enlisted or incorporated in the school's objectives by the school in terms of her own and her husband's participation in this activity, since many exercises required considerable parental help and investment of time, as well as ticks and signatures at critical points, which were scrutinised by the school. Quizzed by the researcher as to whether or not she felt sufficiently involved with the school, her exasperation is clear, as she implies that she feels that she is already doing a great deal of the work that she believes should be done in school. The tension caused by these high and perhaps unrealistic expectations of the school are revealed in her comments:

"I suppose I am really [involved enough], because I mean, they go to school to learn, right, but I mean, this is what I am saying with Gordon, he seems to get more work home with him than he seems to do at school. So I mean, as far as I am concerned, I think I do. I haven't got time to do any more [laughs] of the work with them."

Where children were not just slow in completing their work, but strongly resisted having the tasks imposed on them, the battles to maintain concentration or to insist on correct completion of tasks wore parents to shreds. Barbara recounts her dealings with her daughter:

"Sometimes it's a bit of a carry on. She will maybe say, 'Oh I don't want to do this', and I say, 'You are not getting out of it. You have to do it'. I will say, 'If you don't do it....' They have a comments book – a homework book – that says what you have to do, and you have to sign it, and I will say, 'Well if you don't ... if you are not wanting to do your homework I will just write a note to the teacher saying that you didn't want to do it blah, blah, blah. Craig – he just gets on with it, nothing seems to bother him. But Rebecca.... Oh, she will have a stromash [tantrum]."

Such uncomfortable interludes reinforce Scanlon and Buckingham's (2004) point about the psychological implications of increased parental involvement in schooling, namely the development of stress and the manifestation of what Elkind (1981) first termed the 'hurried child' syndrome. Reay also talks of the 'emotional capital' involved in assuming a teacherly role (1998).

This intrusion of school into home life also alters the boundary between parent and child roles (Solomon et al, 2002). James and James (2001) have pointed to the net of social control tightening on children's lives. The further intrusion of school into the home through the adoption of parents as partners in education has implications for parenting roles and relations with children. Edwards and Alldred (2000), for example, point to evidence on how working-class children connive to exclude their parents from school-related activities. They make every attempt to keep their home and school lives separate.

Such trends perhaps serve also to discredit parents' own understandings of childhood and children's needs and jeopardise 'natural' parental educational practice. A study of the introduction of preschool education for three- and four-year-olds (Copus et al, 2001) shows how mothers' own intuitive notions of what 'a good day' for a three-year-old should be were quickly replaced with a more schematised curricular notion of how the child should spend the day. In the pilot study reported here many parents expressed a strong view that children needed time to relax and play, especially at weekends, and there was more than a little truculence expressed where homework tasks dripped over into this portion of the family's time together.

> *Int*: "Do you talk about school at all at the weekends?"
>
> *Claudia*: "Not at the weekend. I think school should be left for the week."
>
> *Rosa*: "Umm, I don't. She sometimes ... she'll sometimes speak about it. I don't bring it up. I'll wait to see if she does because I think weekends is ... is her time."

Few parents seem to have felt empowered to represent these views to the school or to individual teachers, however. James and James (2001) feel strongly that the model of parent–child relations and of family values embedded in the parental involvement movement may devalue the practices and values of families who are already marginalised. The net effect, they claim, may be to alienate families and to disadvantage their children further.

Little work has been done on the impact of these additional burdens on women's and men's labour market roles and work–life arrangements. Men's roles in relation to their children are particularly poorly scripted. Such an omission needs to be addressed, particularly in the context of a policy climate that encourages women back into the workplace, even when they are the sole carers of children. Working families, tax credits and the establishment of childcare partnerships all bespeak a society desperately keen to address social exclusion through inclusion in the workforce, yet this appears to run counter with inclusion agendas that posit expanded roles at home for parents.

Talking back?

It seems fairly evident then that policy agendas have shifted the boundary, pushing school tasks, norms and expectations into the very heart of family life and family time, as well as family relationships.

Parents, mostly desperately anxious for their children to perform better than they did themselves at school and to have more life chances, might occasionally resent this intrusion and find it difficult to cope with, but there is little evidence of much overt resistance. So far this does not look very much like partnership, however, although it does perhaps resemble the 'tutelage' that Martin and Vincent (1999) speak of, in which parents are subject to a professional discourse that defines the needs of themselves and their children. That discourse, of course, involves the assumption of universality of values and denies the possibility of plurality of values.

Is there any countervailing evidence that parents or families seek to assert their authority over that of the school? In this section we look at the area of communication with schools. As Ranson et al (2004, p 273) have pointed out:

> Institutional practice reproduces relations of power. The social space that schools establish for parental involvement is limited and typically shaped by deep codes that reinforce professional authority and parental deference – a structuration of legitimate authority that is taken for granted.

It appears to be very difficult to challenge schools therefore, especially on territory where teachers might claim professional expertise. Thus it is rare to find parents challenging a teacher on a matter pertaining to learning or work set. Where they do, a complex process is often engaged in of consultation around other parents, so that no one individual is left exposed, or any child singled out for discriminatory retaliation or disadvantage:

> "Yeah because they are all split into certain groups so I'll phone someone else, one of the mums from her group, and they phone me about it as well." (Ruth)

Where this changes is in areas where parents feel competent, namely regarding the happiness, welfare or general care of their child. On these occasions, the 'softly, softly' approach is abandoned and parents will often attempt to fly into action in seconds. Linda recounted the story of her daughter's accident on an adventure holiday with the school, where the child had fallen out of the top bunk bed. Linda and her partner had been up to the school within minutes of finding out what had happened and fully intended to make further representations:

> "Ooh yes, yeah, we had to because this is really a complaint, isn't it? Because they really have to see to it that if they have a trip like that and taking the kids in accommodation using bunk beds … they have to just be sure there are bars and things like that. Now this is my youngest's turn because he is primary 7. Next year they are going to the same place again, so we are thinking … before they go ahead next year we are going to go and see the head teacher and find out what's the latest improvement at that accommodation … if they did something different now, OK."

Similarly, concerns over their son's happiness invested Rebecca and her husband with a quite different way of talking to the teachers:

> "Oh, well we became really aware that he wasn't happy at school. He was really not wanting to go out in the mornings and he wasn't doing his homework very well. We went up [to the school] and she [teacher] said, 'He's just not happy at all'. We said, 'Don't worry about the homework bit just now or the school work. We need to get the happy bit sorted out first. We talked to him [son] and he admitted that he'd been getting bullied."

Ranson et al (2004) have recently discussed these 'storming parents'. Some alarm has been expressed by teaching unions about unruly or storming parents and, while it is obviously important not to condone parents who are violent or abusive with teachers and headteachers, Ranson et al make the point that it is important to understand what provokes these storming episodes. In the view of these authors, it is "the invasion of the parental domains" which causes most such incidents. Anger expressed at incidents of bullying or events which placed children's care at risk "reveal a sense of demeaned capability and self respect" (p 265).

In our pilot study Kevin's outrage at the school is evident when describing an attack on his son that happened at school and the school's apparent lack of care for the boy:

> *Kevin:* "The — Academy is terrible … my son was attacked twice in one day, both resulting in head injuries and they never took him to hospital and never contacted us. He was interviewed by a

policeman on his own without an adult.... As you know there has got to be an adult present when being interviewed by the police. He came home and told us at night after his school day."

Int: "And what did you do, what was your reaction?"

Kevin: "It was like I 'phoned the school, 'Oh we are sorry but we didn't really know blah, blah, blah', and then the police ... they said, 'Oh the police are going to phone you tomorrow anyway'."

Int: "But you weren't happy with the school's reaction?"

Kevin: "No, no I wasnae. They asked him, 'Are you OK?' And as any 14-year-old guy [would say], 'Oh I'm fine there is nothing wrong with me', They didn't even say, 'Right, we will take you to hospital', or 'Go to the nurse'. And they never even 'phoned. We checked our mobile 'phone; we checked our 'phone at home...."

In fact, the majority of the 'critical incidents' that parents recounted to us in respect of contact with the school revolved around cases of suspected bullying.

Thus while parents may be reluctant to challenge the school on curricular or learning matters and are still deferential to the professional expertise of the teacher, issues of care or children's well-being are seen as legitimate areas in which parents are empowered to make representations to schools and strong ones at that.

Conclusion

'Partnership' with parents has been seen as a key instrument in improving social inclusion and raising educational standards and the rhetoric of this is writ large in many policy documents in education since the accession to power of New Labour in 1997. Curiously, the older doctrines of consumerism that crept into policy in the previous decades have not been abandoned, and may indeed be intensifying as education choice is further pushed to the centre of policy discourse and school models are diversifying through specialist colleges. Such trends have been observed across the whole public sector in the UK and the love affair with markets has not been totally abolished. Lupton (1996) is not alone in finding this somewhat paradoxical. The development of partnership would seem to imply trust and parity between partners, whereas consumerist discourses are likely to encourage competition both between schools and between parents (causing schools to concentrate on achievement indicators rather than, say, the holistic development of children, and parents to focus on league tables and performance rather than on children's individual needs and aptitudes). This may in the long term threaten the wider social goals of equal opportunities and of social inclusion. It is also interesting that children and young people are seldom perceived as agents in these discussions of partnership, a weakness in the sustainability of the models of participation currently preferred.

Despite the fact that 'partnership' might be thought to imply a degree of parity, the majority of partnership initiatives are led and dominated by professionals, and are thus controlling rather than enabling or liberating (Vincent and Tomlinson, 1997).

The effect of this has undoubtedly been to push the boundary between school and family closer to the home. Although a great deal of rhetoric talks about 'drawing parents in', with the implication that the walls of the academy are becoming less high and less daunting, the reality is that many such partnership activities simply seek to extend the orbit of the school into home life and family time. There is a strong normalised expectation now that parents will prepare their children for formal schooling and will support the school's methods and goals through further practice and surveillance of homework activity. It is also clear that the extension of homework (often in considerable amounts) even into primary schools is intended at least in part to harness parents into a form of partnership, whether they are willing or not, and that this 'partnership' is more correctly construed as a form of tutelage – with parents being expected to learn an appropriate set of norms.

The extension of schooling into the home has some profound consequences for relations between children and parents, given that the 'teacherly' role demanded of parents can be emotionally demanding for both parties. Moreover, we know too little about the impact of these new demands on the micro conduct of family life in respect of men's and women's labour market roles:

> The demands of homework provide a way of the school monitoring the running of the household, as well as dictating its schedule. It breaks down the public–private

> divide by bringing the work of the school into the home, with little acknowledgement of its impact on the household. (Standing, 1999, p 489)

What is clear, however, is that those families under the most stress in economic terms will find it hardest to comply with the new demands made on them by the shifting of this boundary. Those in our sample who coped as single parents, but also those where men and women worked complex and alternating shift patterns in order to maximise income and minimise childcare costs, felt the strain most clearly. Most debates about school–home partnerships take insufficient account of the divergence of home contexts and familial 'capacity'. The resources families can draw on are hugely diverse. As well as economic constraints, there are many families that are fractured; fathers who are absent or disengaged; wider kin that are not available, and with illness and care burdens. Families are neither equally resourced nor underpinned by similar infrastructures of support. The participation agenda could be one pressure too many and another source of guilt and perceived failure.

Although the boundary has clearly shifted in respect of the school's power to dictate aspects of childrearing, domestic timetables and parenting practices, parents still reserve a space around the boundary, however, where they feel free to demand appropriate standards of care and concern for their child. Issues around bullying or general care for children's health and well-being fire even the most reticent parents into action to challenge the school. This may take the form of polite but determined enquiry, but – in parents otherwise disempowered – may result in 'storming' behaviour, where people feel that the school has intruded too far into the parental domain and yet failed to fulfil its duty in loco parentis.

References

Ball, S. (1995) 'Parents, schools and markets: the repositioning of youth in United Kingdom education', *Nordic Journal of Youth Research*, vol 3, no 3, pp 68-79.

Bhopal, K. (2000) 'Gender, "race" and power in the research process; South Asian women in east London', in C. Trueman, D.M. Mertens and B. Humphries (eds) *Research and Inequality*, London: UCL Press.

Bourdieu, P. (1977) *Outline of a theory of practice*, Cambridge: Cambridge University Press.

Bristol Royal Infirmary Inquiry (2000) *The inquiry into the management of care of children receiving complex heart surgery at the Bristol Royal Infirmary. Interim report: Removal and retention of human material*, Norwich: The Stationery Office.

Copus, A., Petrie, S., Shucksmith, J., Shucksmith, M., Still, M. and Watt, J. (2001) *Preschool educational provision in rural areas*, A report to the Scottish Executive Education Department, published as Arkleton Occasional Report No 1, Aberdeen: Arkleton Centre for Rural Development Research, University of Aberdeen.

David, M., Edwards, R., Hughes, M. and Ribbens, J. (1993) *Mothers and education: Inside out?*, London: Macmillan.

Dehli, K. (1996) 'Between "markets" and "state"? Engendering education change in the 1990s', *Discourse: Studies in the Cultural Politics of Education*, vol 17, no 3, pp 363-76.

Edwards, R. and Alldred, P. (2000) 'A typology of parental involvement in education centring on children and young people: negotiating familialisation, institutionalisation and individualisation', *British Journal of Sociology of Education*, vol 21, no 3, pp 435-55.

Elkind, D. (1981) *The hurried child: Growing up too fast too soon*, Reading, MA: Addison-Wesley.

Ferlie, E., Pettigrew, A., Ashburner, L. and Fitzgerald, L. (1996) *The new public management in action*, Oxford: Oxford University Press.

Gewirtz, S. (2001) 'Cloning the Blairs: New Labour's programme for the re-socialisation of working-class parents', *Journal of Education Policy*, vol 16, no 4, pp 365-78.

James, A. and James, A. (2001) 'Tightening the net: children, community and control', *British Journal of Sociology*, vol 52, pp 211-28.

Lareau, A. (1989) *Home advantage: Social class and parental involvement in elementary education*, Stoke-on-Trent: Trentham Books.

Lupton, D. (1996) 'Your life in their hands: trust and the medical encounter', in V. James and J. Gabe (eds) *Health and the sociology of emotions*, Oxford: Blackwell.

McNamara, O., Hustler, D., Stronach, I., Rodrigo, M., Beresford, E. and Botcherby, S. (2000) 'Room to manoeuvre: mobilising the "active partner" in home–school relations', *British Educational Research Journal*, vol 26, no 4, pp 473-89.

Martin, J. and Vincent, C. (1999) 'Parental voice: an exploration', *International Studies in Sociology of Education*, vol 9, no 2, pp 133-54.

Mason, J. (1996) *Qualitative research*, London: Sage Publications.

Peterson, A. and Lupton, D. (1996) *The new public health: Health and self in the age of risk*, London: Sage Publications.

Ranson, S., Martin, J. and Vincent, C. (2004) 'Storming parents, schools and communicative inaction', *British Journal of Sociology of Education*, vol 25, no 3, pp 259-74.

Reay, D. (1998) *Class work: Mother's involvement in their children's primary schooling*, London: UCL Press.

Ribbens, J. (1993) 'Having a word with the teacher: ongoing negotiations across home-school boundaries', in M. David, R. Edwards, M. Hughes and J. Ribbens (eds) *Mothers and education: Inside out?*, London: Macmillan.

Royal Liverpool Children's Inquiry (2001) *The Royal Liverpool Children's Inquiry Report*, London: The Stationery Office.

Scanlon, M. and Buckingham, D. (2004) 'Home learning and the educational marketplace', *Oxford Review of Education*, vol 30, no 2, pp 287-303.

Solomon, Y., Warin, R. and Lewis, C. (2002) 'Helping with homework: homework as a site of tension for parents and teenagers', *British Educational Research Journal*, vol 28, no 4, pp 603-22.

Standing, K. (1999) 'Lone mothers and "parental" involvement: a contradiction in policy?', *Journal of Social Policy*, vol 28, no 3, pp 479-95.

Toomey, D.M. (1989) 'How home–school relations policies can increase educational inequality', *Australian Journal of Education*, vol 37, pp 284-98.

Vincent, C. and Tomlinson, S. (1997) 'Home–school relationships: the "swarming of disciplinary mechanisms"?, *British Educational Research Journal*, vol 23, pp 361-77.

Walkerdine, V. and Lucey, H. (1989) *Democracy in the kitchen*, London: Virago.

Part Two: Children, families and relationships

Children – our future! The last decade has witnessed a growth in the amount of policy and service initiatives aimed at supporting the health and well-being of children and their families. Much of this work has been based on the assumption that offering a child as good an upbringing as possible has positive outcomes for the child, their family, their community and governments and society in general. The rights of the child have also received welcome attention with wider debates on balancing child and parental rights over a range of issues, not least of which has been disciplining potentially risky or dangerous behaviours.

This part of the book builds on the data and ideas considered in Part One. The following three chapters start from the perspective of the child or children involved in a research study or through a critical review of recent work on childhood, families and boundaries. The focus is very much on the experiences of children and what these might mean for policy and practice work as well as future research. The first chapter, by Hill (Chapter Five), draws attention to children's own creation of boundaries, then considers parents' perspectives and subsequently gives brief attention to family boundaries. Hill engages with a range of literature offering a comprehensive and in-depth review of theoretical and empirical work on childhood, families and boundaries. The chapter reflects on how children and parents negotiate crucial distinctions as regards the familiar and trusted, on the one hand, and the strange or threatening, on the other. Boundaries established among relationships and spaces in children's lives are fluid at any one time and evolve as time goes by. The boundaries created mediate the exchange of ideas, emotion, trust and practical assistance. In his conclusions Hill suggests the need to integrate understandings of children in their own right and as located within relationships. He also notes previous limited engagement in research and policy work on notions of boundaries, children and families asserting that the boundary metaphor offers a new and potentially useful dimension to researching childhood and family life.

Sweeting and Seaman (Chapter Six) present data from two studies that illustrate the complexity of decisions in respect of whether or not certain individuals form part of 'the family'. In order to explore this they consider non-resident birth fathers. They examine problems faced by those researchers who seek to place 'families' in categories. Through exploring methodological issues, as well as data, they illuminate several key themes, including the difficulty of defining family and family boundaries, as potentially represented by the material space of household. Noting the strengths and weaknesses of quantitative and qualitative approaches to data collection on relationships, they contend that almost all studies with a focus on family structure tend to ignore the potential importance of parents and parenting relationships outwith the household. Certainly these relationships are important and relevant to many children and yet can be marginalised in research design and data collection. To consider relationships outside the household allows for the intricacy and fluidity of the family across household boundaries to be documented and recognised.

Parental drug and alcohol misuse challenges the parent–child boundary that is generally created, sustained and enforced through norms, roles, individual practices and social institutions. The relationship between parent and child is often portrayed, not without reason, as one of the few remaining social bonds whose boundaries have a weight of obligation and permanence about them. Partners may become ex-partners, friends become lovers, lovers become friends, but children are always children and parents are always parents. However, empirical studies of family life show that these boundaries, although vested with so much emotional energy and material resources, are malleable and breakable. In Chapter Seven, Bancroft, Wilson, Cunningham-Burley, Masters and Backett-Milburn report on data from interviews conducted with 38 young people between the ages of 15 and 27 who had experienced parental substance misuse for a substantial period in their childhoods. Interestingly, they found that the ways in which children experience care can result in a re-defining of who is a parent. This is a fluid definition as a substance-using parent 'reparents', and may attempt to re-establish emotional bonds, or as the young person themselves becomes a parent. Boundaries between roles are thus reshaped, out of necessity and choice.

Childhood is experienced differentially across social class, localities and time. These chapters offer new and stimulating data and ideas on the dynamic nature of childhood. Authors also locate their work in the context of families and relationships, reflecting on the potential relevance to policy and practice. Thus, the boundary metaphor aids investigation and consideration of children, families and relationships.

FIVE

Children's boundaries: within and beyond families

Malcolm Hill

Introduction

In recent theorising about childhood both regulation and agency are said to be greater now than in the past. Some writers have emphasised how much of children's lives is controlled, yet others – and sometimes the same people – also stress that children have choice and influence over their own environments and development. The apparent paradox derives in part from attention to different timescales and domains, as children are more constrained in some contexts than others. Taking a long-term perspective, childhood is now seen as more regulated than in the past, especially through the creation of schools and, more recently, preschool and leisure institutions (Hendrick, 1997; James et al, 1998; Prout, 2001), although arguably there has also been a limited trend to encourage children's individual choices and collective participation through such measures as school councils (Alderson, 2000). During the last 50 years, such trends as the growth in road traffic and loosening of community ties are seen to have increased parental control of children's space outside the home (Hillman, 1993). Yet within the (western) home, relations are generally thought to have become more democratic in recent times (Mayall, 1994; Dahlberg, 1996; Mayall, 2002). In a postmodern context, children are seen as having to manage greater change and diversity than in previous eras, while also having greater scope for influencing many aspects of their own upbringing, since adults are less able than formerly to impose their own definitions and models (du Bois-Reymond et al, 1993). Young people are, it is argued, less constrained by ascribed roles and socioeconomic determinants of life paths, so they are more able and more inclined to create their own individual biographies (Beck and Beck-Gernsheim, 2001).

The notion of boundary is highly relevant to these trends, as a concept that helps illuminate the extent and limits of children's own choices with respect to relationships and space and a means of describing a key feature of parental control of children. Boundary is not a term used explicitly from children's own accounts of their lives, but is a helpful way of considering the ways in which they manage key relationships and spaces in their lives. The most common explicit application of the word 'boundary' in the academic and professional literatures has been in relation to children embedded in families and other social institutions. Internal family boundaries are seen to demarcate groupings of individuals within the family, while the negotiation of external family boundaries is seen as crucial in shaping interactions, identity and individual security. In that context children have been regarded less as individual agents and more as objects of study in ecological developmental psychology (for example, Bronfenbrenner, 1979) or in their role as family members in family systems and family therapy models (for example, Minuchin, 1974).

This chapter begins with attention to children's own creation of boundaries, then considers parents' perspectives and finally gives brief attention to family boundaries. The conclusion suggests the need to integrate understandings of children in their own right and as located within nested relationships.

Children's boundaries of identity, family and trust

This section considers *inferred personal and affectual boundaries*, which have meaning to children as social actors (Morgan, 1996), in the sense that they structure everyday relationships and activities by demarcating the close, familiar or trusted from the more distant and risky. They are inferred, because on the whole children themselves rarely describe their lives explicitly in this way, but their behaviour and responses to questions or discussion point to the significance of such a demarcation. Boundary notions have been explored for many years in developmental psychology and psychodynamic theory – and taken up by geographers over the last decade (Aitken, 1998). Recent social research has produced considerable relevant information, as a result of its interest in children's everyday and lifecourse choices in negotiating different and largely adult-oriented or controlled contexts (Brannen, 1999).

As the name suggests, ego psychology is concerned with the self and how it changes from infancy onwards (Erikson, 1963). Very young babies are thought to experience the world in a fairly undifferentiated way, having neither a separate sense of self from their sensed environment nor an awareness of different elements in that environment. Gradually, a sense of self develops that includes understanding of the limits and integrity of the infant's body, as well as a growing distinction of self and other in the mental and emotional domains (Kristeva, 1982, cited in Sibley, 1998). According to Winnicott (1971), for young children this does not involve the creation of a rigid boundary but use of 'transitional space', an intermediate zone between the self and the external world. Here, with the reassurance of parental proximity or familiar objects, children play and experiment. Aitken and Herman (1997) suggest that transitional space is a key locus for individual and cultural creativity.

The early stages of establishing boundaries around the self and establishing an identity are affected by the child's gender, especially when care is primarily by someone of the same sex (for girls) or the opposite sex (for boys) (Wetherell, 1997). In psychodynamic theories, the process of boundary development is not a neutral process, since the child associates positive and negative feelings with aspects of self and people, places and objects in the environment (Winnicott, 1965; Aitken, 2001). Emotions about what is good or bad are transmitted both ways across the boundaries between self and other. For example, a disliked aspect of oneself may be displaced onto someone else (projection) or vice versa (introjection). One consequence of trying to maintain a protective boundary around oneself may be that negative feelings are deflected onto others, sometimes particular individuals, sometimes whole groups thereby feeding gang processes, racism or sectarianism, for instance (Sibley, 1995).

Hence the notion of boundary is closely linked to ideas about identity. A child's sense of self relates in part to the body (gender, age, size, say) (see, for example, James, 1993), but it also entails external or social identity, namely the groupings an individual sees himself or herself as belonging to. These may range from family or friendship groups to national or even supranational identification. Thus children are part of 'we groups' distinguished from others who are different or do not belong. Psychological approaches to identity have traditionally conceptualised this in terms of a phased progression towards a relatively fixed identity achieved in late adolescence, while until recently sociology tended to define identity in terms of ascribed categories such as class and ethnicity. Recent theory tends to portray identity as multiple, provisional and changing, consistent with the idea that individuals often set fluid boundaries around the cultures and groups they feel connections with (Fook, 2002; Hopkins 2004).

A number of studies have explored where children place the boundaries around their ideas of what constitutes a family and more specifically who they regard as part of their family (Morrow, 1998). Children usually include in their family those they live with and close consanguineal kin, but may also add others they feel close to. Besides co-residence, choices about where to place the boundary of inclusion are affected by frequency of contact, strength of feelings and nature of the feelings, positive or negative (Brannen and Heptinstall, 2003). Children vary in the extent to which they include extended kin like grandparents, whether living in or beyond the household. Those from certain minority ethnic backgrounds with an emphasis on joint kin households and activities tend to embrace a wider range of relatives. It is quite common for children to include pets and unrelated people they feel close to (Levin, 1995; O'Brien et al, 1996; Brannen et al, 2000).

When children experience major family and household changes, they reconfigure the boundaries between those they feel to be family or trusted and those who are or have become less close (Jensen and McKee, 2003). Some children see their family as strongly divided with a marked internal boundary (Hill et al, 1995). Children who live separately from one or both parents exercise choices about whether to include the separated parent(s) or the 'second' parent(s) and perhaps siblings they have acquired through remarriage, fostering or adoption. In such circumstances children may say they have 'two fathers' (for instance, by birth and stepparenthood) or two mums (a foster mother and a birth mother, say) (Hill et al, 1989; Heptinstall et al, 2001). Also children may retain ties to half- and stepsiblings they are separated from, which are stronger than adults realise (Kosonen, 2002). Even street children who are not visibly living with any kind of family nevertheless often see themselves as part of their birth family, both emotionally and economically (Beazley, 2000).

Boundaries surround not only families, but also the home. Several writers have noted how the distinction between the private world of the home and that public world outside is increasingly artificial. The media and computers bring the world at large into the home. Also children themselves often recognise an intermediate space close to their homes, which can offer a desirable mix of security and opportunities for freedom (Kelley et al, 1997; Harden, 2000).

Boundaries of trust within and outside the home are central in children's lives. Access to trusted relationships is widely seen to bring an array of benefits for children, including happiness, security, self-esteem, social capital and the capacity to overcome adversity (Newman,

2004). Many children make a key distinction between familiar people and strangers, reinforced by the attention given to stranger danger by parents, teachers and the media (Kelley et al, 1997; Borland et al, 1998). There is much evidence that children and young people hold differentiated views of key people in their networks, with parents (particularly mothers) and friends usually being the main confidants (Catan et al, 1997; Ghate and Daniels, 1997; Borland et al, 1998; Hill, 1999). When families are the sites of violence or neglect, then trust within the family is threatened or destroyed, so children's capacity to cope may depend on their ability to extend their boundaries of trust to other figures such as teachers or youth workers. The kinds of criteria children typically use when choosing when and if to seek or accept help include kindness, being listened to, having confidences respected, being taken seriously and perceiving action that responds to the child's own concerns (Hill, 1999; Wade and Smart, 2002). Trust becomes particularly important when children have problems they feel sensitive about or a status experienced as stigmatising, such as being fostered or adopted, having a disability or a parent with a mental health problem (Hill et al, 1989; Armstrong et al, 2000; Sinclair et al, 2001).

Allan (1996) has concluded from a number of studies that adults of middle-class backgrounds are more oriented to extending relationships across different settings, whereas working-class sociability has traditionally been more confined to discrete contexts. Children living in poverty can find it hard to make and sustain friendships because they do not have the material resources necessary to engage in shared travel and activities or to adhere to peer norms with regards to dress and possessions (Middleton et al, 1995; Ridge, 2002).

Children demarcate places as well as people as safe and trusted or as risky in ways that shape their use and avoidance of space. Danger may be perceived in the nature of the physical environment, but fears are also affected by human presence (rival gangs, racial divides, drug addicts, controlling adults and so on) and time (especially hours of darkness) (Hart, 1979; Moore, 1986; Webster, 1996; Tucker, 2003).

Parent–child negotiations of boundary setting

Certain professionals and academics use the word 'boundary' as a shorthand for all the rules that parents set where children are expected not to go beyond a limit of time, space, activity or personal contact (see, for example, Hood et al, 1996; Borland et al, 1998; Brannen et al,

2000; Backett-Milburn and Harden, forthcoming). A recent review of psychological research on parenting summarised that "warm/ supportive parents tend to provide firm and consistent boundaries" (O'Connor, 2002, p 557). Beyond the boundaries are actually or potentially risky or threatening people and places, or – in relation to behaviour – harmful consequences. It is not clear how many parents themselves use this term, although some undoubtedly do: "You've got to have a little bit of boundary, you know" (mother, cited by Brannen et al, 2000, p 181). It is a significant component in the discourses of some who are in close contact with professionals, such as foster carers (Walker et al, 2002).

Parents set boundaries around such matters as where children may go, alone or accompanied, what time they should be home and how they ought to behave. With increasing age, but to variable extents, children 'challenge these boundaries' and seek to renegotiate them. Even parents who perceive themselves as giving their children much freedom have 'bottom lines', which they seek to enforce strictly. The explicit motivations and rationales for such boundaries include children's needs for care and safety, but there are also elements of encouraging the child to fit with (adult) community norms and securing a controlled home environment that suits adults' wants or needs (Sibley, 1995; Brannen et al, 2000).

Parents who live in neighbourhoods that they perceive to be dangerous tend to place more restrictions on their children's activities (Borland et al, 1998; Russell et al, 2002). Some parents place an emphasis on stating clear boundaries that children are directed to adhere to, while others are more willing to negotiate with their children both about the nature of the boundaries and the ways of dealing with transgressions (du Bois-Reymond et al, 1993; Brannen et al, 2000). In the psychology literature, it is suggested that parents follow consistent styles, with some tending to be directive or to favour negotiation across all types of boundary setting (for instance, rules concerning personal care and privacy, home life, school, leisure, time keeping, behaviour and peer associations) (Maccoby and Martin, 1983). Many parents' accounts indicate that they seek to encourage their children to internalise ideas about safe and appropriate people, behaviour and areas, such that the children generate their own boundaries without the need for the parents to impose them (du Bois-Reymond et al, 1993; Borland et al, 1998).

It appears that most children and young people broadly accept their parents' rights to set limits and, for the most part, abide by the particular boundaries set (Coleman and Hendry, 1992; du Bois-

Reymond et al, 1993). Equally, they employ a variety of strategies that enable them to push the boundaries back, either in general or by appeal to exceptional circumstances. For instance, Christensen et al (2000) found that children exploited their movements in and out of the home to create periods they had control over. An exchange may be negotiated, whereby conformity on most issues is used to bargain for autonomy on some matters. Harden et al (2000) described children agreeing to carry out domestic duties in return for a parental concession. Other research has shown that children, to varying degrees, contest with parents their use of time outdoors and so are active contributors to the rules that are established (Valentine, 1997; Matthews et al, 2000; Valentine, 2004). Other strategies include secrecy, lying, moods and collusion with friends or siblings (Kelley et al, 1997). Current research in progress by this author and colleagues has highlighted how parents nowadays use mobile phones as a means of control at a distance for trying to keeping their children safe, while some young people adapt this form of communication to gain more freedom for themselves.

Family systems perspectives on boundaries

The most explicit and long-standing application of the concept of boundary with regard to children has been within family systems and family therapy thinking, which has also influenced professional work more broadly, as in relation to child protection. This approach stresses the interconnectedness of all family members, sometimes to such an extent that children's agency and the external world are left out of the picture. Early formulations usually focused on family households of conventional form (although with problematic interactions in the family therapy sphere), but nowadays greater recognition is given to family diversity.

According to Dallos and Draper (1998), families control power, intimacy, personal space and privacy through boundary setting and maintenance. Boundaries are established between individuals and grouping within the family, as well as between the family and the outside world. One kind of *internal* boundary lies between the self and family membership or shared activity (Dallos, 1997), whereas another occurs between different subsystems (pairs or groups of family members). Two types of subsystem boundaries are identified. The first type is based on the biological distinctions of age and gender, which are seen to shape natural or desirable groupings within families. For instance, a boundary is recognised between an adult or parental subsystem and a dependent child subsystem. This is seen as a universal feature of families, although the precise meaning of the adult–child division is shaped by culture, time and place. The second type of boundary is between particularistic alliances. These develop on a short-term or longer-term basis, often in situations of conflict, as when two siblings gang up on a third or when a child seeks the support of one parent to influence the other parent.

When families grow, split or rejoin, a systems approach emphasises how boundaries have to be renegotiated. This may mean that the certain individuals' family membership may be contested or depend on the viewpoint. When a couple with children separate, each parent may seek to set a boundary excluding the other and including one or more of the children, whose own boundary preferences may vary among siblings and over time. Thus a stepparent may not be accepted as a family member by a child, while a father who has left home may be seen as having left the family by his wife or partner, but not necessarily by his child(ren). The arrival of half- or stepsiblings can challenge previous expectations (Berger, 2000), while the departure of older children to independent living may result in realignments among the remaining family members.

Differentiation within families is acknowledged through the concept of internal boundaries but there is also a tendency to describe the family as operating as a single collective unit, with uniform wishes and goals, thereby disguising questions of which family member(s) may determine family decisions, rules and actions and whose needs and interests these may serve. In family systems theorising, children are generally shadowy figures with little direct input to family processes, although their needs as perceived by experts are a central consideration and they are often foregrounded as displaying emotions or behaviour that mirrors a crucial feature of family dynamics. Typically, a child's 'symptom' is redefined as signifying family dysfunction. This reframing of the problem makes the child central to family processes, yet risks marginalising the child as individual and participant in extra-familial realms.

Families are depicted as having *external* boundaries with varying degrees of semi-permeability. Gehring et al (1998) define such a boundary in terms of rules to determine who belongs within a family and who does not. Relationships within the family system are seen as more intense and intimate, compared with those outside (Barker, 1998). People behave differently to those inside the boundary and often have shared beliefs about how to behave towards those outside. Boundaries control exchange and closeness. Families vary in their beliefs about the appropriate levels of exposure of their private world to and influence or interference by the outside public world. Each family determines how often and in what way members interact with the outside world to take advantage of opportunities and resources (for example, employment) and to respond to demands made (that the children attend school, for example), as well as to protect itself from unwanted external interference. Aspects of the boundary maintenance processes may include rules about self-presentation and the allocation of roles to different individuals to deal with particular external interactions (Minuchin, 1974; Nichols et al, 2000). The manner in which this occurs both reflects and creates family identities (Dallos, 1997).

Family therapy and boundaries

Family therapies refer to encounters between one or more professionals and family members with the intention of resolving or ameliorating some kind of problem related to family dynamics. Apart from occasional attempts to involve extended kin and even other key social network members (Marsh and Crow, 1998; Hill, 2002), family therapy has normally been focused on the nuclear families, although increasingly with attention to their interactions with the nexus of helping agencies. There have been several evolving schools of thought, but most have used, to a larger or smaller extent, systems ideas to understand the dynamic relationship between (a) the connectedness among family members and their individual autonomy and (b) the changing balance in family relationships according to the evolving needs of family members. Prominent among the foci of assessment and treatment are "subsystems, interpersonal boundaries and relationships" (Vetere, 1999, p 148). Most of the different schools draw on systems ideas about internal and external boundaries.

A strong component is the view that *within families* a clear or strong boundary should separate the generations. In other words, (young) children should not be expected to undertake 'adult' functions – taken to include sexual activity, financial provision, emotional labour, major physical care taking, resolving martial problems. Families should have a clear boundary between the adult subsystem and the child subsystem (Barker, 1998). Thus, a key aim of family therapy may be that adults 'take back' responsibilities or worries they have placed on children. The therapist may exclude the children from the room when parents discuss their own conflicts (Dallos and Draper, 1998).

A slightly different point, deriving from Minuchin (1974), is that individuals (adult or child) need boundaries that reconcile closeness with separate identity. Thus it is problematic if relationships become enmeshed (members are too closely involved in each other's problems) or disengaged (members lead largely separate lives). Structural therapy aims to strengthen boundaries between people when they are enmeshed and to weaken boundaries when they are too detached (Gehring et al, 1998).

A further claim is that families also need 'clear' external boundaries. 'Dysfunctional' families are seen as having either rigid or chaotic boundaries, whereas 'non-clinical' families have definite but flexible boundaries. An impervious boundary implies social isolation (Barker, 1998).

Other professionals and boundary setting

Only a small minority of professionals working with families embrace a full family therapy approach, although some others have been influenced by its concepts and techniques. Professionals tend to operate with the concept of boundaries in relation to two issues, namely managing children's behaviour and keeping children safe.

With respect to behaviour, this can arise when parents have difficulties in 'controlling' their children, who are acting in ways that cause concern to parents themselves, neighbours or to outside agencies (school, the police, for instance). Such parents are thought to need help in setting firm and clear boundaries for their children (see, for instance, Lanyado, 1999). Also, when parents provide 'explanations for the settings of rules and boundaries', this correlates with 'positive outcomes' for the children (Coleman, 2001, p 29). Especially as children grow older, they are regarded as having a thrust towards extending their horizons and the activities and spaces over which they have autonomy (especially within a western or postmodern context of individualisation), while parents are characterised as needing to provide guidance and restraint for the sake of the child's safety, the protection of others or the parent's own piece of mind (Borland et al, 1998; Russell et al, 2002). Parents, of course, are not necessarily objective in their assessment of what are appropriate boundaries, which is influenced by their own biographies and interests (Lanyado, 1999).

When professionals refer to the need for clear and socially acceptable boundaries, this is linked to the notion of family rules. The argument is that parents should, first, make explicit to their children what the rules are concerning the limits or boundaries of acceptable behaviour, second, make clear what are the consequences of unacceptable behaviour and, third, enforce those consequences consistently. This approach draws not only on family systems notions of boundary, but also psychological research on effective parenting and social learning theories (Herbert, 1998). The boundary or limit may apply to behaviour (shouting or aggression, say), time (for example, coming home by an agreed hour), place (not going to certain places, for example) or people (not associating with 'undesirables', say). Not uncommonly the boundary will embody a combination of several dimensions, such as rules not to associate with certain individuals at night when they are going to a disapproved place, not to swear in the presence of a sensitive older person or not to go to a party or club without adult supervision or transport. Thus some behaviours or activities may be absolutely off limits in a particular family (for instance, physical violence), whereas the (un)acceptability of others is contingent on the interaction with the socio-spatial-temporal context.

At one extreme of applying such ideas, children are excluded from processes of defining the problem and planned solutions. They are treated as reactive in that they are expected to conform to the rules and boundaries that are set or else face negative consequences (Gough, 1999). More commonly, children are engaged in the negotiations, but may only have influence on the margins (to modify rules about time keeping, for instance). For some professionals, it is sufficient and effective to focus on the child's behaviour, as construed by the adults, with little or no attention to the child's definitions of the problem, the social or situational contexts contributing to the production of the behaviour or the personal history that might help account for the difficulties. Others combine boundary setting with attention to the child's emotional and social needs and with negotiations about the young person's wishes. These contrasting approaches are evident in different types of fostering schemes that have developed for young people with histories of family conflict and/or involvement in crime (Walker et al, 2002).

Whereas boundary management of behaviour affects young people characterised as troublesome, in relation to child abuse and child protection the issues correspond to perceptions of children as vulnerable and innocent. With reference to boundary setting in professional interventions where parents are thought to have harmed their children, Beckett (2003) suggests that aims and ground rules should be agreed with parents. This "is based on the idea that parents have crossed some boundary of acceptable parental behaviour, and the aim of the work is to re-establish that boundary" (Beckett, 2003, p 37). A key application of the boundary idea involves the notions of appropriate intergenerational boundaries and personal boundaries. Sex between adults and children is seen by most commentators to be a complete transgression of a generational separation of sex, as an activity that is meant to be confined to adults and is harmful to children (Lanyado, 1999). Few dissent from this perspective in relation to pre-pubertal children, although the moral imperative to protect children and evidence about harm have been challenged (Evans, 1993). As with children's participatory rights, more uncertainty exists as young people move through the teen years. Regardless of age, sex between parental figures and children additionally crosses near universal taboos.

A further issue in which intergenerational boundaries have been described as unacceptably crossed has been with respect to children performing practical and sometimes emotional tasks for or on behalf of their disabled or ill parents. During the 1990s this situation was crystallised and problematised through the concept of 'young carers', a term that many of the children themselves do not like (Dearden and Becker, 2001; Banks et al, 2002).

Conclusions

This chapter has reviewed evidence about how children and parents negotiate crucial distinctions as regards the familiar and trusted, on the one hand, and the strange or threatening, on the other. As with political frontiers (Newman and Paasi, 1998), children, parents and families demarcate the 'we' from the 'other'. However, the boundaries established among relationships and spaces in children's lives are fluid at any one time and evolve as time goes by. The boundaries created mediate the exchange of ideas, emotion, trust and practical assistance.

While there is a growing literature on these processes, the idea of boundary has been rarely applied or developed explicitly. In contrast, overt reference to boundaries has been prominent in family systems perspectives and family therapy. However, here the term boundary is mostly used descriptively as a simple demarcation between different spheres of family and social life, with little development of ideas about the nature of the boundary or positionality. An exception is the work of Aitken (2000, 2001), who has developed the psychodynamic concept of 'transitional space' representing border areas, where children explore, experiment and interact across boundaries among the safe/familiar and new or less familiar experiences, people and places.

Hence there is a need to link and develop child-centred and family-centred approaches to boundary phenomena and to conceptualise these further, in ways that incorporate both children's agency and their embeddedness within family relations. This should be rooted in the constructions of children, parents and other key adults in their lives, since so far (including this chapter) the term has been normally imposed by academics and professionals to group how they themselves see families and organise their own understandings about children's and parents' perceptions. Boundary thinking about children within and beyond their families will involve mapping from children's points of view the key spaces in their environment and the interactive processes and accounts that underpin children's evaluations and usage of social spaces in their lives and the borders and frontier zones between them. These have thus far been largely conceptualised by academics 'from above' (Bronfenbrenner, 1979; Moss and Petrie, 2002; Brannen and Moss, 2003), so the boundaries between adult theories and the views of children also need to be made more permeable.

Likewise policies and services could be more attuned to family members' perspectives on boundaries as these portray interactions of place, time and behaviour that create spaces seen to provide safety and opportunity *or* physical and lifestyle dangers (Seaman, 2004). Young people in urban and rural areas have repeatedly highlighted the importance of neighbourhood design, child-friendly transport and accessible leisure facilities as crucial for their social inclusion in varied ways, alongside adult attitudes that respect children's agency (Hill et al, 2004; Seaman, 2004). This requires not only the availability of adult supervised facilities promoting the development of human and social capital, but also safe transitional spaces, where innovation and self-regulation can occur (Aitken and Herman, 1997).

References

Aitken, S. (1998) *Family fantasies and community space*, Piscataway, NJ: Rutgers University Press.

Aitken, S. (2000) 'Play, rights and borders', in S.L. Holloway and G. Valentine (eds) *Children's geographies*, London: Routledge.

Aitken, S. (2001) *Geographies of young people*, London: Routledge.

Aitken, S. and Herman, T. (1997) 'Gender, power and crib geography: transition spaces and potential places', *Gender, Place and Culture*, vol 4, pp 63-88.

Alderson, P. (2000) 'Practising democracy in two inner city schools', in A. Osler (ed) *Citizenship and democracy in schools*, Stoke-on-Trent: Trentham Books.

Allan, G. (1996) *Kinship and friendship in modern Britain*, Oxford: Oxford University Press.

Armstrong, C., Hill, M. and Secker, J. (2000) Young people's perceptions of mental health, *Children and Society*, vol 14, pp 60-72.

Backett-Milburn, K. and Harden, J. (2004) 'How children and their families construct and negotiate risk, safety and danger', *Childhood*, vol 11, no 4, pp 429-77.

Banks, P., Gallagher, E., Hill, M. and Riddell, S. (2002) *Literature review of identification, needs assessment and service provision for young carers and their families*, Edinburgh: Scottish Executive Central Research Unit.

Barker, P. (1998) *Basic family therapy*, Oxford: Blackwell Science.

Beazley, H. (2000) 'Home sweet home', in S.L. Holloway and G. Valentine (eds) *Children's geographies*, London: Routledge.

Beck, U. and Beck-Gernsheim, E. (2001) *Individualisation*, London: Sage Publications.

Beckett, C. (2003) *Child protection: An introduction*, London: Sage Publications.

Berger, R. (2000) 'Remarried families of 2000', in W.C. Nichols, M.A. Pace-Nichols, D.S. Becvar and A.Y. Napier (eds) *Handbook of family development and intervention*, New York, NY: John Wiley & Sons.

Borland, M., Laybourn, A., Hill, M. and Brown, J. (1998) *Middle childhood*, London: Jessica Kingsley.

Brannen, J. (1999) 'Reconsidering children and childhood: sociological and policy perspectives', in E.B. Silva and C. Smart (eds) *The new family?*, London: Sage Publications.

Brannen, J. and Heptinstall, E. (2003) 'Concepts of care and children's contribution to family life', in J. Brannen and P. Moss (eds) *Rethinking children's care*, Buckingham: Open University Press.

Brannen, J. and Moss, P. (2003) *Rethinking children's care*, Buckingham: Open University Press.

Brannen, J., Heptinstall, E. and Bhopal, K. (2000) *Connecting children*, London: Routledge/Falmer.

Bronfenbrenner, U. (1979) *The ecology of human development*, Cambridge, MA: Harvard University Press.

Catan, L., Coleman, J. and Dennison, C. (1997) *Getting through*, Brighton: Trust for the Study of Adolescence.

Christensen, P., James, A. and Jenks, C. (2000) 'Home and movement', in S.L. Holloway and G. Valentine (eds) *Children's geographies*, London: Routledge.

Coleman, J. (2001) 'The needs of parents and children', in J. Coleman and D. Roker (eds) *Supporting parents of teenagers*, London: Jessica Kingsley.

Coleman, J.C. and Hendry, L. (1992) *The nature of adolescence*, London: Routledge.

Dahlberg, G. (1996) 'Negotiating modern childrearing and family life in Sweden', in J. Brannen and R. Edwards (eds) *Perspectives on parenting and childhood: Looking back and moving forward*, London: South Bank University.

Dallos, R. (1997) 'Constructing family life: family belief systems', in J. Muncie, M. Wetherell, M. Langan, R. Dallos and A. Cochrane (eds) *Understanding the family*, London: Sage Publications.

Dallos, R. and Draper, R. (1998) *An introduction to family therapy*, Buckingham: Open University Press.

Dearden, C. and Becker, S. (2001) 'Young carers: needs, rights and assessments', in J. Horvath (ed) *The child's world*, London: Jessica Kingsley.

du Bois-Reymond, M., Buchner, P. and Krueger, H.-H. (1993) 'Modern family as everyday negotiation: continuities and discontinuities in parent–child relationships', *Childhood*, vol 1, pp 87-99.

Erikson, E.H. (1963) *Childhood and society*, Harmondsworth: Penguin.

Evans, D.T. (1993) *Sexual citizenship*, London: Routledge.

Fook, J. (2002) *Social work: Critical theory and practice*, London: Sage Publications.

Gehring, T.M., Debry, M. and Smith, P.K. (1998) *The family system test: FAST*, London: Brunner-Routledge.

Ghate, D. and Daniels, A. (1997) *Talking about my generation*, London: NSPCC.

Gough, D. (1999) 'Social learning and behavioural approaches to work with children and families', in M. Hill (ed) *Effective ways of working with children and families*, London: Jessica Kingsley.

Harden, J. (2000) 'There's no place like home', *Childhood*, vol 7, pp 43-59.

Harden, J., Backett-Milburn, K., Scott, S. and Jackson, S. (2000) 'Scary faces, scary places', *Health Education Journal*, vol 59, pp 12-22.

Hart, R. (1979) *Children's experience of place*, New York, NY: Irvington.

Hendrick, H. (1997) *Children, childhood and English society 1880-1990*, Cambridge: Cambridge University Press.

Heptinstall, E., Bhopal, K. and Brannen, J. (2001) 'Adjusting to a foster family: children's perspectives', *Adoption and fostering*, vol 25, pp 6-17.

Herbert, M. (1998) *Clinical child psychology*, Chichester: John Wiley & Sons.

Hill, M. (1999) 'What's the problem? Who can help? The perspectives of children and young people on their well-being and on helping professionals, *Journal of Social Work Practice*, vol 13, pp 135-45.

Hill, M. (2002) 'Network assessments and diagrams: a flexible friend for social work practice and education, *Journal of Social Work*, vol 2, no 2, pp 233-54.

Hill, M., Lambert, L. and Triseliotis, J. (1989) *Achieving adoption with love and money*, London: National Children's Bureau.

Hill, M., Laybourn, A. and Borland, M. (1995) *Children's well being*, Glasgow: University of Glasgow Report for Health Education Board for Scotland.

Hill, M., Davis, J., Prout, A. and Tisdall, K. (2004) 'Moving the participation agenda forward', *Children and Society*, vol 18, pp 77-96.

Hillman, M. (1993) *Children, transport and the quality of life*, London: Policy Studies Institute.

Hood, S., Kelley, P., Mayall, B., Okley, A. and Morrell, R. (1996) *Children, parents and risk*, London: Institute of Education.

Hopkins, P. (2004) 'Young Muslim men in Scotland: inclusion and exclusions', *Children's Geographies*, vol 2, no 2, pp 257-72.

James, A. (1993) *Childhood identities*, Edinburgh: Edinburgh University Press.

James, A., Jenks, C. and Prout, A. (1998) *Theorising childhood*, Cambridge: Polity Press.

Jensen, A.-M. and McKee, L. (2003) *Children and the changing family*, London: Routledge-Falmer.

Kelley, P., Mayall, B. and Hood, S. (1997) 'Children's accounts of risk', *Childhood*, vol 4, pp 305-24.

Kosonen, M. (2002) *Foster children's sibling relationships in middle childhood*, Glasgow: University of Glasgow Press.

Kristeva, J. (1982) *Powers of horror*, New York, NY: Columbia University Press.

Lanyado, M. (1999) '"It's just an ordinary pain": thoughts on joy and heartache in puberty and early adolescence', in D. Hindle and M.V. Smith (eds) *Personality development*, London: Routledge.

Levin, I. (1995) 'Children's perceptions of their family', *Annale dell'Istituto di Dirritto e Procedura penale.*

Maccoby, E.E. and Martin, J.A. (1983) 'Socialisation in the context of the family: parent–child interaction', in E.M. Hetherington (ed) *Handbook of child psychology: Socialisation, personality and social development*, New York, NY: John Wiley & Sons.

Marsh, P. and Crow, G. (1998) *Family group conferences in child welfare*, Oxford: Blackwell.

Matthews, H., Limb, M. and Taylor, M. (2000) 'The "street as third-space"', in S.L. Holloway and G. Valentine (eds) *Children's geographies*, London: Routledge.

Mayall, B. (1994) *Negotiating health: Primary school children at home and school*, London: Cassell.

Mayall, B. (2002) *Towards a sociology of childhood*, Buckingham: Open University Press.

Middleton, S., Ashworth, K. and Walker, R. (1995) *Family fortunes*, London: CPAG.

Minuchin, S. (1974) *Families and family therapy*, Cambridge, MA: Harvard University Press.

Moore, R.C. (1986) *Children's domain: Play and place in child development*, London: Croom Helm.

Morgan, D.H.J. (1996) *Family connections*, Cambridge: Polity Press.

Morrow, V. (1998) *Understanding families: Children's perspectives*, London: National Children's Bureau.

Moss, P. and Petrie, P. (2002) *From children's services to children's spaces*, London: Routledge.

Newman, D. and Paasi, A. (1998) 'Fences and neighbours in the postmodern world: boundary narratives in political geography', *Progress in Human Geography*, vol 22, pp 186-207.

Newman, T. (2004) *What works in building resilience*, Barkingside: Barnardo's.

Nichols, W.C., Pace-Nichols, M.A., Becvar, D.S. and Napier, A.Y. (2000) *Handbook of family development and intervention*, New York, NY: John Wiley & Sons.

O'Brien, M., Aldred, P. and Jones, D. (1996) 'Children's constructions of family and kinships', in J. Brannen and M. O'Brien (eds) *Children in families*, London: Falmer Press.

O'Connor, T. (2002) 'The "effects" of parenting reconsidered: findings, challenges and applications', *Journal of Child Psychology and Psychiatry*, vol 43, pp 555-72.

Prout, A. (2001) *The future of childhood*, Dublin: The Children's Research Centre.

Ridge, T. (2002) *Childhood poverty and social exclusion*, Bristol: The Policy Press.

Russell, A., Mize, J. and Bissaker, K. (2002) 'Parent–child relationships', in P.K. Smith and C.H. Hart (eds) *Blackwell handbook of childhood social development*, Oxford: Blackwell.

Seaman, P. (2004) 'Parents' evaluations of risk and safety in their communities: parenting responses and implications for the study of social capital', *Scottish Journal of Youth Issues*, vol 7, pp 53-70.

Sibley, D. (1995) *Geographies of exclusion*, London: Routledge.

Sibley, D. (1998) 'Families and domestic routines: constructing the boundaries of childhood', in S. Pile and N. Thrift (eds) *Mapping the subject: Geographies of cultural transformation*, London: Routledge.

Sinclair, I., Wilson, K. and Gibbs, I. (2001) '"A life more ordinary': what children want from foster placements', *Adoption and Fostering*, vol 25, pp 17-26.

Tucker, F. (2003) 'Sameness or difference: exploring girls use of recreational spaces', *Children's geographies*, vol 1, pp 111-24.

Valentine, G. (1997) '"Oh yes I can". "Oh no you can't": children and parents' understanding of kids' competence to negotiate public space safely', *Antipode*, vol 29, no 1, pp 65-89.

Valentine, G. (2004) *Public space and the culture of childhood*, Aldershot: Ashgate.

Vetere, A. (1999) 'Family therapy', in M. Hill (ed) *Effective ways of working with children and families*, London: Jessica Kingsley.

Wade, A. and Smart, C. (2002) *Facing family change: Children's circumstances, strategies and resources*, York: Joseph Rowntree Foundation.

Walker, M., Hill, M. and Triseliotis, J. (2002) *Testing the limits of foster care*, London: British Agencies for Adoption and Fostering.

Webster, C. (1996) 'Local heroes, violent racism, localism and spacism among Asian and white people', *Youth and Policy*, vol 53, pp 15-27.

Wetherell, M. (1997) 'The psychoanalytic approach to family life', in J. Muncie, M. Wetherell, M. Langan, R. Dallos and A. Cochrange (eds) *Understanding the family*, London: Sage Publications.

Winnicott, D.W. (1965) *The child, the family and the outside world*, Harmondsworth: Penguin.

Winnicott, D.W. (1971) *Playing and reality*, London: Tavistock.

SIX

Family within and beyond the household boundary: children's constructions of who they live with

Helen Sweeting and Peter Seaman

Introduction

This chapter presents data from two studies that illustrate the complexity of decisions in respect of whether or not certain individuals form part of 'the family'. In this case, the individuals in question are non-resident birth fathers. Our perspective is primarily methodological and our focus is the problems faced by those researchers who seek to place 'families' in categories. However, these data illustrate several of this book's key themes, including the difficulty of defining family and family boundaries, particularly as potentially represented by the material space of household.

The notion of 'family boundary', derived from family systems theory, refers to the invisible set of rules determining who, when and how members participate in family life (Minuchin, 1974). 'Boundary ambiguity' therefore occurs when family members are uncertain about who is in and out, and who is performing what tasks (Boss and Greenberg, 1984). Since such boundaries may be physical or psychological, a non-resident birth father who, for example, continues to provide input in respect of decisions about a child's upbringing or education, may remain psychologically present while physically absent (Taanila et al, 2002). Shifts in family structure require a reorganisation of boundaries and clarification of new roles and expectations (Cole and Cole, 1999). Previous literature has focused on this in respect of individual family members, since it has been suggested that lack of clarity, or disparity between physical and psychological presence or absence, is stressful and related to poorer family functioning (Boss and Greenberg, 1984). However, the fluid nature of family boundaries is also an issue for policymakers and practitioners.

Researching family structure

Quantitative researchers with an interest in family life are a further group for whom the fluid nature of family boundaries is an issue, since they generally wish to define various family characteristics within a narrow range of predetermined categories for analytical purposes. For example, studies that focus on the family structure of children and young people usually ask respondents to tick a number of boxes ('mother', 'father', 'stepmother', stepfather', 'father's girlfriend', and so on) in order to indicate which adults they live with. These responses are then used to divide their sample into two (those with two resident parents compared with those with one – for example, Green et al, 1990) or three groups, created by further splitting the former category (those residing with two birth parents, compared with those with one birth parent plus a new partner forming a 'step' or 'reconstituted' household – Sweeting et al, 1998, for example). In this chapter we focus on two issues raised by such methods. The first of these is the subjectivity of respondents' perceptions of their family structure, the second is the difficulty of mapping these perceptions onto researchers' predefined categories. Illustrative data are drawn from two studies conducted with children, young people and their parents, one quantitative (the West of Scotland 11 to 16 Study) the other qualitative (Young People's Family Life).

Subjectivity in respect of family structure

One consequence of the fact that family members may each "live in rather different worlds" (Olson and McCubbin, 1983, p 220), and hold somewhat different perceptions of their family, is that two people from the same family might describe a third person in quite different ways. The question of the validity of a single family member's perceptions of family relationships and dynamics is now well acknowledged (Tein et al, 1994). However, it may be that even family structure has a larger subjective component than tends to be assumed. For example, a comparison of two waves of the US National Survey of Families and Households, separated by five years, found significant discrepancies in adults' reports of sibling number (White, 1998).

Another area where we might expect to find discrepancies over time or between individuals (both children and adults) is the category they select to describe a resident parent's new partner (termed here, for simplicity, the 'stepparent' even though this may be unofficial) once they enter the household as a cohabitee or following marriage. Whether or not they are accepted by children as a parent will vary according to a number of factors (Allan and Crow, 2001). These include the children's age, their relationship with and the length of time they have lived apart from the birth parent, the length of time they have known and lived with the stepparent, the stepparent's role in the household and the perceived desires of the resident parent. While adults in stepfamilies may seek to normalise their domestic arrangements and present themselves as an 'ordinary' family, this may be difficult. A stepfamily, is for example, most likely to self-define, and be defined, as 'not really a step family' when the couple has been together since the stepchildren were young (Burgoyne and Clark, 1984) and when the non-residential parent plays no part in their lives.

Mapping respondents' perceptions onto researchers' predefined categories

A second issue raised by the 'who do you live with' tickbox approach is that researchers' predefined categories may be quite different from those perceived by individual respondents. An illustration of this can be found in the way that the great majority of those with an interest in family structure restrict themselves to relationships between members who are co-resident in the same household. In this they are like almost all censuses and surveys in assuming that 'family' and 'household' can be treated as interchangeable because they coincide. However, the greater variety and changeability of modern family life means that for increasing numbers of research participants the fact is that they do not (Marsh and Arber, 1992; Haskey, 2000; Peplar, 2002). One consequence of this has been an expanding literature on 'family practices' (Morgan, 1996, 1999), or the active participation and commitment required to 'do' as opposed to 'be' in a family (Morrow, 1998; Silva and Smart, 1999; Allan and Crow, 2001). Accompanying this is the growing recognition that by compiling information only on family members living in the same household, some potentially important players may be being excluded. For instance, a 'one parent household' may for many purposes be a 'two parent family' via the involvement of a parent figure absent from the household (Crow and Hardey, 1992; Allan and Crow, 2001).

One example of the 'one parent household'/'two parent family' is visiting or 'living-apart-together' unions where partners do not share a single residence (Murphy, 1996). Another, of significance for growing numbers of children and young people, is the situation of 'parenting across households' (Maclean and Eekelar, 1997), which can occur after parental separation or divorce. Clearly, the degree of involvement from the non-resident parent, usually the father, can vary enormously. At one extreme are those who maintain direct and active involvement in all aspects of their children's daily lives, at the other those who have little or no involvement with their children, with a spectrum of visiting relationships associated with reduced parental authority in between. The first of these arrangements has been described as 'shared care' (Bradshaw et al, 1999), 'co-parenting' (Smart and Neale, 1999) or 'active joint parenting' (Allan and Crow, 2001), the others as 'solo-' and 'custodial-parenting' respectively (Smart and Neale, 1999).

A number of authors note the changes in both understandings of parenting and policy (termed the 'new orthodoxy' by Maclean and Eekelar, 1997, p 50) that occurred in the 1980s, culminating in the 1989 Children Act and 1995 Children (Scotland) Act. Prior to this the assumption was that "the best solution to divorce was remarriage" (Smart and Neale, 1999, p 70) since it not only provided children with a substitute father but also allowed the birth father to focus on a new family. With its aim of promoting the position and best interests of the child, the Children Act recognised divorce as the ending of the marriage but not of parenting; indeed the Children (Scotland) Act specifically outlines that a parent has both responsibilities and rights "if the child is not living with him, to maintain personal relations and direct contact with the child on a regular basis … in so far as compliance … is practicable and in the best interests of the child". The result has been "a legal situation wherein divorce no longer altered parents' legal relationship to their children … to this way of thinking there is no reason to imagine that the parent/child relationship should be harmed or reduced because of adverse spouse relationships" (Smart, 1999, pp 101-2). While shared, co- or joint parenting is in accord with the Children Act ethos, there are clear emotional as well as physical costs associated with any attempt to maintain the nuclear family across households and following the breakdown of a marital or cohabiting relationship

(Smart and Neale, 1999). It is more likely to occur when the parents were previously married (rather than cohabiting – Maclean and Eekelar, 1997) and when the non-resident parent lives alone or with a new partner but no children (Bradshaw et al, 1999).

For many children and young people, an additional complicating factor is that others apart from the resident and non-resident parents may also fulfil parenting functions, something which is likely to be more commonplace in one parent or solo parenting situations. The result is to further stretch the number of households in which they experience family practices such as being met from school, given treats or put to bed (Moore and Beazley, 1996). Although these people, along with non-resident parents, may be an important part of a child or young person's life, they are unlikely to feature in the 'your home and family' section of a structured questionnaire. In the remainder of this chapter we present data from two studies, one quantitative, the other qualitative, in order to illustrate these issues.

Research studies

The first of these was the baseline survey of the West of Scotland 11 to 16 Study: Teenage Health, a longitudinal, school-based study of health and health behaviours in a cohort of children resident in and around Glasgow city (West and Sweeting, 1996). This study provides our quantitative data on 'living with dad'. During classroom sessions conducted in 1994-95, 2,586 11-year-olds in 135 primary schools completed health and lifestyle questionnaires that included a section on their family. Nurses helped with questionnaire completion if necessary, and confirmed the family section with the child at the end. Questionnaires about earlier health history, family background and social position, delivered by children to their parents, were completed and returned via the school in respect of 86% of the sample (n = 2,237). The second study, Young People's Family Life, which forms the source of our qualitative data on 'parenting across households', was conducted in the same geographical area. It focused on the experience, enactment and understanding of family life, and its role in the transition to adulthood (Seaman, 2003). Its data were derived from joint and individual interviews conducted in 1997-99 with young people (aged 13-17) and their parent figures from both one and two parent households (11 of each).

Living with dad

In order to ascertain family structure in the 11 to 16 Study, the *children's* self-complete questionnaire asked which of the following adults they stayed (note that this is local terminology meaning 'live') with 'at home': 'my mum'; 'my dad'; 'my stepmum'; 'my stepdad'; 'another woman who is not my mum'; and 'another man who is not my dad'. They were then asked, 'If you do not stay with your mum or your dad, why is this?' with the (non-exclusive) options:'they are separated'; 'my mum is not alive'; 'my dad is not alive'; and 'another reason'. The section of the *parental* questionnaire focusing on the mother and father figure asked their relationship to the study child, with the options 'natural (birth)'; 'legal adoption'; 'step'; 'father's girlfriend/ mother's boyfriend'; 'other'; and 'no mother/father figure'. If the child was not living with the birth parent, parents were asked the reason, the child's age at separation, and frequency of contact. If the child was living with another parental figure, the parental questionnaire asked the child's age when the current figure took responsibility.

Initial inspection of responses to these items demonstrated a relatively large number of parent–child discrepancies (note that all analyses reported here were restricted to those for whom a parental questionnaire was available). The resulting data-cleaning[1] exercise did not assume that descriptions of family structure from the parent were superior to those of the 11-year-old child. Rather, it aimed to reconcile child–parent responses in respect of family structure by modifying either a child's, parent's or both questionnaires, depending on the nature of the disagreement. For example, a parent may have omitted details of a cohabitee when their child had specifically noted their presence; alternatively a child may have omitted a cohabitee when the parent had provided details of this person's relationship to the child and its duration.

Following reconciliation of discrepancies, a quarter (530) of the sample of children were classified as not currently living with their birth father. However, re-examination of the *initial* (uncleaned) data from these children revealed that while 453 had noted this to be the case on their questionnaire, 77 (15%) of them had reported that they *did* live with 'dad', thus disagreeing with information obtained from the parent relating both to members of the household and current father figure (and sometimes also with their own subsequent responses in respect of, for example, parental separation). Analyses were therefore conducted on all those classified as not currently living with their birth father in order to compare those who reported

Table 6.1: Children for whom the balance of data suggested they were not living with a birth father

	(a) Those living with father figure *other than birth father*		(b) Those living with *no father figure*	
Child reports birth father ...	**absent**	**present**	**absent**	**present**
Current father figure				
adoptive	0.7	35.2		
step	57.7	53.7		
mother's boyfriend	29.6	7.4		
other	12.0	3.7		
(Total n)	(142)	(54)		
	χ^2 =56.6, ***			
Age when current father figure took responsibility				
0-2 years	11.9	52.9		
3-5 years	21.4	23.5		
6-8 years	42.1	21.6		
9-11 years	24.6	2.0		
(Total n)	(126)	(51)		
	χ^2 = 40.3, ***			
Reason not with birth father				
death	6.3	0.0	9.1	4.8
illness/disability	0.0	0.0	0.4	0.0
separation	14.1	13.0	39.3	81.0
divorce	66.9	35.2	36.0	9.5
never lived with	7.7	46.3	13.1	4.8
other reason	4.9	5.6	2.2	0.0
(Total n)	(142)	(54)	(275)	(21)
	χ^2 = 41.9, ***		χ^2 = 14.1, *	
Age separated from birth father(excludes those who never lived with birth father)				
0-2 years	33.6	69.0	24.4	11.8
3-5 years	33.6	24.1	24.0	17.6
6-8 years	27.3	6.9	36.9	17.6
9-11 years	5.5	0.0	14.7	52.9
(Total n)	(128)	(29)	(217)	(17)
	χ^2 = 13.8, **		χ^2 = 16.1, **	
Frequency of seeing birth father				
weekly	34.8	7.4	35.0	88.2
monthly	7.6	0.0	6.0	0.0
less often	18.9	3.7	19.7	5.9
never	38.6	88.9	39.3	5.9
(Total n)	(132)	(54)	(234)	(17)
	χ^2 = 39.1, ***		χ^2 = 19.0, ***	

Note: * = p < 0.05; ** < 0.01; *** < 0.001.
Source: West and Sweeting (1996)

on the questionnaire that they *did not live with 'dad'* with those reporting that they *did*. The results are shown in Table 6.1.

The first set of comparisons (analyses 'a') refer to the children (n = 196) whose parental questionnaire reported that they lived with a father figure other than the birth father (that is, those with an adoptive or stepfather, mother's boyfriend or other father figure). As Table 6.1 demonstrates, those who (apparently incorrectly, given the alternative options available to them) reported that they *did* live with 'dad' differed significantly from those who did not in a number of respects. They were much more likely to live with an adoptive father (rather than mother's boyfriend or other father figure), and he was more likely to have taken responsibility at an early stage of their life. This group were also more likely to have never lived with their birth father and less likely to have experienced his loss via parental divorce. Almost none of this group had any contact with their birth father, and among those who had ever lived with him, were more likely to have been separated under three years of age. Since it is possible that these differences might be accounted for by those children living with adoptive parents, the analyses were repeated, excluding this group. The results were unchanged; almost all those reporting 'dad's' presence had been living with a stepfather since they were aged five or younger, had never lived with their birth father or been separated before the age of two and had no current contact with him. For this group, the current father figure *was* 'dad' – indeed some may have been unaware that this was not the case: a note written by one of the nurses involved in fieldwork reads: "Headmistress informed me he is adopted, but that he doesn't know it."

In contrast, analyses 'b' focus only on those children (n = 334) whose parental questionnaire reported that they did *not* currently live with *any* father figure. What were the characteristics of those who nevertheless reported that they did live with 'dad'? This group were more likely to have experienced his loss via parental separation (rather than the more 'final' divorce, death or never having lived with). This event was more likely to have occurred recently and almost all remained in regular (weekly or more frequent) contact with him. For this group, the birth father ('dad') was still an important part of their lives, indeed it is possible that some did live with him on a part-time basis, although our questionnaire did not allow for this 'two homes' situation. The continuing relationship with 'dad' was exemplified by a mother in the study, who in response to the question 'How is the person now acting as the father related to the study child?', ticked the option 'natural (birth) father', adding a note to the effect that 'natural father is still acting father although he doesn't live in family home', followed by responses describing parental divorce and weekly contact between him and her child.

Parenting across households

As family members in the qualitative Young People's Family Life study talked of the perceived tasks of families, two key issues emerged: those of expressivity and discipline, both of which could in some circumstances transcend a one parent household structure. The clearest description of this came from a 14-year-old, living with his mother following his parents' separation two-and-a-half years previously. Although his parents had very little contact, the boy lived within a couple of miles of his father and visited him every second week. Here he outlines his perception of his parents complementary *expressive* roles:

> "I can talk to my mum about more personal things than I can my dad, but I can talk to my dad, if I am not getting on with my mum I can go and talk to him about that … I can't talk to her about man things, she doesn't really know about that, I talk to my dad about stuff like that … girls and that."

His understanding of parental discipline is similarly of complementary, or additive roles:

> "If your ma cannae get through to you, your dad might get through to you.… Normally my ma tells me not to take drugs and alcohol and that, but when my dad says it, it just goes into my brain more, because two of them are telling me and not just one of them, and because my dad knows people who take drugs and he's seen what has happened and he says it's a no-no."

For this boy it appeared that two parents, even if one was non-resident, equalled twice the discipline; the sentiments expressed in the expression 'wait 'till your father gets home' held weight even though his father's home was different from his own. An interesting slant is that this example also demonstrates different perceptions of the degree of the non-resident parent's involvement with his son. While the infrequent contact between his mother and father is consistent with Smart and Neale's (1999) definition of 'solo parenting', his own account of his relationship with his father would suggest much greater involvement. Indeed, his descriptions are in complete accord with the notion that, as a father from another household put it, children and young people need '*one of each type*' of parent, which would suggest that he perceives himself as experiencing 'co-parenting'.

The complexity of potential parenting inputs from outwith the household was also evident. The significance of the following interaction is that *Gordon* is not a blood relation of the 15-year-old speaker, but the father of his seven-year-old brother, although, just as importantly, not his mother's current partner:

> "If you had a problem, who would you turn to first?"
> "It would probably be Gordon."
> "Right, why would you go to him first?"
> "Because he's not part of the family but is more of a friend than he is a parent. I would rather go to my mum, and then Gordon. My dad, I'm not so sure about, he doesn't really like answering questions."

In another example, a mother living with her three teenage girls and younger son said:

> "I think we're a very girly household and Drew has particular problems in that, being the only boy and sometimes my male friends are very aware of it and they'll come particularly to chat to him, ask him boys' stuff and such. They sort of single him out for special attention and I really appreciate that."

What these examples demonstrate is that alternatives to the input of resident fathers are available. What they do not show, however, is how satisfactory these alternatives are, although one might assume that some input is generally better than none at all, and indeed in some cases, may be preferable to that of the birth father himself.

Discussion

The fact that studies of children and young people tend to find that differences between groups divided on the basis of family structure are greater than those within groups is now widely accepted, with, for instance, "some experiencing problems and others adjusting well or even showing improvements in behaviour" following divorce (Amato, 1993, p 23). Adjustment within different family structures will obviously depend on a wide range of factors (Richards, 1996). One factor that quantitative studies cannot account for is the way in which particular individuals (within or outwith the household) are perceived, since the understandings of individual respondents may not correspond with those of the researchers. Related to this is a factor that almost all studies with a focus on family structure tend to ignore, namely the potential importance of parents and parenting relationships outwith the household.

Within the quantitative data presented here, it is, of course, possible that child–parent discrepancies simply reflect *unintentional errors* on the part of the children. As Amato and Ochiltree (1987, p 669) note: "[B]eliefs about the immaturity, shyness, and distractibility of young children suggest that they may be unable to provide reliable and valid interview data". It is for this reason that, for example, the UK General Household Survey interviews are confined to people aged 16 and over. Alternatively, such a response by a child or young person may be quite *intentional*, perhaps providing the answer that they perceive to be most socially desirable or as leading to fewer subsequent questions abut potentially difficult issues such as parental breakup or death.

However, the fact that there was a clear pattern to the 'incorrect' responses suggests that they were neither the result of carelessness nor intentional errors, but instead represent children's perceptions of the situation with regard to their father figure. The household situation of those living with a non-birth father figure who they described as 'dad' tended to be consistent with those whom others have described as 'not really a stepfamily' or 'just an ordinary family' (Burgoyne and Clark, 1984; Allan and Crow, 2001). In contrast, the circumstances of the 11-year-olds who apparently had no resident father figure but who nevertheless described themselves as living with 'dad' were more like those whom others have depicted as experiencing shared, co- or joint parenting (Bradshaw et al, 1999; Smart and Neale, 1999; Allan and Crow, 2001; Welsh et al, 2004).

Respondents are "active participants in defining their own families ... discrepancies may yield meaningful insights ... the bottom line is that discrepancies are not necessarily errors from some true score and should not necessarily be discarded or corrected" (White, 1998, p 732). Just as previous authors have found in respect of family process (for example, Ohannessian et al, 1995), child–parent discrepancies in descriptions of family structure may have meaning and be attributable to differing perceptions. One explanation for this might be found in Giddens' (1991, 1992) commentary on the contemporary experience and construction of significant relationships, incorporated within his analysis of 'reflexive modernity'. Both Giddens' account of the reflexively experienced 'pure relationship' and the issues posed by the data here arise when the traditional markers defining a relationship have shifted and no longer hold steady. Both involve individuals having to reorganise their own experiences and biographies into a coherent narrative or trajectory. In Giddens' (1992, p 6) account, intimate relations (the relations between partners that would form the conjugal bond at the heart of a traditional nuclear or extended family) have become "internally referent". Primary relationships become pure relationships that are "no longer anchored in criteria outside that relationship itself – such as criteria of kinship, social duty or traditional obligation ... (requiring) to be effectively controlled over the long term, against the backdrop of external transitions and transformations". While their parents live in a "separating and divorcing society", forming relationships on the basis "until further notice, that each gains sufficient benefit from the relation to make its continuance worthwhile" (Giddens, 1992, pp 61-3), children are attempting to forge understandings of their relationships between themselves and significant adults within these conditions. In perceiving a permanence that transcends the transience of residential status, they are actively constructing their family against a backdrop of traditional standards and expectations and a reality of flux and change.

From a methodological standpoint, the need to assume that individual participants all understand a question in the same way and mean the same thing by the answer they choose is a well-recognised problem for quantitative studies which of necessity employ limited numbers of predetermined categories (Moser and Kalton, 1971). As we have argued, we might expect young people to have understandings of their primary relationships that objective scientific instruments, derived from traditional, and therefore externally referent models of family life, would have difficulty capturing. Although it may be possible to considerably reduce the difficulties in respect of parent figures by providing very clear definitions, the growing diversity in family situations and hence increasing distinction between household and family means that quantitative research with an interest in family structure is messy and is likely to become more so. However, unless it can adapt to modern family forms, its results will be both more open to dispute and less relevant.

The 2001/2002 World Health Organisation Health Behaviour in School-Aged Children survey, which was conducted in 35 countries, has tried to recognise this. The mandatory 'family' section was designed in two columns, allowing respondents in more complex family set-ups to list the people in each home and indicate the amount of time they spend there. In addition, a question on communication with family members included 'stepfather' (or mother's boyfriend) as well as 'father' (plus the equivalent for mother figures) with the option 'don't have or see this person' (Pedersen et al, 2001). The aims were not only to give a better picture of family life, but also to increase the sensitivity of the questionnaire by making it more likely that all respondents could find an option that described their circumstances (Pedersen et al, 2004). Analyses will clearly be complicated, but this may be the direction that future studies with an interest in the family structure of children and young people have to take. In doing so, they will be paying some heed to the intricacy and fluidity of the family and recognising that the relationships it represents transcribe the household boundary.

Note

[1] Data cleaning refers to the process of reducing errors in quantitative datasets prior to analysis. Such errors may be made by respondents (for example, ticking the 'wrong' box or entering an 'impossible' number), data coders (for example, incorrect interpretation and thus classification of a response) or those responsible for data entry (for example, typing errors).

References

Allan, G. and Crow, G. (2001) *Families, households and society*, Basingstoke: Palgrave.

Amato, P. (1993) 'Children's adjustment to divorce: theories, hypotheses and empirical support', *Journal of Marriage and the Family*, vol 55, pp 23-38.

Amato, P. and Ochiltree, G. (1987) 'Interviewing children about their families: a note on data quality', *Journal of Marriage and the Family*, vol 49, pp 669-75.

Boss, P. and Greenberg, J. (1984) 'Family boundary ambiguity: a new variable in family stress theory', *Family Process*, vol 23, pp 535-46.

Bradshaw, J., Stimson, C., Skinner, C. and Williams, J. (1999) *Absent fathers?*, London: Routledge.

Burgoyne, J. and Clark, D. (1984) *Making a go of it*, London: Routledge and Kegan Paul.

Cole, C. and Cole, A. (1999) 'Boundary ambiguities that bind former spouses together after the children leave home in post-divorce families', *Family Relations*, vol 48, pp 271-2.

Crow, G. and Hardey, M. (1992) 'Diversity and ambiguity among lone-parent households in modern Britain', in C. Marsh and S. Arber (eds) *Families and households: Divisions and change*, Basingstoke: Macmillan.

Giddens, A. (1991) *Modernity and self-identity: Self and society in the late modern age*, Cambridge: Polity Press.

Giddens, A. (1992) *The transformation of intimacy: Sexuality, love and eroticism in modern societies*, Cambridge: Polity Press.

Green, G., Macintyre, S., West, P. and Ecob, R. (1990) 'Do children of lone parents smoke more because their mothers do?', *British Journal of Addiction*, vol 85, pp 1497-500.

Haskey, J. (2000) 'Demographic issues in 1975 and 2000', *Population Trends*, vol 100, pp 20-31.

Maclean, M. and Eekelar, J. (1997) *The parental obligation: A study of parenthood across households*, Oxford: Hart.

Marsh, S. and Arber, S. (1992) 'Research on families and households in modern Britain: an introductory essay', in C. Marsh and S. Arber (eds) *Families and households: Divisions and change*, Basingstoke: Macmillan.

Minuchin, S. (1974) *Families and family therapy*, Cambridge, MA: Harvard University Press.

Moore, M. and Beazley, S. (1996) 'Split family life', in M. Moore, J. Sixsmith and K. Knowles (eds) *Children's reflections on family life*, London: Falmer.

Morgan, D. (1996) *Family connections*, Cambridge: Polity Press.

Morgan, D. (1999) 'Risk and family practices: accounting for change and fluidity in family life', in E. Sillva and C. Smart (eds) *The 'new' family?*, London: Sage Publications.

Morrow, V. (1998) *Understanding families: Children's perspectives*, London: National Children's Bureau.

Moser, C. and Kalton, G. (1971) *Survey methods in social investigation* (2nd edn, reprinted 1993), Aldershot: Dartmouth.

Murphy, M. (1996) 'Family and household issues', in A. Dale (ed) *Looking towards the 2001 Census*, Occasional Paper 46, London: OPCS.

Ohannessian, C., Lerner, R., Lerner, J. and Von Eye, A. (1995) 'Discrepancies in adolescents' and parents' perceptions of family functioning and adolescent emotional adjustment', *Journal of Early Adolescence*, vol 15, pp 490-516.

Olson, D. and McCubbin, H. (1983) *Families: What makes them work*, Beverly Hills, CA: Sage Publications.

Pedersen, M., Granado Alcon, M., Rodriguez, C. and Smith, R. (2004) 'Family', in C. Currie, C. Roberts, A. Morgan, R. Smith, W. Settertobulte, O. Samdal and V. Rasmussen (eds) *Youth people's health in context: Health behaviour in school-aged children (HBSC) study: International report from the 2001/2002 survey*, Copenhagen: WHO Regional Office for Europe.

Pedersen, M., Granado Alcon, M., Borup, I., Zaborskis, A., Vollebergh, W., Smith, B. and Marklund, U. (2001) 'Family culture: focus area rationale', in C. Currie, O. Samdal, W. Boyce and B. Smith (eds) *Health behaviour in school-aged children: A world health organisation cross-national study: Research protocol for the 2001/2002 survey*, Edinburgh: University of Edinburgh, Child and Adolescent Health Research Unit.

Peplar, M. (2002) *Family matters: A history of ideas about family since 1945*, London: Longman.

Richards, M. (1996) 'The needs of children at separation and divorce', paper presented at the BT Forum: Family Law Consultation, Leeds Castle, Kent.

Seaman, P. (2003) 'Connecting experiences: young people's family life as a unifying entity', Glasgow: unpublished PhD thesis University of Glasgow.

Silva, E. and Smart, C. (1999) 'The "new" practices and politics of family life', in E. Silva and C. Smart (eds) *The 'new' family?*, London: Sage Publications.

Smart, C. (1999) 'The "new" parenthood: Fathers and mothers after divorce', in E. Sillva and C. Smart (eds.) *The 'new' family?*, London: Sage Publications.

Smart, C. and Neale, B. (1999) *Family fragments?*, Cambridge: Polity Press.

Sweeting, H., West, P. and Richards, M. (1998) 'Teenage family life, lifestyles and life chances: associations with family structure, conflict with parents and joint family activity, *International Journal of Law, Policy and the Family*, vol 12, pp 15-46.

Taanila, A., Laitinen, E., Moilanen, I. and Jarvelin, M. (2002) 'Effects of family interaction on the child's behaviour in single-parent or reconstituted families', *Family Process*, vol 41, pp 693-708.

Tein, J., Roosa, M. and Michaels, M. (1994) 'Agreement between parent and child reports on parental behaviors', *Journal of Marriage and the Family*, vol 56, pp 341-55.

Welsh, E., Buchanan, A., Flouri, E. and Lewis, J. (2004). *Involved fathering and child well-being: Fathers' involvement with secondary school age children*, York: Joseph Rowntree Foundation.

West, P. and Sweeting, H. (1996) *Background, rationale and design of the west of Scotland 11 to 16 Study*, Working Paper No 52, Glasgow: MRC Medical Sociology Unit.

White, L. (1998) 'Who's counting? Quasi-facts and stepfamilies in reports of number of siblings' *Journal of Marriage and the Family*, vol 60, pp 725-33.

SEVEN

Children managing parental drug and alcohol misuse: challenging parent–child boundaries

Angus Bancroft, Sarah Wilson, Sarah Cunningham-Burley, Hugh Masters and Kathryn Backett-Milburn

Introduction

The parent–child boundary is created, sustained and enforced through norms, roles, individual practices and social institutions. It has symbolic resonance partly because the relationship between parent and child is often portrayed, not without reason, as one of the few remaining social bonds whose boundaries have a weight of obligation and permanence about them (Beck, 1994). Partners may become ex-partners, friends become lovers, lovers become friends, but children are always children and parents are always parents. However, empirical studies of family life show that these boundaries, although vested with so much emotional energy and material resources, are malleable and breakable. Circumstances in which this has been explored include family breakup and reformation (Smart et al, 2001), situations where children take on caring roles (Becker et al, 1998), and parental substance misuse (Bekir et al, 1993), the subject of this chapter.

Parental substance misuse is transgressive, both of boundaries within the family and in how the problem is constructed. Boundaries of the family can be reworked – for some in our study, 'the family' was redefined to exclude some members of the original family and include others, for instance aunts and uncles, neighbours, or service workers. Problems of substance misuse in the family are usually assumed to emanate from the behaviour of adolescents and young people, rather than parents. Children and other family members then have to deal with its doubly transgressive nature.

In this chapter we explore the challenges to and reshaping of parent–child boundaries in young people's accounts of the impact of parental substance misuse on them. We examine four dimensions along which parent–child boundaries are shaped. These are: roles and responsibilities; risk; knowledge; and space/time. The experience of parental substance misuse can be usefully examined in terms of them, but they can also be used for thinking through other disruptions that impact on family life, including parental separation, conflict, illness and so on, as well as more normalised but potentially problematic experiences, such as lifecourse transition. The taken for granted realities of family life can be revealed in these circumstances, for example, the assumptions around expected roles and responsibilities can be challenged by the dynamics of substance misuse. For this research we interviewed 38 young people between the ages of 15 and 27 who had experienced parental substance misuse for a substantial period in their childhoods. The young people were interviewed by a research fellow with extensive experience of interviewing on sensitive topics (Sarah Wilson). Full details can be found in the project report (Bancroft et al, 2004).

Roles and responsibilities

Research into the impact of parental health and emotional problems on roles and responsibilities within the family is mainly situated in the fields of social care and in psychology (Tunnard, 2004). Work in social care has highlighted the needs of young carers, focusing for the most part on children who care for parents with an illness or disability (Aldridge and Becker, 1993). Psychological research has used the concept of the 'parentified child' to describe children who assume responsibility for their parents' emotional state, along with caring for parents and others in the family such as younger siblings (Earley and Cushway, 2002). The parentified child can take on controlling, enabling and decision-making functions as well as practical caring work.

Substance misuse is acknowledged within both these literatures, but it tends to be peripheral to them. There are differences between the circumstances of children caring for parents with a mental or physical illness or disability, and those of children parenting due to parental substance misuse. There are issues of stigma, legitimacy, secrecy and disclosure that are especially salient in these circumstances. For instance, unlike physical illness, which is clearly bounded in society as a pathology in terms of the sick role, substance use is common, to some extent normative, and in the case of alcohol, nearly universal in our society. Hence there is ambivalence of acknowledgement – of children recognising what the problem is and of parents and others acknowledging it. The parentified child is also not the whole story in our study – respondents intermittently adopted some parenting roles and responsibilities, and at times also withdrew from the home to avoid parents. There were several elements to the impact of parental substance misuse on roles and responsibilities, not all of which were present in all the accounts that we gathered. Parents could withdraw from some or most aspects of an adult, parental role; they could demand that children collude in various ways; but they could also continue to be seen by respondents as loving and caring.

Not being 'adult'

In some respondents' accounts, parents were described as not behaving like adults, as regressing in their behaviour, when using substances. This appeared to be more the case for alcohol use, perhaps because of its association with the gregarious or aggressive abandonment of inhibitions:

> "Nuh they're more like a bigger child theirself. He'd act the way I used to act when I was fourteen getting pissed [drunk] wi' my mates and that. Stoating aboot steaming, 'way hey! F – you! I'm the world, come and take on me' and all that eh." (Sophie, 19, father alcohol misuser)

The parent could also be seen by the young person as 'attention seeking' when in this state. Some of the respondents felt their parent would rely on them to satisfy their emotional needs, in a way that was perceived as disruptive. For example, one young woman was frequently woken up at night by her drunk mother in order to chat. This was sometimes seen as a hassle, sometimes as a more onerous emotional burden, more, in their eyes, than a parent should demand of a child. Parents who treated the child as a constantly on-call source of emotional support were a source of disturbance and those who were perceived to use the child for their own emotional ends were seen as violating a fundamental obligation and placing unwanted demands on children:

> "And he sorta agreed he'll help me if I can help him, ken get off the drink. But I done it for a couple of weeks and it was just, he wasnae really bothered. It was just an excuse to get somebody else back in the house....

> Because I'm his –his bairn ... but he wasnae for stopping the drink or anything so I just left. I couldnae, couldnae handle it. That's how I left first time." (Lana, 20, father alcohol misuser)

With Lana, the words 'I'm his bairn' signified how in her eyes there should be another set of obligations between them that were not apparent in her father's behaviour. A perhaps more jarring violation of expected obligations was when a parent stole money:

> "And just when I was about to leave [city] and go back up on the bus, I got out my wallet and there was only fourteen quid there. What my dad had done is he took all the money and just left my bus fare. So when I came up here I lost my digs [accommodation]." (Ian, 23, mother and father alcohol misuser)

Ian spoke of this in a very matter of fact manner, as one more way in which his parents impinged on him even when he was no longer living with him.

Colluding and boundary maintenance

Young people described how they could have to engage in boundary work, maintaining boundaries of what they thought family life should be like or just would play along with a drunken parent's happy state because it was pleasurable to see that parent happy:

> "So I was still up probably at oneish. And sometimes if you were up and he came in, you didn't know. You can't leave because he wants everybody to be happy because he comes in. So you're, so then like you have to stay. And so it's like really, it's like it's like a game you know? I can remember, because you've got to pretend. I mean obviously you, it's like you don't live in this constant state of alcohol. You know it's like you pretend that – that everything, you're having a good time because dad's there and he's in a good mood." (Ellie, 19, father alcohol misuser)

Maintenance of a parent's mood or responding to and managing their emotional demands is one aspect of the 'parentified child' role described in the literature. Another is taking over parental responsibilities and many of our respondents' accounts focused on more practical concerns: parents not getting children up for school, not cooking, not cleaning, not providing in other ways. This withdrawal of the parent from some of the practical aspects of the parental role often required a response from the child. Children could have to shop, cook, clean the house and care for younger brothers and sisters. Some had to look after their parents' personal needs, for instance ensuring that they washed properly, or protecting parents from themselves.

Enforcing disciplinary boundaries was another aspect of this blurring of parent/child responsibilities:

> *Sarah Wilson*: "And did she act like a mother, in a sense, but did she sort of like try and enforce discipline or?"
>
> *Alexis*: "Nah."
>
> *SW*: "No."
>
> *Alexis*: "Like when she was drinking? ... Nah. It was me that had to do that...."
>
> *SW*; "And what did you, what did you do when your mum was drunk?"
>
> *Alexis*: "Gave up [laughs]. Sent her tae her bed or something then just [sat] doonstairs and watched telly.... Made sure Jill and Gordon [sister and brother, anonymised] were fine first. Made sure they've had something tae eat. And then just leave it." (Alexis, 17, mother alcohol, heroin, poppers misuser)

In this example, Alexis felt she had to enforce discipline over her younger brother and sister and, to some extent, enforce boundaries with her mother also. She resented her siblings using their mother's intoxication to exploit her for money. From her point of view this was not good, putting more strain on the family income and representing a breakdown in parenting.

The interviews revealed that children were active in developing, but also placing limits on, their adoption of a parenting role. From the young people's accounts, it appeared that nobody asked them to take on the tasks and responsibilities which they did. In our interpretation, there was a learning process, in which they adopted some strategies and not others, through trial and error and observation of others.

Trial and error appeared to be in evidence in, for instance, the management of parents' substance use. Some respondents reported throwing out drugs and alcohol in an attempt to control their parents' habit. Taking this action could end up either provoking violence from the parent, or meaning that that parent borrowed money to buy more, putting the family further into debt:

> *Allan*: "I done that. I flung the alcohol bottle away and I ended up wi' a broken arm."
> *SW*: "So she – she hit you?"
> *Allan*: "Aye."
> *SW*: "How old were you when that happened?"
> *Allan*: "I poured – eh I was fourteen. And I poured, I threw seventy, seventy ounce bottle o' vodka down the sink. She broke my arm wi' a sledgehammer." (Allan, 17, mother alcohol misuser)

The recollections of many of our sample suggested that these attempts to manage parents' substance use directly were not successful.

Parental absence under the influence of substance use happened to some in our sample. This is often seen in the literature as the most extreme violation of parenting norms, as simple abandonment, and caused distress and worry for almost all of those in our sample who experienced it. In contrast, in this instance, which was unique among the young people we spoke to, Emma reflects on how parental absence came as some relief and helped her to restore some sense of stability to her life:

> "Just that she went away for four days and we could have a normal hoose, me and my sister, my wee sister. Not a normal hoose, because I shouldnae have tae cook meals and get my sister up for school. And iron uniforms at fourteen year old. So." (Emma, 21, mother alcohol misuser)

Some young people described how their parents resumed responsibility when recovering from the worst effects of substance misuse. One respondent was ambivalent about this re-establishing of parent–child boundaries:

Alexis: "Mm, it's just a, like recently started changing. My mum's started like taking her ane responsibilities back [laughs]."
SW: "Yeah? How do you find that?"
Alexis: "It's hard to adjust. ... It's like I'm used tae daen all the tidying and the cooking and like telling Jill and Gordon when tae be in and who no tae hang aboot wi' and who no, where no to go and stuff like that. And my mum's started daen that and we kinda, it's like a kinda conflict between us noo because she's saying, like, "you're seventeen, I'm the mum". [...] Aye, it was hard, but then like I'd been daen it that long I kinda adjusted into the role. That's why it's hard to like, like it's she taken it away fae me." (Alexis, 17, mother alcohol, heroin, poppers misuser)

Her ambivalence reflected the extent to which she had worked herself into a parenting role, in her view.

Parents continuing to 'be there'

Not all the parents in the study with substance use problems were considered by the respondents to be have been prevented from fulfilling a parenting role all the time; some said their parent had been a good parent. Sometimes this simply meant there being food on the table:

> "Eh, she was – she was alright. Still a good ma, still made sure there was eh food on the table and that. Ken she a'ways made sure that we had our dinner and there was always messages [shopping] and that there." (Dan, 21, mother and two stepfathers heroin misusers)

Some parents were recognised as continuing to 'do their best' despite the substance misuse:

> "My dad's always been there for me and he's said he always will be, so if ever anything happened to me or Keri [sister] or my mum, because like no matter how drunk he was it's like he'd always make sure we were OK before he was." (Abby, 16, father alcohol, mother amphetamines misuser)

In the case of Abby, just quoted, statements of 'being there' reassured her that her father was still part of her life as a parent. Her parents were separated, and this may have made it more practical for her father to present himself as 'being there' for her, her mother and her sister, since he was not called on to be an actively engaged parent as frequently as he might otherwise have been. She also withdrew from her father when he was drunk, which she was able to do as she did not live with him – this fact made it easier for her to create a boundary between her and her father's substance use, which helped to maintain the boundaries of their relationship as parent and child, or perhaps more accurately, as father and daughter.

That said, it was apparent from the interviews that a sense that there was love between parent and child could make up for a lot, and could help the child separate the person of their parent from the problems of substance use:

> "Well the past, I would say, would be that I think, I think whatever problems mum and dad both had, they still, like, loved us and they still want us to be a family and it was a strong sense of, like, they knew what, they knew what was best, or they were good people at heart, you know. It's just, whatever, things got in the way. So there's always a strong sense of, like, of that." (Ellie, 19, father alcohol misuser)

Some young people gave the impression of loving their parents more than their parents could love them. Comments such as 'I'll be waiting' were akin to statements of parental love for a rebellious, estranged child. Some of our respondents awaited the return of the prodigal parent.

Risk and knowledge

Risk is something that every parent and child has to incorporate into the boundaries of their relationship. As mentioned earlier, children are imbued with many expectations as objects of the last primary relationship. They are also treated in research, policy and in the media as continuously 'at risk', often from parents themselves (Kelley and Mayall, 1998). Research into parental substance misuse often lies within the latter paradigm, treating children as 'at risk' from exposure to substance use and associated problems such as neglect and violence. Here we explore risk in the accounts of respondents from a different perspective, looking at how risk boundaries were altered in the context of substance misuse, and how knowledge boundaries were protected by children as a potential source of risk to them.

Risk from parents could be one aspect of the violation of roles and responsibilities discussed above. For instance, a parent who drove while drunk could be a danger to others in the car. Parents' substance misuse could also create dangers inside the home:

> "But when they're drunk, you know, they werenie really you know. They were, they were always putting me in jeopardy, you know. ... So they were. You know, one day I nearly died in the hoose because my mum and dad left the bloody, the bottle o' milk ... they put a bottle of milk [a baby's bottle] in a pot of boiling water to heat it up ... and they fell asleep and then the next thing I remember my – my nana ... came in the hoose and eh she had to get somebody to boot the door in because there was smoke coming oot the letterbox. And the whole hoose was just smoke and I couldnae breathe you know. I ended up collapsing, you know. Just, it was always something every day." (Ian, 23, mother and father alcohol misusers)

The accounts of our respondents showed how parents could be a risk to the respondents, but also to younger siblings. This was a source of concern for respondents, especially towards those still at home after the respondent had left and could no longer be on site to look out for them.

Another theme that came through strongly was of parents as being at risk to themselves. Risk to parents was described as coming from violent or destructive partners and from the effects of substance misuse. Children sometimes had to watch out for parents. One young woman reported that she stayed up when her father was asleep drunk, turning him over in his sleep in case he was sick and choked. Respondents who described this felt they could not manage or limit their parents' substance use and so had to try and limit its effect, and the risk to themselves and parents.

Risk was also constructed in terms of boundaries of knowledge. Many parents who are substance users attempt to hide their use from children, usually without success. Children can feel that they are obliged to play along with this fiction (Barnard and Barlow, 2003). Respondents described a process of gradual coming to awareness of parents as having a substance misuse problem. Some described parents' attempts at concealing their substance use from them, usually with cynicism:

> "Sometimes they'd hide it, you know. They'd usually hide it when they start drinking and say they're sober and start.... You go intae the room, you hear the can going 'psshh'. But they go [coughing noise] you know. It's like that, aye okay right. So that's them drinking again. And sometimes they'd try and be civilised and be normal and pour it into a glass and sit like that. But after a few o' them, they end up drunk and go – then that's it." (Allan, 17, mother alcohol misuser)

In some circumstances respondents in our study were aware that they had to maintain knowledge boundaries against 'outsiders', such as police and social workers and also within the family. There was some sense of risk of family disruption; that they might be taken away from their parents. The awareness or suspicion that others in the community or at school knew about their parents' substance use resulted in feelings of being exposed and judged. Boundaries of risk and knowledge are constituted with parent–child relationships. Substance misuse creates risks that children are faced with, risks from and to parents, and the risk that those knowledge boundaries outwith their control might be broken.

Space and time

Boundaries of space and time were present in respondents' accounts. Family life takes place in settings in which children have more or less power. Some settings may be recognised or constructed as 'belonging' more to one or other family member. Many of these settings are contested. Substance misuse would occur in particular settings – this could be the family home, or outside it, at other people's houses or in the pub. It could be perceived as taking over the life of the family if it involved shifting a family occasion to an inappropriate setting:

> "Right, no we were supposed to go to McDonald's one time and he wanted a drink so we had to go to another pub place for a meal because he wanted to drink." (Abby, 16, father alcohol, mother amphetamines misuser)

Parents could use their control over a setting to protect their children from knowledge about their substance use, as this young man's mother tried to:

> "But eh when I was, right up till I was fourteen I was never really in the room or I was kept, ken, through – in the bedroom. You're chased, you're chased through, ken." (Dan, 21, mother and two stepfathers heroin misusers)

From our interviews it was apparent that children could also use space to avoid parents under the influence of substance misuse. They might retreat to their bedroom or leave the home. Whether they were able to do this depended on factors such as their age and whether there were others in the home they felt needed their protection. They sometimes felt compelled to police the home setting as part of maintaining boundaries, for instance not taking friends home:

> *SW*: "And when your dad was there would you take friends home?"
> *Tanya*: "Nuh."
> *SW*: "No? Okay. And that was because of him?"
> *Tanya*: "Aye. Just in case he would be embarrassing or ken."
> *SW*: "Would he be embarrassing?"
> *Tanya*: "Probably, aye." (Tanya, 17, father alcohol, street valium misuser)

Time was another dimension in which substance misuse was associated with boundaries being broken. This could involve parents being perceived to have an alcohol problem because they were drinking outside the bounds of normal drinking time, for instance in the morning or afternoon, or if they disrupted children's sleep time. Parents are usually held to be the family members responsible for maintaining boundaries around their children's use of space and time. Disruptive or delinquent children are defined in part by their scorn for these boundaries (Cromer, 2004). In this instance, children had to take on some of the work of maintaining boundaries of space and time which substance-misusing parents broke.

Discussion

Boundaries shape the impact and meaning of substance use. Substance use only becomes 'misuse' within a societal context, a context which implies that there is normalised or non-problematic use and sets the boundary between the two (Young, 1971). This boundary is itself liable to change as some behaviours are pathologised and others normalised (Parker et al, 2002). Legal, socioeconomic, cultural and institutional contexts also construct boundaries around 'parenting', 'mothering', 'fathering' and the 'child'. They shape the experience of parenting and the child's relationship with parents and other family, friends and neighbours, and services. A significant aspect of the experience of parental substance misuse is the breaking or challenging of parent–child boundaries (Velleman and Orford, 1993; Barnard and McKeganey, 2004). The various dimensions discussed in this chapter are shaped partly by the actions of parents and children, and others close to them, but also in terms of other factors and contexts, such as the substances used, gender, social class, and services.

There was much similarity in the experiences of young people affected by drug, alcohol and polysubstance use, but there were also important divergences. Boundaries of knowledge appeared to differ with drug and alcohol use. Alcohol use could be more public, being legal and more socially acceptable. However, this made the risk of exposure greater if the parent was seen drunk by others in the community. Felt stigma was greater with drug use and some of our respondents reported that, as children, they were sometimes explicitly told, 'don't tell'. The illegal nature of drugs, which meant exposure to a criminal subculture, and greater difficulty obtaining the drugs, required a commitment of time, money and energy. The particular intoxicating effect of different substances, although impossible to isolate from learnt impact and context, also shaped how parents behaved, as when alcohol was felt to 'immature' parents.

Social class and economic circumstances also constituted an important context. Most respondents in our sample were from less well-off backgrounds. However, six respondents came from middle-class backgrounds. Substance misuse was held by some respondents to be at the root of parents being unemployed or finding it difficult to obtain work. Middle-class families could draw on greater resources to ensure substance misuse is hidden and to soften some of the impact. Then, the parental role of 'providing' could be easier to maintain, although sometimes at the expense of becoming indebted to other members of the family.

Gendered constructions shape parent and child roles in general and these underlay the young people's accounts of their lives. Where fathers were users, mothers were reported to take on a more providing/authority role. Respondents recounted how, as children, they felt responsibility for the protection of mothers who had a drug problem. This was particularly the case when a mother's uptake of drug use was associated with the presence of a drug-using boyfriend. This could be felt to be doubly violating – putting the mother at risk, and taking her away from the child.

From what respondents told us, it appeared that most did not have contact with social services when living with the substance-using parent, although this is something that we as researchers could not know for certain. As highlighted, the need to maintain boundaries of knowledge meant that social service intervention could be viewed with trepidation by them.

It seemed that for many of our respondents there was some ambivalence about the 'childcarer' or 'parentified' role. It was marked by shifting, permeable boundaries, stigma and ambivalence. Young carers are often treated as having a well-defined role – that of carer – here, children were, often it seemed, just trying to get on with things.

The ways in which families and family members respond to substance use highlights how 'family' can be a malleable, flexible term that is reshaped actively by its members. In situations where children experience 'care' as coming more constantly from a close friend than a parent then they may redefine what 'parent' means, who is their parent and what they expect from them. This definition will change over their lifecourse, as a substance-using parent 'reparents', attempts are made to re-establish emotional bonds or as the young person themself becomes a parent. Boundaries between roles are thus reshaped, out of necessity and choice. Children and other family members are active agents in this reshaping; but this is restricted by the choices of others, and by the social and material resources they can draw upon.

Conclusion

The accounts of neglect given in many of our interviews, and in other research, can lead to the impression that there is a fundamental clash between being a parent and being a substance user and that children are passive victims in the face of the acts of morally reprehensible 'risk producers'. It is certainly the case that drug and alcohol use change the dynamics of family life. However, from our research we have also seen that children are reflective individuals, whose decisions and actions contribute to the reshaping of parent–child boundaries. This happens in four dimensions that we have picked out. First, roles and responsibilities shift and mutate; children pick up some roles and take on some responsibilities for themselves and others. They can be adopting a parentified role, acting from necessity and a desire for some kind of normality in the home. Second, substance misuse produces risks *for* them – risks to others that they have to manage – and risks *to* them. Research and policy often focus on the latter, but the former were also very important, frequently involving parents being at risk. Third, risk could also come from knowledge boundaries being threatened or broken. Fourth, particular space/time-bounded settings could be used by children as respites, but could also have to be guarded by children as part of maintaining knowledge boundaries. There was no simple story of 'deparented' parents and 'parentified' children, rather a complex of permeable, shifting boundaries between parents and children.

Acknowledgement

We would like to thank the Joseph Rowntree Foundation, which funded this research.

References

Aldridge, J. and Becker, S. (1993) *Children who care: Inside the world of young carers*, Loughborough: Loughborough University Press.

Bancroft, A., Wilson, S., Cunningham-Burley, C., Backett-Milburn, K. and Masters, H. (2004) 'Resilience and transition: the experiences of older children of drug- and alcohol-misusing parents', York: Joseph Rowntree Foundation.

Barnard, M. and Barlow, J. (2003) 'Discovering parental drug dependence: silence and disclosure', *Children and Society*, vol 17, no 1, pp 45-56.

Barnard, M. and McKeganey, N. (2004) 'The impact of parental problem drug use in children: what is the problem and what can be done to help?', *Addiction*, vol 99, no 5, pp 552-9.

Beck, U. (1994) *Risk society: Towards a new modernity*, London: Sage Publications.

Becker, S., Aldridge, J. and Dearden, C. (1998) *Young carers and their families*, Oxford: Blackwell.

Bekir, P., McLellan, T., Childress, A.R. and Gariti, P. (1993) 'Role reversals in families of substance misusers: a transgenerational phenomenon', *International Journal of the Addictions*, vol 28, no 7, pp 613-30.

Cromer, G. (2004) ' "Children from good homes": moral panics about middle-class delinquency', *British Journal of Criminology*, vol 44, pp 391-400.

Earley, L. and Cushway, D. (2002) 'The parentified child', *Clinical Child Psychology and Psychiatry*, vol 7, no 2, pp 163-78.

Kelley, P. and Mayall, B. (1998) 'Children, parents and risk', *Health and Social Care in the Community*, vol 6, no 1, pp 16-24.

Parker, H., Williams, L. and Aldridge, J. (2002) 'The normalization of "sensible" recreational drug use: further evidence from the North West England Longitudinal Study', *Sociology*, vol 36, no 4, pp 941-64.

Smart, C., Neale, B. and Wade, A. (2001) *The changing experience of childhood: Families and divorce*, Cambridge: Polity Press.

Tunnard, J. (2004) *Parental mental health problems: Key messages from research, policy and practice*, Dartington: Research in Practice.

Velleman, R. and Orford, J. (1993) 'The importance of family discord in explaining childhood problems in the children of problem drinkers', *Addiction Research*, vol 1, pp 39-57.

Young, J. (1971) *The drugtakers: The social meaning of drug use*, London: MacGibbon and Kee.

Part Three: Health, illness and well-being

Issues relating to health, illness and well-being affect individuals, their families, wider relationships, communities and societies. The boundaries within families, for example, as expressed through gendered roles, or between families and the wider community may all be challenged and redrawn in response to threats to health and well-being. The maintenance of well-being itself may require boundary construction, to ensure time for self or leisure is maintained despite caring and work commitments.

The three chapters comprising this part of the book focus on very different aspects of health, illness and well-being. The first chapter, by Backett-Milburn, Airey and McKie, provides a gendered, lifecourse perspective on health, medicine and well-being. Well-being, it is argued, may be a useful concept through which to challenge conventional boundaries around ageing, health and illness. The chapter focuses on a study of women in their fifties and examines how the boundaries of caring and providing intersect with lifecourse stage, biographical history and social and familial circumstances. The experience of ageing can only be understood within that wider context and, at this time of life, boundaries around families and relationships seem to be both sustained and challenged. For example, changing patterns of employment suggest new boundaries between work and home; respondents in the study also reported a sense of a freeing up of time for their own interests, challenging traditional boundaries and expectations around women's ageing. However, caring responsibilities across the generations invoke more traditionally gendered roles; ambiguity and ambivalence were present in the women's accounts of this time in their lives. Wider personal relationships were described as important sources of support and knowledge about the ageing process, signifying changing dynamics between family and friends.

The chapter by Weaks, Wilkinson and Davidson (Chapter Nine) focuses more specifically on the effect of a particular disease diagnosis on relationships within a longer-term marriage. Two case studies are presented where one partner, in both cases a man, has been diagnosed with dementia. The authors take a social constructionist perspective in relation to the definition and impact of dementia and concentrate on how boundaries and relationships are co-constructed through the illness trajectory. Dementia challenges established roles and boundaries; in both case study couples, different roles within the marriage were created, sometimes quickly and sometimes gradually. In one case, Angus and Mary, new roles seemed to be rather imposed by the partner without dementia, effectively excluding the affected spouse from meaningful engagement in family decision making. This seemed to result in Angus seeking new social contacts outside the family through a support group for people affected by dementia. A boundary of exclusion constructed within the family was challenged by the creation of new relationships outside the family. By contrast, for Peter and Ruth, a boundary seemed to be constructed around the family to protect Peter from the outside and the revelation of his diagnosis to others. A gradual process of renegotiation of this practice occurred, which enabled Peter to cross that boundary and take his diagnosis into his social relationships outside the family in a supportive and meaningful way.

The final chapter in this section takes a very different approach to issues relating to health and well-being through a focus on violence. The prevalence of domestic violence indicates that the family and home are not bounded safe havens; communal violence means that neither families nor communities are protective. McKie and Lombard draw on two case studies of inter-communal violence, one from research by Bringa in Bosnia and the other from research by Connolly and Healy in Northern Ireland. McKie and Lombard construct an argument that boundaries are drawn and redrawn between history, memories and public institutions in ways that can form the basis for inter-communal violence. The relationship between families and communities can be reconstructed to create outsiders of former friends and neighbours. These new boundaries of inclusion and exclusion can perpetuate conflict both within and between families and communities. Boundary work here is portrayed as oppressive; physical boundaries, for example, create and perpetuate sectarianism and collective memories constructed to reinforce difference and hatred. Families stand at the interface of communal violence, reproducing boundaries of exclusion and inclusion.

All three chapters suggest that boundaries are actively constructed, reconstructed and transgressed as people, through their families, relationships and communities, manage their day-to-day lives whether in times of peace or conflict. The construction of boundaries can be an act of preservation, for example of identity or well-being. Boundaries can also be acts of oppression through exclusionary practices on an individual or communal level. The boundary metaphor successfully transcends time and place and can analytically link diverse studies of health, illness and well-being.

EIGHT

Intersections of health and well-being in women's lives and relationships at mid-life

Kathryn Backett-Milburn, Laura Airey and Linda McKie

Introduction

Luhmann (1982, p 232) has asserted that the "evolution or modernization of society has often been described as a process of increasing system differentiation and pluralization". One dimension of these dynamic processes is the acquisition and constant renegotiation of 'boundary roles'. Boundary roles are those that have potential to transform social relations and cultural practices through drawing ideas and experiences across arenas (Luhmann, 1982, p 236). For example, the woman who engages in paid employment while retaining the main responsibility for domestic and caring work may be in such a role. Thus she may identify herself as a worker and a carer and as someone who must manage the boundaries of the public and private. This fluid or porous boundary has the potential to transform her sense of self and shift the perceptions of others. In this chapter, we discuss some of the key issues that frame women's health and well-being at mid-life to explore these ideas further. In particular, we concentrate on how health and well-being intersect with women's structural and familial circumstances, and their views and experiences of caring roles. We illustrate our arguments by drawing on a qualitative study of women in their fifties carried out by the authors.

Gilleard and Higgs comment that "times change and ageing too is changed by time". They assert that the contemporary experience of ageing now encompasses a greater diversity in cohort, class and gendered relations than existed for previous generations and that these social and demographic changes "render less possible any common cultural position than can be popularly represented as 'ageing'"

(Gilleard and Higgs, 2000, p 8). One feature of this changing ageing process is that the fifties may be differentially experienced by social class and gender and reflect an increasingly complex and diverse experience of social and economic structures (Arber and Ginn, 1995; Benson, 1997; Sulkunen et al, 1997; Gilleard and Higgs, 2000). In these respects, changing experiences of ageing may challenge the boundaries between expectations of personal and social life at mid-life and the often contradictory realities facing individuals.

For some women this period in their lives may be experienced as a transitional time, with opportunities for themselves, perhaps also involving a changing sense of identity or a greater sense of self-confidence (Granville, 2000). However, for many, their fifties can also be characterised by uncertainty and change in their personal relationships and family lives. For example, there may be increasing experience of life events, such as bereavement, divorce, children leaving home, adult children staying or returning home, the arrival of grandchildren and caring responsibilities for elderly parents or chronically ill relatives and friends (Finch, 1989; Featherstone, 1995; Cunningham-Burley and Backett-Milburn, 1998). Demographic trends point to rising numbers of 50-something women experiencing separation and divorce; figures from the 2001 Census in the UK indicate that 16% of women in their fifties are divorced, which represents a threefold increase compared to 30 years ago (ESRC, 2001; National Statistics Online[a]). The divorce rate for those in their fifties is likely to increase over the next decade, impacting particularly on women's futures in and out of employment, their economic circumstances and their relationships with others (ESRC, 2001). Such social trends mean that boundaries are shifting around families and relationships as women negotiate changes and continuities in their personal circumstances.

Boundaries between home and work are also being renegotiated since, at the turn of the 21st century, women in their fifties are experiencing profound and diverse changes in the expectations of work and family commitments, specific to their gender (Apter, 1995; Granville, 2000). Employment rates for mid-life women have risen. According to the Labour Force Survey, the employment rate for women aged between 50 and retirement age (that is, 60, at present) reached 67% in winter 2003/04, up from 59% a decade ago (National Statistics Online[b]). These trends seem set to continue, given the increasing concerns about pension provision in both the state and private sectors. Paradoxically, however, increasing labour force participation may also result in the realities of adverse career or job prospects becoming more apparent to mid-life women, and financial or leisure planning for retirement, or early retirement, becoming an increasing concern (Deem, 1996; Hirsch, 2000; ESRC, 2000).

These wider structural changes notwithstanding, women continue to have the main responsibility for the organisation if not the conduct of caring work and traditional assumptions about the relationship between femininity and caring remain relatively intact (McKie et al, 2002). For women in their fifties these responsibilities can also encompass growing children, stepchildren and older relatives (Lister, 1997; Cancian and Oliker, 2000). Figures from the 2001 Census in the UK indicate that almost a quarter of women aged 50-64 are involved in providing unpaid care; however, studies of caregiving suggest that the proportion of the over-fifties who provide some form of care may be as high as 1 in 2 (Mooney et al, 2002; Phillips et al, 2002). Therefore, for women at this point in the lifecourse, changing conceptualisations of employment and caring work intersect with shifting patterns of dependency and independence (Arber and Cooper, 2000), necessitating redrawing of the boundaries around self, citizenship and social responsibility.

Changing conceptualisations of women's health and ageing at mid-life

While social and economic changes may be shaping the broader diverse contexts of women's lives at mid-life, in turn these affect and are affected by cultural meanings attached to this point in the lifecourse (Bernard et al, 2000). Here, the notion of well-being provides a heuristically appropriate concept that helps to avoid traditional connotations of inevitable decline at this point in the lifecourse (Gullette, 1997). Well-being has been defined as addressing the conditions of human flourishing (Sen, 1993), thus offering a more dynamic and potentially more positive standpoint to enable women to account for ageing. A review of well-being has shown its pluralistic potential as it crosses disciplinary boundaries, is seen to be culturally responsive and incorporates functional and existential features as well as addressing issues of both structure and agency (Cronin de Chavez, 2005). Thinking about well-being may therefore be one way of challenging conventional boundaries around ageing, health and illness by focusing on notions of personal agency and active ageing.

Experiences of health and illness are central to understandings of mid-life and the ageing process. Research on the importance of lay theorising has pointed to the relevance of social and cultural contexts in understanding conceptualisations of health and health-relevant behaviour (Milburn, 1996; Watson et al, 1996). Moreover, qualitative research has shown that the meaning of lifestyle, in its relationship to health behaviour and body practices, is culturally embedded in beliefs concerning what is appropriate at certain stages of life (Backett and Davison, 1995). In this finding, awareness of ageing is a reflexive product of self-comparison (personal biography, relationships and everyday life) with lay epidemiology and wider cultural images. By the fifties there may be a level of 'knowingness' about self, health and the body but physical changes also become more obvious and less deniable (Cunningham-Burley and Backett-Milburn, 1998).

How women view and experience their bodies is also important in developing an understanding of this period in the lifecourse (Davis, 1997; Nettleton and Watson, 1998; Backett-Milburn and McKie, 2001). Issues of health, illness and healthcare have tended to form a major component of research and debates about the ageing population (BMJ, 1997; Wadsworth, 1997). International studies of women and ageing have also shown that women have different healthcare needs from men, indicating the need for an appropriately gendered approach to these needs and relevant services (Tannenbaum et al, 2003). However, in general, research has been dominated by a biomedical perspective, to the neglect of the body as the site of gendered, biographical experience, culturally mediated and socially located.

The biomedical perspective is increasingly being challenged by researchers, especially feminists, who argue that, in western culture, mid-life women are characterised essentially as menopausal bodies who are emotional, unstable and potentially out of control (Lupton, 1998; Green, 2001). As such they become the primary target of 'medicalisation', which, it is argued, renders women as passive recipients of treatment (Greer, 1991; Komesaroff et al, 1997). Other sociological critiques of the biomedical model show that women's experiences of the menopause are quite different in other cultural contexts (Locke, 1998) and that their healthcare and healthcare practices intersect not just with gendered issues but also with other social divisions, such as class and ethnicity (Guillemin, 1999). More recently, however, there has been a renewed focus on women's own agency in these processes. This is based on an acknowledgment that health-maintaining practices are not 'stand alone' but are made sense of and taken up by women in terms of their own lives and experiences. Moreover, some researchers have argued that, far from being victims, women themselves seek out health technologies and treatments, treating these as 'lifestyle choices' to challenge conventional boundaries around ageing and to create opportunities to 'reinvent' themselves (Griffiths, 1999).

The metaphor of boundaries and Luhmann's (1982, p 236) notion of boundary roles, offers the potential to explore the dynamic, shifting and gendered experiences of women at mid-life. Importantly, the notions of boundaries offer hybridity as they may be transgressed through a range of experiences including growing older, dissolution of families and the re-formation of family groupings. We explore these ideas further in the following sections where we present the study and findings.

The study

This qualitative study explored health and well-being issues with women in their fifties from a diverse range of social circumstances. Nineteen women took part in the study; 11 in discussion groups and eight in individual interviews. Interviews and discussions groups were taped and transcribed. The authors undertook the analysis as a team and in this chapter we report findings that illuminate issues on roles, identities and boundaries drawn from women's accounts of their experiences, views of their current situation and ideas about the future. (See Airey et al, 2004, for an extended account of the data analysis.) Topics included: women's views and thoughts about being in their fifties; current experiences of day-to-day life; perceptions of changes and continuities in their lives over time; current experiences of health and well-being; and thoughts/plans for the future.

Women's views of being in their fifties: transgressing and renegotiating boundaries around physical change and ageing

Our study found many instances of women speaking about facing and renegotiating the shifting boundaries around self and identity, personal and home life and the challenges of work and health. Overall, respondents were reasonably positive about life in their fifties; many women viewed this stage in their lives as a time to expand their horizons and 'get the most out of life'. In some respects, therefore, our findings concur with the work of Gullette (1997) in the US who argued that mid-life women are 'declining to decline', challenging and transgressing traditional boundaries and expectations regarding women's ageing and associated social changes. However, our data also indicate that women's opportunities to lead a satisfying life in their fifties are related to various aspects of their life circumstances. In particular, family roles and relationships, employment opportunities and anticipation of retirement emerged as key influences upon the nature and quality of the women's everyday lives (for a fuller discussion of work and employment issues, see Airey et al, 2004).

For women at mid-life the menopause marked the boundaries between childbearing and post-childbearing stages of their lives. While biomedical developments are now challenging this physical transition, for most women it is still assumed to herald familial, social and personal change and, perhaps, to be seen as one continuing signifier of the boundaries between early and later family life. Interestingly, however, issues around the menopause itself were not central to these mid-life respondents' accounts, even though they were specifically raised at a certain point in the interviews. This is not to say that the menopause was not discussed during the interviews; rather, its salience was minimal compared to other aspects of everyday life, such as issues around family and work. Indeed, even in the context of discussions about health and illness, apart from an occasional mention of osteoporosis, concerns and issues other than the menopause dominated women's accounts. Moreover, where wider, sometimes serious, issues of health and well-being had intruded into some respondents' lives, these were generally presented as things to be dealt with and kept on top of, rather than as an inevitable part of the ageing process with implications of further deterioration. For example, when one member of discussion group B reported that she had just been diagnosed with high blood pressure, she commented, laughing as she spoke: "Until last week I thought I was perfect; very high blood pressure, which I thought, 'oh fizz, just fight that'".

Whose life is it anyway? Renegotiating the boundaries around family roles and relationships and personal well-being at mid-life

It was evident from respondents' accounts that, for most, family relationships continued to be central to their everyday lives and were highly valued. However, such values could also be seen regularly to jar with changing boundaries around identity and ageing. For many in our sample, their fifties had been characterised by life events associated with family situations, such as children leaving home, adult children staying or returning home, the arrival of grandchildren, the onset of caring responsibilities for elderly parents or other relatives, and divorce or bereavement. Sixteen of the 19 respondents were mothers. While none of the women interviewed were currently involved in looking after her own children full time, the continued importance of mothering – and of caregiving within the context of mother–child relationships – was a strong thread running through their accounts.

A vivid sense of continuing parental responsibility and obligation pervaded the interviews. Although many respondents talked about how they now had a 'more equal' relationship with their children, it was also evident they provided emotional and financial support to their children, even as their children entered their thirties; 'caring about' rather than 'caring for' their children. Only a small minority indicated, however, that their families were their sole and chief concern; Alice was unusual in saying: "I just live for my grandchildren, they're my life now." Nevertheless, almost all the mothers expressed continuing worries and concerns for their children – as one woman said:

> "Ye've heard the old sayin', I mean, really, ye worry aboot yer family until the day that ye die. But the worries that ye had when they were growin' up is entirely different from, ye know, what ye have when they're adults." (Maggie)

However, most respondents, while acknowledging the continued salience of their gendered caring roles, also tended to regard themselves as being at a point in their lives when they should be able to develop and pursue their own goals, rather than spending their time undertaking caring activities. This sentiment is clearly illustrated by the following comment:

> "I've had my children and I've brought them up. I've done my best for them and it's my turn now. I'm living life for me. I'm enjoying it, this is my time." (Frances)

There was diversity in the sample regarding the extent to which respondents seemed actually able to realise these aspirations; many respondents' lives were still bounded by the opportunity constraints of class and economic circumstances. For some, the sense of their fifties being 'time for me' was expressed through their participation in paid employment, while others spoke of developing hobbies, spending more time with friends or going travelling. However, the interviews showed that opportunities for women in their fifties to 'widen their horizons' and focus on their own well-being, once their childcare responsibilities diminished, were constrained by other aspects of their social circumstances, for example their financial situations. Further, the fifties might see the onset of new caring demands and obligations, such as the need to provide support to elderly parents or grandchildren. Sometimes, for this 'pivot generation', this might also entail responsibilities for supporting both, thus having to negotiate lifecourse boundaries between being a parent and supporting a parent.

Renegotiating the boundaries between continuing caring roles and fostering their own personal development and well-being were ever-present challenges described by many in this sample. This was illustrated by a few respondents explicitly stating their intention *not* to be drawn into providing care to any grandchildren that they might have in the future. However, all those women who were already grandmothers were in fact involved in looking after their grandchildren in some form or another. This suggests that, while women may indeed express the wish to pursue their own goals throughout their fifties and beyond, in reality it may be more difficult than anticipated for them to stand back from emergent caring demands within the family. For many of our respondents then, the tensions and intersections involved in reconciling and negotiating personal and familial well-being provided a continuing moral and cultural challenge at mid-life.

Falling to bits but keeping it together: making sense of health and well-being in mid-life

Our study showed that an important aspect of caring for self at mid-life was the ability to look after one's physical health and emotional well-being. This involved negotiating the boundaries between understandings of the ageing process and one's embodied experience within this. It was evident that making sense of the ageing process in this way involved at once acknowledging bodily changes but also seeing these as shared and therefore rendered less personally problematic. Family and other social relationships provided cultural referents for this process, perhaps in slightly different ways. Here it seems that boundaries around personal health, work and family caring may be shifting to reflect the increasing importance of friendships and non-familial relationships in contemporary society. From this small piece of research, it seemed that while the lay epidemiology of health and health problems primarily involved families as referents and resources, the lay epidemiology of well-being and ageing drew very much on friendships and wider social relationships, as the following section shows.

Embodied changes and social relationships: redrawing boundaries around ageing

A common theme within respondents' discussions of health in their fifties related to a growing awareness of bodily changes (other than those associated with the menopause) at mid-life. Although women might state that they felt the same inside as they did in their twenties or thirties, their embodied experience told them something different – that they were 'ageing'. For instance, respondents commented on specific physical and mental changes they had noticed: greying hair, deteriorating eyesight, difficulties in remembering words, stiff or creaky joints, sagging stomachs and wrinkled skin. Several remarked that they had less energy in their fifties compared to previous decades. This was often described in terms of 'slowing down' or 'running out of steam'. Some explained that they were less able to live at the same pace or do as many things as they had done in their twenties and thirties, for example when they were bringing up children.

What was particularly interesting about this discourse of embodied change, however, was how respondents drew on various cultural resources to make sense of these processes. In many respects, respondents' reported and observed discussions with other mid-life women about these changes seemed both to normalise such changes and, to a certain extent, then to see these as 'not ageing'. Resistance to and management or downplaying of changes were common themes in our data, since these were not expected by respondents to be dominant in their lives or to threaten their personal development and well-being. One woman illustrated this well when she said:

> "Yes, that's a thing, trying to remember words. You know it's in there, and it does come out eventually, or someone's name, and it's at the end of the day … but who cares? It's not a big issue though it is? It's not. It could be so much worse […] and you don't feel so bothered because you know everyone is going through the same thing." (Jenny)

Our data do not show mid-life women describing their lives as dominated by embodied concerns and changes. Rather, women made efforts in the interviews to downplay these changes: by laughing them off; by pointing out that these things happen to everybody; and by emphasising that these changes could be accommodated within daily life because they did not interfere with everyday functioning. As a respondent in discussion group B explained:

> "I want to widen my life. That's what I'm looking for. I want to brighten it because every time, because when I look in the mirror, I see what's happening and I don't want to see it. I want to widen it." (Sandra)

Such changes were perhaps not experienced as part of health but rather of well-being; and social relationships, particularly with peers, provided the main resource through which culturally relevant sense could be made of them. If, as is suggested by these data, the fifties were, for many, now more about potential opportunities for self rather than winding down into old age, such shared cultural discourses seemed one important mechanism for accommodating potentially threatening embodied change. Although probably all of our sample would have agreed with Jill, who remarked that, "bits of your body keep going wrong", examples were frequently given of conversations with friends and acquaintances which both reaffirmed embodied change as a shared experience and challenged its functional relevance. It seems that, at mid-life, wider personal relationships provide an important means through which boundaries are being redrawn around identity and the ageing process.

Health, illness and family: maintaining boundaries around help, responsibilities and understandings

In addition to expressing an awareness that their bodies were now displaying signs of ageing, a common theme in these mid-life women's accounts of health and illness was the need to look after their health now that they were in their fifties. Respondents' accounts of illness experiences tended to be interwoven with references to the part played by family members. In some cases, this was actual involvement in dealing with illness, for instance by suggesting medical treatment (a sister suggesting being checked out for cancer, a husband insisting on hospital treatment) or in commenting on and sometimes helping with ways of improving health or recovery from illness (daughters helping with visits to the gym). In other cases, family experiences and responsibilities were often referred to as reasons for respondents to be concerned about their health, for instance, worrying about consequences for dependants if anything happened to them or hoping for good enough health to be able to enjoy grandchildren.

Several women in our sample were now experiencing specific health problems. Again, wider cultural discourses, such as personal responsibility for health, had prompted some into making changes to their lifestyle behaviours, notably exercise and diet, with the aim of keeping particular health conditions under control. Others, however, whose interviews suggested that they were aware of such discourses, said that they found lifestyle changes difficult to sustain, as the following quotation shows:

> "Well I suppose. I think women in their fifties are really lookin' quite alright now. A lot better than they did years ago. I mean, when I was a wee girl somebody in their 40s looked old, or somebody in their thirties looked old. But I think women have got more goin' for them now because maybe they've got that wee bit extra money. Likes o' years ago, maybe when ma mother was young, they didnae have enough money to spend on maybe goin' tae the hairdressers, maybe, eh, like we can go out an' maybe spend a wee bit money on face creams, even if it's just moisturiser, maybe eat better, ye know, maybe like more fruit. But sometimes I don't eat as healthy as I should be eatin'. Other times I do.... As I say, I don't smoke an' things." (Valerie)

As has been found in other studies, family history often provided an important resource for making sense of health and illness (Hunt et al, 2000). Again, however, the tone in which such connections were explained was often one implying that, although in some ways these illnesses were not unexpected, nevertheless how respondents then experienced and managed them might be somewhat different.

Making sense of health problems in mid-life involved looking backwards as well as forwards. For many respondents this involved making reference to family members or responsibilities. However, several women challenged the inevitability of family history or, at least, the inevitability of the course of a particular illness experience. There was diversity among the sample group in terms of how women made sense of their health problems at mid-life and their intersections with family; decline or degeneration, as perhaps witnessed in previous generations, was no longer taken for granted. A couple of women referred to chronic health problems that they had had for several decades, noting that now they were into their fifties, it was more difficult to deal with these problems. However, even though the likelihood that individuals will experience chronic health problems increases throughout the fifties, a few respondents reported feeling quite shocked when problems such as high blood pressure, gall bladder problems and diabetes had started at mid-life. Indeed, one or two women went so far as to say that they did not think that their health problems were related to their age.

As with notions of embodied change and well-being, cultural definitions of ageing also appeared to be influencing how these women responded to health problems at mid-life. This study suggests that there were ambivalences about acknowledging any links between ageing and ill health. Even illnesses that were perceived as inherited could now be viewed by this cohort of women in their fifties as having a potentially different and, for them, often a more optimistic trajectory. Furthermore, it seemed that 'ageing' was viewed very negatively by almost everyone in the sample. Almost all of the women defined ageing in terms of physical and mental incapacity and expressed the opinion that 'ageing' was not a label that currently applied to them personally. There were many examples of respondents talking about resisting the signs and symptoms of ageing:

> "I've had one or two blips in my life recently, em, a couple of years ago I had to have a hip replacement and for quite a while before that, I was really quite immobile and that made me feel old and I didn't want to be old and I looked in the mirror. I got up one morning and looked in the mirror and my hair was turning grey and I felt miserable cos I couldn't walk and I couldn't get about the same as I used to and I thought, what can I do to help myself? And I went to my hairdresser and got my hair dyed and that made me feel better." (Grace)

It could be that, while mid-life women may consider it acceptable to joke about embodied changes such as failing eyesight or greying hair, shared with others, it may be a different matter to acknowledge that with age may come more serious health problems, which family histories or family responsibilities can render more problematic. To make explicit connections between the experience of health problems and one's age may be to identify oneself as 'ageing'; this in turn may give rise to unwelcome connotations, namely, those associated with being on some kind of slippery slope towards incapacity and, ultimately, death. For this sample of women in their fifties it was therefore important to continue to see good health as a resource (or illness as a manageable threat) that was necessary to make best use of the rest of their lives. This links to the opportunities that most of these respondents saw this time of life as offering them and the shifting boundaries many identified around personal well-being and personal responsibilities, for instance, for their families.

Concluding comments

Concern about ageing western societies has led to an increase in research and theorising of later adulthood (Arber and Ginn, 1995; ESRC, 2000; Phillipson et al, 2001). In the UK, however, there have been relatively few empirical studies of middle adulthood (Blaikie, 1997; Bernard et al, 2000; Gilleard and Higgs, 2000). In particular, how women are perceiving, managing and constructing their middle years has been under-researched in comparison to the focus on work, economic and retirement-related issues, until relatively recently predominantly characterised as affecting men. Some social trends affecting mid-life women are now being highlighted, notably the effects of demographic and labour market trends on their health, employment and financial circumstances and the increased medical surveillance of their bodies (Lupton, 1998; Hirsch, 2003).

The findings of the study reported here seek to address the gaps in research and policy debates on women and relationships at mid-life. Familial and social relationships, employment and other commitments were interwoven throughout the interviews as women accounted for issues of health and well-being. Through our analysis of data we also found many ambivalences and ambiguities around the roles and expectations of these mid-life women, reflecting in part the shifting cultural and structural boundaries and roles they had to negotiate (Luhmann, 1982).

Notions of life stages as sites of distinction coexist alongside the discursive experiences of life in the fifties. The impact of social and economic changes, including divorce, reformation of partnerships, step-parenting, grandparenting, increased longevity and eldercare, creates biographical disruption from what might be considered commonly anticipated life stages. For example, women in their fifties might be expected to have completed close proximity parenting for their children but might be caring for parents and grandchildren. Some women are progressing through their lifecourse in what might be considered this linear, standardised pattern, while others are grappling with a range of issues on care, health and relationships across generations.

Gendered boundaries are prevalent and dynamic. Despite changes in the role of, and opportunities for, women in their fifties, the workings of gender power and inequality are evident. Thus, while opportunities for women in the fifties grow, boundaries have to be negotiated and transgressed in a gendered world. Tensions continue between caring roles and personal development. These tensions are likely to increase. Shifts in the provision of welfare from state to mixed economy provision premised on greater individual and familial responsibilities place pressures on women and families to manage and resource informal care, health and domestic work.

Women have a strong sense of self and speak of varied aspects of active ageing. They have expectations about increased longevity, health and well-being and healthcare services. When they experience ill health, boundaries are placed around symptoms and, while these are discussed, women are keen to get on with life (and their own lives) as best they can. The goal is attaining and maintaining the notion of 'normal' involvement in family life, employment and other activities (however a woman chooses to define that). At times their bodies become sites of resistance as women (re)negotiate their role, identities and health status against the backdrop of commonly held notions about life stages.

References

Airey, L., McKie, L. and Backett-Milburn, K. (2004) 'Women in their fifties: continuities and ambiguities in work, caring and well-being', paper presented at the CRFR International Conference: 'Work-life balance across the lifecourse', Edinburgh: Centre for Research on Families and Relationships (www.crfr.ac.uk).

Apter, T. (1995) *Secret paths: Women in the new midlife*, New York, NY: W.W. Norton and Co.

Arber, S. and Cooper, H. (2000) 'Socio-economic change and inequalities in health across the lifecourse', in E. Annandale and K. Hunt (eds) *Gender inequalities in health*, Buckingham: Open University Press.

Arber, S. and Ginn, J. (1995) *Connecting gender and ageing*, Buckingham: Open University Press.

Backett, K. and Davison, C. (1995) 'Lifecourse and lifestyle: the social and cultural location of health behaviours', *Social Science and Medicine*, vol 40, no 5, pp 629-38.

Backett-Milburn K. and McKie, L. (eds) (2001) *Constructing gendered bodies*, Basingstoke: Palgrave.

Benson, J. (1997) *Prime time: The middle aged in twentieth century Britain*, London: Longman.

Bernard, M., Phillips, J., Machin, L. and Harding Davies, V. (2000) *Women ageing: Challenging identities, challenging myths*, London and New York: Routledge.

Blaikie, A. (1997) 'Age consciousness and modernity: social construction of retirement', *Self, Agency and Society*, vol 1, pp 9-26.

BMJ (British Medical Journal) (1997) 'Aging: a subject that must be at the top of the world agendas', *British Medical Journal*, vol 315, pp 1029-30, special issue.

Cancian, F. and Oliker, S. (2000) *Caring and gender*, London: Pine Forge Press.

Cronin de Chavez, A., Backett-Milburn, K., Parry, O. and Platt, S. (2005) 'Understanding and researching well-being: its usage in different disciplines and potential for health research and health promotion, *Health Education Journal*, vol 64, no 1, pp 70-87.

Cunningham-Burley, S. and Backett-Milburn, K. (1998) 'The body, health and the middle years', in S. Nettleton and J. Watson (eds) *The body in everyday life*, London: Routledge.

Davis, K. (ed) (1997) *Embodied practices*, London: Sage Publications.

Deem, R. (1996) 'No time for a rest? An exploration of women's work, engendered leisure and holidays', *Time and Society*, vol 5, no 1, pp 5-25.

ESRC (Economic and Social Research Council) (2000) *ESRC growing older programme*, www.shef.ac.uk/uni/projects/gop/

ESRC (Economic and Social Research Council) (2001) *Fit and fifty report*, www.esrc.ac.uk/esrccontent/PublicationsList/fifty/demo.html.

Featherstone, M. (1995) *Undoing culture: Globalization, postmodernism and identity*, London: Sage Publications.

Featherstone, M. and Turner, B.S. (eds) (1991) *The body: Social process and cultural theory*, London: Sage Publications.

Finch, J. (1989) *Family obligations and social change*, Cambridge: Polity Press.

Gilleard, C. and Higgs, P. (2000) *Cultures of ageing: Self, citizen and the body*, Harlow: Pearson Education.

Granville, G. (2000) 'Developing a mature identity: a feminist exploration of the meaning of menopause, PhD thesis, University of Keele.

Greer, J. (1991) *The change: Women, ageing and the menopause*, London: Hamish Hamiliton.

Green, E. (2001) 'Leaky bodies or drying husks? Menopause, health and embodied experience', in S. Clough and J. White (eds) *Women's leisure experiences: Ages, stages and roles*, Leisure Studies Association Publication 70, Eastbourne: University of Brighton.

Griffiths, F. (1999) 'Women's control and choice regarding HRT', *Social Science and Medicine*, vol 49, pp 469-81.

Guillemin, M.N. (1999) 'Managing menopause: a critical feminist engagement', *Scandinavian Journal of Public Health*, vol 27, pp 273-8.

Gullette, M. (1997) *Declining to decline: Cultural combat and the politics of the midlife*, London: University Press of Virginia.

Hirsch, D. (ed) (2000) *Life after 50: Issues for policy and research*, York: Joseph Rowntree Foundation.

Hirsch, D. (2003) 'Crossroads after 50: improving choices in work and retirement', in *Foundations: Analysis informing change*, December 2003, York: Joseph Rowntree Foundation.

Hunt, K., Emslie, C. and Watt, G. (2000) 'Barriers rooted in biography: how interpretations of family patterns of heart disease and early life experiences may undermine behavioural change in mid-life', in H. Graham (ed) *Understanding health inequalities*, Buckingham: Open University Press.

Komesaroff, P., Rothfield, P. and Daly, J. (eds) (1997) *Reinterpreting menopause: Cultural and philosophical issues*, London: Routledge.

Lister, R. (1997) *Citizenship: Feminist perspectives*, London, Macmillan.

Locke, M. (1998) 'Anomalous ageing: managing the postmenopausal body', *Body and Society*, vol 4, no 1, pp 35-61.

Luhmann, N. (1982) *The differentiation of society*, New York, NY: Columbia University Press.

Lupton, D. (1998) 'Going on with the flow: some central discourses in conceptualising and articulating the embodiment of emotional states', in S. Nettleton and J. Watson (eds) *The body in everyday life*, London: Routledge.

McKie, L., Gregory, S. and Bowlby, S. (2002) 'Shadow times: the temporal and spatial frameworks of caring and working', *Sociology*, vol 36, no 4, pp 897-924.

Milburn, K. (1996) 'The importance of lay theorising for health promotion research and practice', *Health Promotion International*, vol 11, no 1, pp 41-6.

Mooney, A., Statham, J. and Simon, A. (2002) *The pivot generation: Informal care and work after fifty*, Bristol/York: The Policy Press/Joseph Rowntree Foundation.

National Statistics Online(a), http://statistics.gov.uk/statloose/ssdataset.asp?vlnk=8631&More=Y

National Statistics Online(b), http://statistics.gov.uk/cci/nugget_print. asp?ID=878

Nettleton, S. and Watson, J. (eds) (1998) *The body in everyday life*, London: Routledge.

Phillips, J., Bernard, M. and Chittenden, M. (2002) *Juggling work and care: The experiences of working carers of older adults*, Bristol/York: The Policy Press/Joseph Rowntree Foundation.

Phillipson, C., Bernard, M., Phillips, J. and Ogg, J. (2001) *The family and community life of older people: Social networks and social support in three urban areas*, London and New York: Routledge.

Sen, A. (1993) 'Capability and well-being', in M. Nussbaum and A. Sen (eds) *The quality of life*, Oxford: Clarendon Press (World Institute of Development Economics).

Sulkunen, P., Holmwood, J., Radner, H. and Schulze, G. (eds) (1997) *Constructing the new consumer society*, London: Macmillan.

Tannenbaum, C.B., Nasmith, L. and Mayo, N. (2003) 'Understanding older women's health care concerns: a qualitative study', *Journal of Women and Aging*, vol 15, no 1, pp 3-16.

Wadsworth, M.E.J. (1997) 'Health inequalities in the life course perspective', *Social Science and Medicine*, vol 44, pp 850-69.

Watson, J., Cunningham-Burley, S., Watson, N. and Milburn, K. (1996) 'Lay theorising about the "body" and implications for health promotion', *Health Education Research: Theory and Practice*, vol 1, no 2, pp 161-72.

NINE

Families, relationships and the impact of dementia – insights into the 'ties that bind'

Dot Weaks, Heather Wilkinson and Shirley Davidson

Introduction

The impact of a diagnosis of dementia reaches far beyond the person to whom it is given. It permeates through the family system and to relationships outside the boundaries of the family. While illness brings a unique set of stressors to challenge relationship bonds, including chronicity, unpredictability and social stigma (Lyons et al, 1995), the very nature of dementia is such that a diagnosis results in major tensions and trials within family relationships. Smith et al (2001) reported that dementia pervaded every part of couples' relationships, for both caregiver and the person with dementia, including spiritual, legal, financial, housing, medical and emotional needs and concerns. In many relationships, the boundaries of roles and responsibilities can be fairly fixed, especially within a spousal relationship, where one partner may take responsibility for managing household budgets, while the other may take responsibility for external house maintenance. When one partner has dementia, many of these task-oriented roles require to be renegotiated and the notion of fixed, bounded demarcation of responsibility changes. Although a person may be experiencing changes in their day-to-day functioning, it is not until a diagnosis is given that the notion of a different self-identity is triggered and the processes of identity renegotiation become evident. Following diagnosis, there will also be a 'crossing of boundaries', as roles and identities are reconstructed and reconfigured, for example from 'person' to 'person with dementia'; from 'person' to 'patient' and from spouse to 'dependent relative'. By drawing upon the experiences of two married couples, we explore the impact of living with dementia and how they negotiate complex processes to support their identities and roles within their relationships following one spouse being diagnosed with dementia. The nature of caring, based on notions of reciprocity, obligation, intimacy and commitment will also be highlighted. We focus on the processes, both positive and negative, within the spousal relationship that are brought into engagement following a diagnosis of dementia and suggest that it is essential to understanding family relationships that they are viewed as grounded in dynamic processes of role negotiation. In trying to understand these processes, we draw on exchange and equity theory, continuity theory and biographical disruption.

The work reported here presents insights into the changes within the relationships of two married couples, when one partner has a diagnosis of early dementia. We begin with a section on dementia, including our social constructionist perspective, moving on to explore the impact of dementia on relationships; these early sections are followed by more data-focused sections based on our two case study couples, drawn from ongoing research projects, where we highlight the processes of change within these relationships before a discussion on the role of care in relationships for people with dementia. We conclude that an understanding of the impact of dementia on all relationships, and a practice-based supportive framework to support relationships, are essential to creating a more positive and supportive social model of care.[1]

Dementia

Within western society there are a number of discourses that offer an explanation for the changes experienced by a person who has dementia, including psychological, sociological and medical perspectives. The predominant discourse relating to dementia is that of medicine, wherein it is explained as a syndrome causing disruption to higher cortical functioning and according to the World Health Organisation (ICD10, WHO, cited in Burns et al, 2002, p 3) disturbs "memory, thinking, orientation, comprehension, calculation, learning capacity, language, and judgement. Consciousness is not clouded". This medical perspective leads to models of disease and behavioural management rather than an understanding of the person and their experience from a wider perspective. These models, however, are limited in as much as they each offer only one way of understanding an extremely complex process.

By adopting a social constructionist perspective, we seek to enhance the understanding of how people act together to co-construct their changing roles and identities following an early diagnosis of dementia. Harding and Palfrey (1997) suggest that this is a two-stage process, the first involving the messages that a person receives from society about dementia. These include the perception that it is a mental illness, with inherent stigma attached and that it is predominant among the elderly. The next stage involves the recipient of these messages construing his or her identity as a person with dementia. Burr (2003) identified certain features fundamental to the social constructionist perspective, namely that a critical stance has to be adopted towards 'taken for granted', culturally and historically bound ways of understanding the world; that knowledge is co-constructed as a result of people interacting together and is sustained by the continuing social processes. Burr (2003) also claimed that knowledge and social action are inextricably linked to each other; for example, it used to be rare for people with dementia to be informed of their diagnosis. It is only since the mid-1980s that society has recognised that a person with dementia has a right to know about that diagnosis (Fearnley et al, 1997). Especially since the development of new pharmacological treatments for Alzheimer's disease (a type of dementia), people have expectations of prescribed treatment following diagnosis, and dementia is beginning to be seen as 'treatable',[2] as opposed to a syndrome of old age where 'nothing can be done'.

There is little to be found in the literature about how people with dementia themselves define the diagnosis or experience the psycho-social impact of the diagnosis and the following period. However, Gloria Sterin, herself diagnosed with Alzheimer's disease, highlighted the meaning and impact of the word itself. For her, the psychological consequences of labelling someone with dementia were extremely powerful; it had the implications of rendering someone as mindless, and "without a mind, one is not really fully human … in fact, not human at all" (Sterin, 2002, p 7). Once the label had been given, she found that people reacted differently to her than they had previously, some withdrawing, some with dismissal and disrespect and some with an excess of kindness. Sterin was experiencing what Goffman (1963) refers to as stigma, defined as "a special kind of relationship between attribute and stereotype" (p 14). Stigmatisation is a process by which the normal identity is spoilt by the reaction of others to the knowledge of the disease with which one has been labelled. The taken for granted assumption by western society that a person labelled with dementia is unable to participate in and contribute to relationships and wider society requires a critical stance in order to challenge this assumption. The analysis of our data presented in the form of case studies will highlight the ability of people with an early diagnosis of dementia to push the boundaries of such taken for granted assumptions, illustrating through key themes the changes in role and identity that were undertaken in order for them to continue to lead a meaningful life, and sustain meaningful, changed relationships.

Research into dementia and relationships

Until the 1990s, the medical model dominated dementia research and care (Downs, 1997), while research on the psychosocial aspects of dementia concentrated on the accounts of carers/caregivers, their burden, stress and coping strategies. The impact of this disease process on relationships has been explored in some depth from the perspective of the spouse (Poth and Steffen, 2000; Bauer et al, 2001; Gallagher-Thompson et al, 2001; Kaplan, 2001; Quayhagen and Quayhagen, 2001; Rankin et al, 2001; Eloniemi-Sulkava et al, 2002; de Vugt et al, 2003; Heru et al, 2004), adult and adolescent children (Davies et al, 2000; Perry, 2004) and primary caregivers (Smith et al, 2001; Teel and Carson, 2003). The personal perspectives of people with dementia themselves have been less common, although there has been evidence of more proactivity in research, writing, and campaigning to have their voices heard (Davis, 1989; McGowin, 1993; Bryden, 2002; Friedell, 2002; McKillop, 2002; Robinson, 2002). Yet, as the 21st century advances, there has still been little exploration of the impact of dementia on daily living from the perspective of the person with dementia. Wright's (1993) study stands out as having addressed the perspectives of people with dementia; this included both parties in the marital relationship and compared couples in which one person was affected by Alzheimer's disease with 'relatively healthy' couples. The sample in this US study was experiencing early- to middle-stage dementia. She found the relationships were 'profoundly different' for each of the two groups. The healthy group enjoyed mutual companionship, high affectional and regular sexual expression, shared responsibilities and low degrees of tension while the hallmark was an increasing respect and reciprocity. Conversely, for the individuals with Alzheimer's disease and their spouses, what had once been shared responsibilities now became the responsibility of the caregiver spouse, with a resultant increase in tension. There was no longer the same degree of reciprocity. The view of the relationship from the perspective of the person with dementia differed from that of the caregiver spouse; it was experienced as less problematic, with less evidence of tension. Both partners remained committed to continuing their marital relationship, described by Wright (1993) as a 'committed-dependent' relationship.

Other studies have mainly highlighted the impact of dementia on the caregiver spouse, addressing such issues as marital interaction (Gallagher-Thompson et al, 2001), the impact on marital relationships (Baikie, 2002), caring at home versus caring in an institution (Hirschfeld, 2003) and the couplehood of spouses of institutionalised persons with Alzheimer's disease (Kaplan, 2001). These studies highlighted a loss of emotional support from spouse, a reduction in quality of verbal interaction, changes in intimacy and satisfaction with the marital relationship and a lowering of morale. Most couples moved along a continuum of couplehood from strongly feeling part of a 'we' to feeling strongly about being 'I' and much depended on where the couple started out, prior to the onset of dementia.

The qualitative study reported in this chapter focused on the experience and views of the case study participants. Analysis used grounded theory as an inductive approach to data collection (Martin and Turner, 1986). The data were transcribed and each transcript was open coded separately, noting categories of significance. These were then interchecked and re-examined to adjust the coding as appropriate and to remove any redundancies. The coded individual interviews were then compared to each other and theory from these data generated based on the patterns, common themes and categories that emerged (Strauss and Corbin, 1990). Therefore, the specific experiences of case study participants were not analysed according to a priori assumptions but rather the emergent themes and general patterns in order to develop the theoretical framework for understanding their experience. This highlighted key themes of reciprocity, continuity, co-construction of self-identity and renegotiating roles.

Case studies

Case study research invites us to seek understanding of each case, both for its commonalities and uniqueness. The case study can be defined as a 'bounded system' and people are seen as prospective cases (Stake, 1995). In an attempt to capture the unique and familiar, we acknowledge that "everybody's story is different because no two people have the same personality, the same personal history, the same web of relationships or the same pattern of health" (Goldsmith, 2004, p 57). Our cases reflect a narrative approach in order to hear the story of the changes that have taken place in people's lives since their diagnosis of dementia. To enable the reader to learn how our case study people function in the ongoing change processes within their present relationships, we illustrate this with two of our case studies from two ongoing research projects. We highlight the narrative that portrays our key themes relating to reciprocity, continuity, co-constructing of self-identity and renegotiating roles. The first (Wilkinson, 2000)[3] of these studies used qualitative, open interviews with seven couples and six single people with dementia to explore the experience of living with dementia for people in early stages. Each couple was interviewed at least twice and was asked to explore issues around diagnosis, social networks, living with dementia, care and health. The second study (Weaks, 2002)[4] involved qualitative case studies of five couples to explore the impact of dementia on their lives immediately following a diagnosis of dementia and for the six months thereafter, using in-depth interviews and participant observation within an ethnographic study. This study focused mainly on how families initially reacted to and managed the diagnosis and how relationships changed in order to accommodate the diagnosis. The two case study couples have been chosen for their similarities in some respects (they are both long-term married couples with children and have a recent diagnosis of a dementia; their experiences clearly highlight the processes of co-constructing of relationships following the diagnosis) while contrasting in terms of the quality of their relationships and the impact that dementia has had on their relationships.

That family relationships are affected by a family member having dementia is beyond dispute; it is how they are affected that is of interest to the researcher and practitioner. To some extent this will depend on how these relationships functioned prior to one of its members developing dementia and indeed who the members of the 'family' are. The case study individuals with dementia were still very articulate; they were aware of their diagnosis and retained the ability to discuss the impact it had on their lives and their relationships.

The first case study individual, Angus,[5] who was in his fifties, was interviewed four times over a period of one year. He had been diagnosed with dementia about two years prior to the first interview. He had been married to Mary for over 28 years and they had three children, one of whom was still at school. Angus and Mary were interviewed separately and once together.

Interviewing the spouses together had the advantage of allowing the researcher to experience how they interacted and gave a flavour of their relationships with each other. The case of Angus and Mary, however, highlighted the advantages of interviewing each one of the couple separately as well as together, as they confided feelings to the researcher which they had been unwilling to share with their spouse.

Our second man, Peter, was in his late sixties and had been married to Ruth for over 40 years. Research interviews commenced two weeks after Peter had received the diagnosis of Alzheimer's disease. The initial interview with both partners was held separately and thereafter Peter and Ruth were interviewed together monthly over a six-month period, and observed in different situations, interacting in different relationships. The couple had three adult children and five grandchildren. Peter retired from his own business eight years prior to being diagnosed with dementia

It can be seen that the characteristics of the two case study couples appeared to reflect the traditional modernist concept of 'the family' (Jamieson, 1998), which is perhaps a reflection of the age group in question.[6] In such longstanding orthodox family relationships, the respective roles of the partners within the relationship have had time to establish themselves, where there are expectations placed upon them, and predetermined roles are implied, frequently assigned by gender. The case study couples indicated that this was the case; for example, Peter described how he and Ruth had: "Our own spheres of operation. Ruth runs the house, gets the messages in etc and I cut the grass and do that sort of thing, like pruning the roses … it's a very pleasant life." Against this background of stability, it may be expected that any changes wrought by dementia will be all the more identifiable. These once pre-determined bounded roles within the family relationship, and within the social network, are challenged by their construction of the dementia.

The study previously referred to (Wright, 1993) identified a diminution of reciprocity between couples after the onset of dementia. This theme of reciprocity, mutuality and equality in a relationship is one of the most significant running through the literature (Baikie, 2002; Eloniemi-Sulkava et al, 2002; de Vugt et al, 2003; Hirschfeld, 2003). The presence of these elements in a relationship are indicators of its quality and durability, while their absence is highlighted as the main reason for partners to leave a relationship (Lyons et al, 1995) and having the strongest influence in the decision as to whether a partner enters full-time nursing home care or not (Hirschfield, 2003). Knowledge about the quality of marital (and family) relationships and how this changes as a result of chronic illness and disability is, however, still relatively limited and we know little about how such relationships are affected by resultant changing roles (Lyons et al, 1995). Lyons et al suggest that the onset of serious illness provides an opportunity to examine exchange and equity theory in marriage, where such theory would predict that relationships are dissolved or their quality reduced or that conflicts result from a loss in exchangeable resources or unfair resource exchange.

In our case studies, the relationship between Angus and Mary, post diagnosis, provided an extreme example of 'reduced quality', bordering on dissolution. Angus's role in the household as husband and father seemed to all intents and purposes to have disappeared. He described how he felt that his wife no longer involved him in decisions to do with the children or other matters in the house. Angus had to struggle to come to terms with the deconstruction of his identity within his 'natural' family. He rather poignantly described Mary as being "a good quality housekeeper … the loving side has just gone". In contrast, his wife Mary (when interviewed alone) described a couple of episodes of difficult and unacceptable behaviour that had taken place. He had never exhibited this type of behaviour before and the first incident had upset both of them. Angus had offered to leave her but she had persuaded him that his action was due to the illness and that "we've got to deal with it". The way the rest of the family did deal with it was to exclude him and he felt that the family who did things "behind his back", did not trust him and were afraid he would embarrass them. The family's expectations of Angus could not be upheld, because of the way his family had created an identity for him as a "dementia patient", who could no longer operate within the boundaries of his earlier roles within the family as father and husband. There was no negotiation and if he were going to survive he had to seek emotional support beyond the 'natural' family. This boundary-breaking work was needed so that Angus could create a self that could contribute to society in a meaningful way. Not only did social outings with an Alzheimer's support group give Angus a refuge from "things in the house just closing in … I just needed to get away out the road and get some peace and quiet" but they were crucial in helping him to create a different self.

Sabat (2002a, 2002b) observes that a person may manifest a variety of social selves. Angus described the "really bitter angry battles" leading up to his receiving a diagnosis of dementia. The time prior to receiving the diagnosis had come to be regarded by Angus as the primary period of illness and distress. Since then, he had constructed a new role, and identity, through his mutually supportive relationships with other people with dementia as part of a support group. He described these relationships with other people with dementia in terms of "we're all equals", "camaraderie", "a sense of humour", highlighting the importance of feelings of equality and reciprocity within relationships. This helped him to co-construct a different self and he found meaning through his day-to-day interactions with his new 'contemporary family'. This was in direct contrast to Peter (see later), who was able to create a continuity of his self-identity with the help of his wife and other close relationships, including his minister, from discussions he had with them about his diagnosis.

Caron et al (2000) noted that, following the impairment to cognitive function that is caused by dementia, the non-affected spouse/caregiver of the person with dementia tends to assume responsibility for household tasks, while responsibility for maintaining social relationships also falls on the non-affected spouse. In our case studies, however, comprising people with as yet limited cognitive impairment, the couples continued to negotiate and/or share these tasks, to a greater or lesser extent. We would acknowledge here that despite the limited cognitive impairment, this was still enough to result in stigmatisation, with questions posed around ability and risk.

Peter's wife provided him with support in order to maintain his reputation as 'reliable' within his social network, by checking his appointments and encouraging him to keep a diary. In contrast, Angus forged new social relationships and, in so doing, created a new role for himself outside the home. The maintenance of established, and the making of new roles and relationships continued to be important to these men, reflecting the findings of Menne et al (2002), in a study of people with an early diagnosis of dementia, who expressed the wish to continue the lifestyle that they had been experiencing previously, despite their diagnoses.

Continuity theory would suggest that, as people age, their core tasks are developing, preserving and maintaining adaptive capacity (Atchley, 1999). This assumes an ability to use feedback from successes and failures in order to develop and modify patterns of behaviour, activities and relationships. Peter reported that he had always been a "private person" and he was loath to share inner thoughts and feelings. This was particularly true when it came to telling other people about his diagnosis of Alzheimer's disease, complicated by his fear of stigma arising from such a diagnosis as he felt that: "If people knew that I was in the stages of dementia, they would shy away from me." In maintaining his previous pattern of behaviour he was impeding the continuance of his social activities, including his role as an elder in church. The relationship between Peter and Ruth appeared to have been a loving relationship, although not without its stresses and tensions, and, as previously stated, operated within the sphere of 'the orthodox family'. When there was discussion about whether they should tell people about the diagnosis, this was the conversation:

> *Peter*: "I don't think we should broadcast it you know...."
>
> *Ruth*: "Neither of us have been the type to broadcast things, neither of us are like that."
>
> *Peter*: "We don't broadcast to each other readily either in some ways!!"
>
> *Ruth*: "If you don't mind, then I can let it out slowly ... I hesitate to say this but in a sort of way I have been protecting you for quite some time ... (becomes emotional)."
>
> *Peter*: "Oh dear, oh dear, dear, dear...."
>
> *Ruth*: "If you forget appointments then I can't say why and I try to...."
>
> *Peter*: "Shield me."
>
> *Ruth*: "To protect you from criticism and I think it would be easier if it was more open."

This conversation highlights Ruth's 'confession' about how she has already adapted in order to accommodate the different needs of Peter. The tensions within this family were highlighted as Ruth was aware of having to change her role in protect Peter. The acknowledgement from Peter that they have not always communicated clearly their needs to each other, coupled with a dawning awareness that this is no longer a useful way to operate, allowed him to use this feedback to find a new way forward in order to adapt to his present situation. This conversation proved to be the trigger for him to share his diagnosis with others, including his minister, from whom he then received a great deal of support. This again reflects the need to go outside the 'natural family' for emotional support. The 'natural family' were geographically distant, and unable to give the 'hands on' support that was required. Arising out of the successful encounter with his minister, Peter was encouraged to share his diagnosis with others in his social network and in so doing, managed, with their feedback, to co-construct a new meaning of his life with the diagnosis of Alzheimer's disease. He reported that "it's far better to be open ... people in general have been extraordinarily sympathetic and helpful". Once he had shared his diagnosis, he was then able to develop a new adaptive strategy in order to get on with his present life: "I would like people to know that it is not the end of life you know, life goes on, I can still play golf, I can still be part of social intercourse et cetera ... you don't need to climb down into a hole and shut the door behind you." He had used groups within his 'contemporary family' to facilitate the boundary work necessary to construct who he was, and this gave him the meaning necessary to know that he continued to be accepted within these groups of people in his church, fellow members of his golf club and retired professional business men (Probus). The significance of his local 'social world' is of paramount importance to Peter in the co-construction of his new identity.

It may be relevant to examine briefly the classic sociological formulation of the notion of chronic illness as 'biographical disruption' (Bury, 1982). According to the 'biographical disruption' model, the ill person rethinks their biography and self-concept, resulting in a mobilisation of resources to respond to the life disruption. Because the effects of dementia may include changes in behaviour, memory loss and a degree of questioning of identity and 'selfhood' (Sabat and Harre, 1992; Charmaz, 2002; Pearce et al, 2002) absent in other chronic illnesses, it is possible that its impact on relationships is different in nature from these illnesses. Being given the diagnosis of dementia was described by Mary as a "relief because things had been so bad". She said that "things had been horrendous for years and it was just getting worse and worse ... totally breaking my heart". By having an explanation for Angus's behaviour, she felt more able to excuse his treatment of her; without this, she would have left him. Her situation, however, following the diagnosis, was similar to that described in Oliver (1983), who commented that, while it could be argued that most carers did not have a choice about taking on their caring commitment, spouses could be seen as having least choice of all. Most wives in her study quoted their marriage vows 'in sickness and in health' and Oliver (1983) posited that ill health and disability are more likely to keep a failing marriage going than the reverse (1983, p 75). Even if a marriage had been on the point of breaking up when illness had been diagnosed, the wife felt that she could not in all conscience abandon a sick person.

Dementia had drastically disrupted Angus's life, shattering his taken for granted assumptions about the world and creating uncertainty about the present and the future. Although families may appear to offer a range of certainties, dementia had broken that certainty barrier. During one interview with Angus, it was clear that he had thought about the 'future' in an apocalyptic sense; in the context of respite care, he was terrified: "You just think, come in for a wee holiday and the door clangs shut and they lock the doors and that's you, you're trapped in there and you can't get out." He carried on: "It might be irrational but [the fear] is there." It could, of course, be said that his fear was not irrational at all – when Mary reminded him that the psychiatrist had told him that a certain psychiatric hospital would not be suitable for him because the people there were "old and very confused", he riposted "maybe I'm not 'not very confused' – I *am* very confused some days. How do I know that that's not permanent? Because you're not aware that you've reached it." However, a year later, Angus told the researcher that he lived day to day or week to week: "I don't look beyond that."

In contrast, in the case of Peter, the period of disruption had been relatively short lived. Initially, on receiving the diagnosis, he reported his reaction to it as thinking that his world had come to an end and said he coped with this by retreating into his shell: "I was stewing in my own juice as it were, and trying to hold it all in, and that just made me miserable, I tried that for a short while and it didn't work, to be honest." In his final interview, he reported that: "I am comfortable with it [telling people about his diagnosis] now, you see I wasn't comfortable with it at the start, that's for sure, because I thought that I was on the slippery slope and that things were going to go down and down and down and I would end up, well, I don't know, an incoherent vegetable and obviously that has not happened so I feel I'm much happier now than I did initially." We would posit that the disruption experienced by both of these men lasted for varying lengths of time and question whether this reflected a temporary glitch in their continuity process.

Peter's reaction to his diagnosis of Alzheimer's disease reflects a story of a disruption in his expectation of life in retirement; the beginning of changes in the reciprocity of the marital relationship, with Ruth taking on more of the day-to-day management of affairs;

and great courage in the way Peter was able to challenge his taken for granted assumptions of how people would react to his telling of the diagnosis. His story also reflects the capacity to co-construct, with others around him, and make meaning of, his life, in the face of adversity, in an attempt to continue enjoying life to the full.

Implications for 'care' in relationships of people with dementia

One of the main implications of living with dementia is that the concept and provision of 'care' becomes a more visible and central aspect of the marital relationship. Underpinning most relationships is a concept of 'care' or 'caring for' each other that is usually invisible and not openly acknowledged or negotiated. However, the onset of illness can create a need for a more formalised concept of care with one person 'caring for' the increasing needs of the person with dementia. The provision of care for people with dementia is based on reliance on the traditional family construct, with spouses providing the main support (Montgomery and Williams, 2001*)*. Positive, and even sometimes negative, family and other social relationships are the key to supporting a person through the disruptions and discontinuities arising out of having dementia. Social trends (Riggs, 2001) indicate that the current reliance on traditional spousal and familial support will not be sustainable, however, so that the reliance on this particular conceptualisation of care may have to change.

Our case studies have shown that the existing boundaries and definition of roles within the family are challenged by dementia. In the case of Peter and Ruth, their relationship seemed to have endured throughout the onset of dementia. Their respective roles within their marriages had changed and would continue to do so, no longer being able to predict, by gender, who was responsible for predetermined roles, but essential elements of understanding, mutuality, communication and commitment remained. With difficulty, they had adapted and were continuing to adapt to the circumstances in which they found themselves. In the case of Angus and Mary, however, their relationship, already tense and fragile, was being further destroyed by the experience of dementia, although the very fact that some aspects of Angus's behaviour could be attributed to dementia placed Mary in the position of feeling unable to leave him. Despite both men having different relationships with their spouses, each of them felt a need to go outside the 'natural family' for emotional support. For Peter, direct access to his 'non-resident' family was impossible because of geographical distance, and for Angus, access was denied because of emotional distance.

These two case studies illustrate a continuing strength in the traditional marriage and its role in providing support and care for people with dementia. Our case studies were, of course, in the early stages of the illness and it may be anticipated that further stresses will be placed on their marriages as time goes on as the capacity for reciprocity fades. The social trends that have been identified in the early 21st century, however, including the increasing diversity of relationships, may have implications for the provision of care and support for people with dementia. Will the same social pressures that existed for spouses to remain bound to each other 'in sickness and in health, for better for worse', as the marriage vows assert, apply to other, non-traditional, relationships, or even to today's concept of marriage when one in three marriages is expected to end in divorce.

Some concluding thoughts

Clearly a diagnosis of dementia brings with it a range of challenges to individual identity and socially constructed roles and relationships. What is evident is that social relationships, as dynamic forms anyway, undergo a process of renegotiation, challenging existing boundaries and forms, resulting in change, either positive or negative, in order to live with dementia. The experiences of the two couples reported here illustrate some of the complex processes they used to renegotiate their relationships. In particular, dementia brings with it a more formalised notion of care as part of overall relationship roles and characteristics. There are challenges to the well-established boundaries within existing relationships with all their motivations and formations as they traverse to relationships operating within a different framework of caring. Our main concern in presenting these data is not to argue for marriage as the main relationship form in which to provide care, but to raise the question of what impact dementia may have on non-traditional relationships. If, as certainly appeared to be the case, it was the commitment created through our couples' understandings of their marriage vows that created the conditions within which they carried on their relationships – in both positive and negative ways – as they learned to live with dementia, then what are the possibilities for individuals who are not in this particular form of relationship? And what and how are their 'ties that bind' formulated and maintained? As society continues to change and more diverse family forms become more common, it is imperative to have a better understanding of how these diverse forms of family and relationships can also be supported to sustain caring and committed relationships.

In an initial attempt to address this question, we make the following suggestions: first, there is an urgent need to understand in more detail what is needed to support and sustain a positive relationship following a diagnosis of dementia (or after any traumatic event). This question has to be addressed for all relationship forms, including individuals who are living alone. Second, the increased understanding brought about by addressing this question will allow for service providers to take new and emerging relationship structures into account when planning for future services. Provision of care and support for the non-traditional as well as the traditional family will be required in order to embrace the diverse needs of the future. Third, as also recommended by Baikie (2002), we perceive there to be a need for professionals working with people with dementia and their families to undergo training in relationship counselling, in order to address the consequences and issues arising from the changing relationships and ensuing distress that is experienced as a result of these changes. We would recommend that this occurs early, at the beginning of the dementia trajectory, when there is the best possibility for preventing many future problems (Weaks et al, forthcoming) rather than waiting to intervene when the relationship is in danger of being challenged beyond repair. We conclude that an understanding of the impact of dementia on relationships is essential to creating a more positive and supportive social model of care.

Notes

[1] It is not the intention of this chapter to examine the provision of services and support for people with dementia and their families, but it is fair to say that the traditional notion of the family means that the boundaries of care are often kept within the family with external sources of support not sought until later.

[2] Pharmacological treatment can delay the progression of dementia in some cases but to date there is no known cure.

[3] Funded by a Royal Society of Edinburgh/Lloyds TSB Personal Research Fellowship 2000-2004.

[4] Funded by Tayside NHS Trust as part of a Research Training Fellowship 2002-2005.

[5] All names and some personal details have been changed to protect identity.

[6] Little research has been carried out in respect of older people in other relationships. See, for example, Heaphy et al, 2003.

References

Atchley, R. (1999) *Continuity and adaptation in aging: Creating positive experiences*, Baltimore, MD: Johns Hopkins University Press.

Baikie, E. (2002) 'The impact of dementia on marital relationships', *Sexual and Relationship Therapy*, vol 17, pp 289-99.

Bauer, M.J., Maddox, M.K., Kirk, L.N., Burns, T. and Kuskowski, M.A. (2001) 'Progressive dementia: personal and relational impact on caregiving wives', *American Journal of Alzheimer's Disease and Other Dementias*, vol 16, no 6, pp 329-34.

Bryden, C. (2002) 'A person-centred approach to counselling, psychotherapy and rehabilitation of people diagnosed with dementia in the early stages', *Dementia*, vol 1, no 2, pp 141-56.

Burns, A., Dening, T. and Lawlor, B. (2002) *Clinical guidelines in old age psychiatry: International classification of diseases (ICD 10)*, London: Martin Dunitz Limited.

Burr, V. (2003) *Social constructionism*, London: Routledge.

Bury, M. (1982) 'Chronic illness as biographical disruption', *Sociology of Health and Illness*, vol 4, no 2, pp 167-82.

Caron, W.A., Pattee, M.D. and Otteson, O.J. (2000) *Alzheimer's disease: The family journey*, Minnesota: North Ridge Press.

Charmaz, K. (2002) 'Stories and silences: disclosures and self in chronic illness', *Qualitative Inquiry*, vol 8, no 2, pp 302-28.

Davies, H.D., Clovis, C.L., Christie, L., Ingram, L., Priddy, J.M. and Tinklenberg, J.R. (2000) 'Stages of resolution: young adult children coping with an Alzheimer's disease parent', *Clinical Gerontologist*, vol 22, pp 43-58.

Davis, R. (1989) *My journey into Alzheimer's disease*, Amersham: Scripture Press.

de Vugt, M.E., Stevens, F., Aalten, P., Richel, L., Jaspers, N., Winkens, I., Jolles, J. and Verhey, F.R.J. (2003) 'Behavioural disturbances in dementia patients and quality of the marital relationship', *International Journal of Geriatric Psychiatry*, vol 18, no 2, pp 149-54.

Downs, M. (1997) 'The emergence of the person in dementia research', *Ageing and Society*, vol 17, pp 597-607.

Eloniemi-Sulkava, U., Notkola, I., Haemaelaeinen, K., Rahkonen, T., Viramo, P., Hentinen, M., Kivelae, S. and Sulkava, R. (2002) 'Spouse caregivers' perceptions of influence of dementia on marriage', *International Psychogeriatrics*, vol 14, pp 47-58.

Fearnley, K., McLennan, J. and Weaks, D. (1997) *The right to know? Sharing the diagnosis of dementia*, Edinburgh: Alzheimer's Scotland/ Action on Dementia.

Friedell, M. (2002) 'Awareness: a personal memoir on the declining quality of life in Alzheimer's', *Dementia*, vol 1, no 3, pp 359-66.

Gallagher-Thompson, D., Dal Canto, P.G., Jacob, T. and Thompson, L.W. (2001) 'A comparison of marital interaction patterns between couples in which the husband does or does not have Alzheimer's disease', *The Journals of Gerontology Series B – Psychological Sciences and Social Sciences*, vol 56, pp S140-S150.

Goffman, E. (1963) *Stigma: Notes on the management of spoiled identity*, London: Penguin.

Goldsmith, M. (2004) *In a strange land: People with dementia and the local church*, Edinburgh: 4M Publications.

Harding, N. and Palfrey, C. (1997) *The social construction of dementia: Confused professionals*, London: Jessica Kingsley.

Heaphy, B., Yip, A.K.T. and Thompson, D. (2003) *Lesbian, gay and bisexual lives over 50 – A report on the project 'The social and policy implications of non-heterosexual ageing'*, Nottingham: York House Publications.

Heru, A., Ryan, C.E. and Iqbal, A. (2004) 'Family functioning in the caregivers of patients with dementia', *International Journal of Geriatric Psychiatry*, vol 19, no 6, pp 533-7.

Hirschfeld, M. (2003) 'Home care versus institutionalization: family caregiving and senile brain disease', *International Journal of Nursing Studies*, vol 40, no 5, pp 463-9.

Jamieson, L. (1998) *Intimacy: Personal relationships in modern societies*, Cambridge: Polity Press.

Kaplan, L. (2001) 'A couple typology for spouses of institutionalized persons with Alzheimer's disease: perceptions of "we"–"I"', *Family Relations: Journal of Applied Family and Child Studies*, vol 50, no 1, pp 87-98.

Lyons, R.F., Sullivan, M.J.L., Ritvo, P.G. and Coyne, J. (1995) *Relationships in chronic illness and disability*, London: Sage Publications.

Martin, P.Y. and Turner, B.A. (1986) 'Grounded theory and organizational research, *Journal of Applied Behavioral Science*, vol 22, no 2, pp 141-57.

McGowin, D.F. (1993) *Living in the labyrinth: A personal journey through the maze of Alzheimer's disease*, Cambridge: Mainsail.

McKillop, J. (2002) 'Did research change anything', in H. Wilkinson (ed) *The perspectives of people with dementia: Research methods and motivations*, London: Jessica Kingsley.

Menne, H., Kinney, J.M. and Morhardt, D.J. (2002) 'Trying to continue to do as much as they can', *Dementia*, vol 1, no 3, pp 367-83.

Montgomery, R.J.V. and Williams, K.N. (2001) 'Implications of differential impacts of care-giving for future research on Alzheimer care', *Ageing and Mental Health*, vol 5, supp no 1, pp 23-34.

Oliver, J. (1983) 'The caring wife', in J. Finch and D. Groves (eds) *A labour of love: Women, work and caring*, London: Routledge and Kegan Paul.

Pearce, A., Clare, l. and Pistrang, N. (2002) 'Managing sense of self: coping in the early stages of Alzheimer's disease', *Dementia*, vol 1, no 2, pp 173 -92.

Perry, J. (2004) 'Daughters giving care to mothers who have dementia: mastering the 3 Rs of (re)calling, (re)learning, (re)adjusting', *Journal of Family Nursing*, vol 10, no 1, pp 50-69.

Poth, T.L. and Steffen, A.M. (2000) 'Anger management for the Alzheimer's caregiver: a case study', *Clinical Gerontologist*, vol 22, no 1, pp 83-6.

Quayhagen, M.P. and Quayhagen, M. (2001) 'Testing of a cognitive stimulation intervention for dementia caregiving dyad', *Neuropsycho-logical Rehabilitation*, vol 11, nos 3-4, pp 319-32.

Rankin, E.D., Haut, M. and Keefover, R.W. (2001) 'Current marital functioning as a mediating factor in depression among spouse caregivers in dementia', *Clinical Gerontologist*, vol 23, nos 3-4, pp 27-44.

Riggs, J.A. (2001) 'The health and long-term policy challenges of Alzheimer's disease', *Ageing and Mental Health*, vol 5, supp no 1, pp 138-45.

Robinson, E. (2002) 'Should people with Alzheimer's take part in research?', in H. Wilkinson (ed) *The perspectives of people with dementia: Research methods and motivations* London: Jessica Kingsley.

Sabat, S.R. (2002a) 'Selfhood and Alzheimer's disease', in P.B. Harris, *The person with Alzheimer's disease*, Baltimore, MD: Johns Hopkins University Press.

Sabat, S.R. (2002b) 'Surviving manifestations of selfhood in Alzheimer's disease', *Dementia*, vol 1, no 1, pp 25-36.

Sabat, S.R. and Harre, R. (1992) 'The construction and deconstruction of self in Alzheimer's disease', *Ageing and Society*, vol 12, pp 444-61.

Smith, A., Lauret, R., Peery, A. and Meuller, T. (2001) 'Caregiver needs: a qualitative exploration', *Clinical Gerontologist*, vol 24, nos 1-2, pp 3-26.

Stake, R.E. (1995) *The art of case study research*, London: Sage Publications.

Sterin, G.J. (2002) 'Essay on a word: a lived experience of Alzheimer's disease', *Dementia*, vol 1, no 1, pp 7-10.

Strauss, A. and Corbin, J. (1990) *Basics of qualitative research*, London: Sage Publications.

Teel, C. and Carson, P. (2003) 'Family experiences in the journey through dementia diagnosis and care', *Journal of Family Nursing*, vol 9, no 1, pp 38-58.

Weaks, D. A. (2002) Research proposal for Tayside Primary Care Trust Research Training Fellowship: 'The psycho-social impact on patients, their families and medical practitioners of early diagnosis of dementia'.

Weaks, D.A., McLeod, J. and Wilkinson, H.A. (2004) *The value of post diagnostic counselling for people with dementia: Perceptions of old age psychiatrists and GPs*, Paper presented at 10th International British Association for Counselling and Psychotherapy, London.

Wilkinson, H. (2000) Funded proposal, University of Edinburgh: 'Social support and the impact of dementia. A qualitative longitudinal study'.

Wright, L.K. (1993) *Alzheimer's disease and marriage*, London: Sage Publications.

TEN

Violence and families: boundaries, memories and identities

Linda McKie and Nancy Lombard

> Violence pervades the lives of many people around the world, and touches all of us in some way. (Brundtland, 2002, p vii)

Introduction

Recent conflicts in Rwanda, Bosnia and Northern Ireland have brought attention to the role of families in inter-communal violence. Acts of inter-communal violence, and the consequences of these, have become more commonly known as ethnic cleansing. Inter-communal violence is characterised by the eruption of violent acts between those who were former neighbours, friends, even relatives and leads to death and injury, with resultant movement of populations. Violence is rationalised on the basis of religious or ethnic differences and the supposed need to exclude those deemed not to belong to a particular group or community. Familial networks, and the interweaving of interpretations of history and memories, help forge collective identities around which a sense of belonging outweighs prior neighbourly connections among families and friends. In this chapter we explore how the boundaries between history, memories and public institutions become contested in and around families, and can form the basis to inter-communal violence.

The chapter opens with a brief overview on violence in and between families. This is followed by a consideration of the role of the home as a location, and the family as a hub, for the creation and moulding of identities. Subsequently, we address recent work on the contested nature of boundaries around memories, history and time. Families can become a conduit for the creation and reinforcement of differences that may be worked out through tensions and violence. At the same time inter-communal violence creates a cultural context in which the prevalence of violence in families, such as domestic violence, increases. The sanctioning of violence becomes evident between and within families. To further these arguments we present two case studies. First, we outline the work of Bringa (1995, 2002) on village and family life in a Muslim community in Bosnia: and, second, we explore a study by Connolly and Healy (2003) on the development of children's attitudes towards 'the troubles' in Northern Ireland. In the concluding comments, we assert that families may be viewed as 'porous'. The boundaries between public and private are dynamic and fluid as those in and around families reflect and (re)interpret ideas and beliefs that are offered as rationalisations for inter-communal violence.

Violence in and between families

Experiences and images of violence pervade our social and cultural life. In the foreword to the World Health Organization *World report on violence and health*, Nelson Mandela (2002, p v) comments that "the twentieth century will be remembered as a century marked by violence". Certainly this has been an era of world wars in which technologies have been adopted and adapted to achieve mass destruction. Today nine out of 10 people who die from the direct or indirect consequences of war are civilians and it is civilians, especially women and girls, who suffer disproportionately from the aftermath of armed conflict (Hynes, 2004). There has also been a notable recognition and documentation of interpersonal violence in familial and intimate relationships, such as domestic violence, and inter-communal conflict in which violence is used to advance ethnic, religious, socioeconomic and political agendas. Violence includes psychological as well as physical abuses and can be experienced through interstate, interpersonal and inter-communal conflicts. Here we focus on the role of families and family practices (Morgan, 1996) in the creation and reinforcement of the last mentioned form of violence, namely inter-communal conflicts.

To place inter-communal violence in context we offer a brief overview (World Health Organization, 2002). It is estimated that each year 1.6 million people worldwide lose their lives to violence. Many more are injured and suffer from a range of physical and psychological problems. Violence between those known to each other is also prevalent with an estimated one in four women in Scotland aged 16 to 64 reporting psychological or physical forms of domestic violence (Scottish Executive, 2000). These data are similar to those reported in many post-industrial societies (McKie and

Hearn, 2004) and, in the aftermath of armed conflict and civil unrest, the incidence of interpersonal and gendered violence may increase (World Health Organization, 2002).

In the case of inter-communal violence conflicts emanate from deep and longstanding tensions between 'communities'. These communities or groups are generally defined in terms of belonging to ethnic or religious identities drawn from interpretations of experiences and histories. This we consider further in the following section. Commonly cited triggers to inter-communal violence include an unequal access to power; a lack of democratic processes; and unequal access to, and distribution of, resources (Carnegie Commission, 1997).

In the reporting of violence there remains a focus on documenting and policing incidents that take place in public spaces; for example, the ongoing concerns about community policing, the development of community safety planning and the surge in CCTV. Certainly inter-communal violence can and does take place in public spaces, often involving the violent acts committed in and around the destruction of the family home of those attacked. The destruction and abuse of bodies and homes through attacking families and neighbourhoods is to annihilate the core of one's identity. However, when inter-communal violence erupts, families can and do support and offer safety to those who might be considered 'other'. Family members may be driven apart, as some do not accept the basis of conflict or refuse to become involved in violent acts. Thus while patterns of inter-communal violence in Rwanda or Bosnia were marked by ethnic cleansing and the redrawing of geographical boundaries between ethno-religious groups, there are examples of families reaching across these boundaries to save neighbours, friends and work colleagues (Hinton, 2002; Hoffman, 2004).

Our home, my family: construction and preservation

Generally, inter-communal violence takes place in and around homes and other physical examples of collective histories, memories and identities such as religious buildings, schools and community centres. The aim is to strike at the entities that make up the collective sense of being of those defined as other. Familial networks and connections are critical to the creation of the sense of belonging or being excluded.

Families are about solidarities and people working collectively to achieve everyday and longer-term sustenance and emotional support. At times they are tense, difficult, and even violent places to be. While the nuclear family continues to be a commonly adopted and adapted model for childrearing, any analysis of families demonstrates a variety of arrangements for parenting and intimate relationships. The formation, breakdown and reformation of families is not an unusual process of family life. Dramatic increases in lone parenting and solo living among younger and older age groups add to the shifting experiences of how we choose to live as we grow up and grow older.

The 'home', the 'household', the 'house' are words that have a deep conceptual meaning for most of us. We return to our home to seek physical and psychological sustenance while attempting to manage the complex interplay and connectedness of the public and private spheres of life (Ribbens-McCarthy and Edwards, 2002). In many families there is one home that takes on the mantle of the 'family home' and adult children, even with children of their own, will speak of 'going home'. This generally means returning to the place and/or relationships of their upbringing. Celebrations of families – weddings, birthdays, anniversaries, religious festivals and Christmas – are often conducted in and around what is considered the 'family home'.

The idea of a space and a place in which to conduct current, past and anticipated partnerships and inter- and intra-generational relationships, is crucial to a post-industrial sense of what it means to be in a state of fusion with others and society in general. Here we draw on the ideas of a place (some type of construction), a space (the floors, rooms or soil on which people live) and the location in which we invest in making plans, the work of 'nurturing' and the promotion of a sense of a group or team: 'our family home'. Through 'dwelling' among things and structures (homes) humans create meaningful things, places and relationships.

Construction is defined as the design and activities of making the building and these are the basis to major aspects of our identities. Observing where we live and our involvement, or otherwise, in the building, refurbishment or decoration of that dwelling creates a context to identities and images of family life. The recent upsurge in television programmes and print media on the design and decoration of homes is evidence of an increased sense that identities and relationships are interwoven with the physical entity of the home and the communities in which we reside.

By contrast the work of preservation "entails not only the keeping of physical objects of particular people intact, but renewing their meaning" (Young, 1997, p 153) in the lives of families:

> The preservation of the things among which one dwells gives people a context for their lives, individuates their histories, gives them items to use in making new projects, and makes them comfortable. When things and works are maintained against destruction, but not in the context of life, they become museum pieces.

The labour of preservation is necessary to meet the needs of others and maintain families as everyday entities and social worlds (Young, 1997; Arendt, 2002). This is labour that is characterised by repetition and includes a multitude of tasks, ranging from the mundane, such as the cleaning of kitchens and bathrooms, to the maintenance of family histories and collective memories by keeping photograph albums, organising events to celebrate birthdays or anniversaries. The histories of 'ordinary' families, as well as the growth in tracing family histories, are examples of growth in the celebration of family life across generations and locations (Samuel, 1999). The raising of children is a form of 'preservation' work and in a global sense this is labour that is typically carried out, organised and/or paid for by women (Ehrenreich and Hochschild, 2002).

To exchange hospitality, memories and stories of personal and family life are practical and symbolic ways of achieving cohesion (Misztal, 2003, p 19). A sense of shared experiences is moulded and shaped through a range of narratives indicative of the current and past family relationships (Misztal, 2003, p 51). Individual memories cannot be divorced from memories that link to broader identities such as those of a religious or ethnic group. And all these draw on, and reinterpret past experiences that include war, civil unrest, and social and economic change: "[G]iven the cruelties of the histories of persons and peoples, remembrance and preservation often consist in the renewal of grief or rage" (Young, 1997, p 154).

Most of us have a disengaged relationship with our familial and ethno-religious history and, as Cohen (2001, p 64) notes, have:

> [An] astonishing capacity to ignore or pretend to ignore what happens in front of their eyes, whether sexual abuse, incest, violence, alcoholism, craziness or plain unhappiness.... The family's distinctive self-image determines which aspects of shared experience can be openly acknowledged and which must remain closed and denied. These rules are governed by the meta-rule that no one must either admit or deny that they exist.

However, for some families and individuals their attachment to familial histories and networks, premised around ethno-religious ideas, can lead to tensions and violence. We now turn to the processes of creating or reworking the notion of self-image and how that image draws on and is drawn upon by public institutions and organisations, at times of inter-communal conflict.

Contested boundaries: families, public institutions and violence

Barbara Misztal, in her book *Theories of social remembering* (2003, p 18), notes the role the family plays in the construction of individual and group memories:

> As long as the family jointly produces and maintains its memory, its cohesion and continuity is ensured. The content of the shared family's narrative, symbolic of family unity across generations, reproduces family traditions, secrets and particular sentiments.

Memories and history intertwine in the creation of a collective past. Yet they differ. History, as an academic discipline, asserts that documentation and data should be critically examined to offer explanations of events. Sometimes these explanations will differ and in postmodernism the discursive accounts of history leave us with 'histories' that must be grounded in the context from which they emerge. Memories tend to mythologise that past, can be arbitrarily selected and appeal to emotions. Combined, memories and histories can collide, and most commonly around familial, ethno-religious identities that may lead to inter-communal tensions and violence.

In times of rapid social change or interstate tensions, nation state, ethnic groups and families may draw on versions of history to create or fuel differences. Mead (1932) asserts that pasts are remembered and reworked in ways that meet the needs of groups; these may include the state, families and other forms of collective identities such as religions or political parties. Memories and histories offer arenas for the contested and some contradictory notions of identities. Early stages of inter-communal conflict classically include numerous charges and countercharges highlighting differences and actual or alleged abuses by one group on another. Memories can become ideologies with limited grounding in available evidence and achieve a status and value that was previously unwarranted. Further, tensions can be fanned through the use of the media (as in the case of Rwanda).

In the following sections we offer two case studies in which social researchers have documented and analysed aspects of inter-communal conflict. Breakdowns in social and familial trust have longer-term consequences that reach across generations, families and histories.

The case studies

To further discussion, a brief review is offered of the work of Tone Bringa, an anthropologist, on Bosnia, and Paul Connolly and Julie Healy, both sociologists, on sectarian violence in Northern Ireland. Case studies provide an opportunity to undertake an empirical investigation of contemporary phenomena in a real life context, using a range of sources of evidence (Robson, 2002, p 178). In both of these case studies, the researchers have considered the social and physical settings in which families inhabit communities and networks.

Historical legacies, ethnic cleansing and evolving global identities (Bringa)

From 1987-88, Tone Bringa undertook long-term field research in a mixed Muslim-Catholic village in central Bosnia, two hours from Sarajevo by road. Bringa's work demonstrated how integration among communities worked and evolved through economic and social relations. For both Catholic and Muslim households, personal and community identity are linked to land, homes and family. There was a 'civic plurality' operating through dialectic. Thus while the state sought to define identity in terms of the Yugoslav nation, villagers defined themselves in terms of ethno-religious groups with cultures and customs passed through generations.

The interplay of the national and local Muslim identities was sustained through the role of women and gender differences. Bringa details how women and households were critical to sustaining ethno-religious identities; for example, families in both communities paid particular attention to the policing of female sexuality as symbolic of family honour and thus status as a 'good' family. Alongside these gendered workings of families ran the economic realities of national and global trends necessitating involvement in changing industrial and post-industrial opportunities. In most recent years, the interplay of the past and present had eroded barriers to the involvement of younger women and men in educational and employment opportunities outside the village.

The village did not experience war until 1992. At that time most of the Muslims thought only outsiders would provoke violent or intimidatory incidents. Yet when outside forces arrived, villagers were horrified to find that some neighbours joined in the killing of Muslims and burning homes, pitting neighbour against neighbour. It was as if neighbours became alien to each other. How did this happen?

In her analysis Tone Bringa (2002, p 194) argues that:

> [A] particular kind of personalised violence [was] directed toward individuals because they belonged to, or were identified with, a specific nationality or ethnic group [and] was the expression of a politically organised attempt at radically redefining categories of belonging.

The notion of 'belonging' was crucial and she details how the 'rhetoric of exclusion' involved the renaming of neighbours, friends, colleagues and even some relatives as foreigners, intruders and enemies. The rhetoric of inclusion also evolved in which public discourses and spaces were redefined as the 'private' spaces of the group in power. Family networks and the home became emotional and physical entities that further marked this notion of 'private spaces'. Political and military processes manipulated fears among both groups such that the physical removal of the excluded seemed to be the conclusion for both groups, especially where violence led to ethnic cleansing. Here is an example of boundary construction and one that drew on and manipulated collective memories in ways that created fears, anger and violence.

Before the recent Bosnian war, everyday life in the village drew on and worked with religious and cultural differences in ways that did not result in particular tensions or violence. Bringa noted ambivalence towards the history of the Second World War. Many atrocities and civil wars that ran parallel to the Second World War were not considered in education or official histories. Rather, post-1945 official history offered two categories, namely the fascists (evil and defeated) and partisans (heroic and victorious but victims). Events or sufferings that fell outside these categories were not publicly acknowledged. The deaths and sufferings of civilians were not commemorated. However, there was a 'cultivation of death' that formed a strong spine in the memories of people, especially men. A celebration of fighting and death led to appeals to mobilisation for a project of restructuring post-Tito Yugoslavia. Cultural and commemorative events kept alive through and between families were central to the maintenance of ethno-religious ideas and solidarities. Yet Bringa's (1995, p 4) work identified ethno-religious groups that lived side by side in localities where socioeconomic strata accounted for more than nationality. In more recent work, Bringa (2002) has detailed how these harmonies were splintered by the rhetoric of nationalism that political and military powers promoted down to the local level. These ideas and fears superseded friendships and relationships and placed renewed focus on collective identities promoted through the interweaving of familial and ethno-religious memories and histories. She notes, sadly, that many of the crimes of mass murder took place with the presence of the international organisations, thus implicating many of us in the implicit perpetration of the rhetoric of peacekeeping. Here we might reflect on the role of external organisations that often fail to address the role of collective memories and histories in the family practices and governmental activities that can result in ethnic violence.

As private interests invade the public domain (Connolly and Healy)

Connolly and Healy (2003) have explored the emergence and development of sectarianism among children with particular reference to age and social class. Earlier studies of children in Northern Ireland had relied on experiments and psychological methods while Connolly and Healy wished to move away from this narrow field by addressing three issues. First, they wished to explore the experiences and attitudes of young people without imposing adult frameworks on their responses. Second, linked to this was their desire to contextualise the attitudes of the young people by using less structured and more qualitative methods. Lastly, Connolly and Healy asserted that by being aware of these concerns their research would not 'essentialise' the experiences of the young people but allow them the space with which to explore and understand their own attitudes.

Children were interviewed across three age groups (3 to 4, 7 to 8 and 10 to 11) in four areas of Belfast, two of which where predominantly working class and two which were predominantly middle class. Here we draw on their reporting of research in working-class localities. Individual interviews were conducted with the youngest children with cultural symbols such as flags and football shirts[1] used as prompts. While their choice of symbol reflected that of their own community, there was little evidence to suggest that the children explicitly understood this representation. This finding could be considered unremarkable in the sense that the children were picking that with which they were most familiar. However, what was of significance to Connolly and Healy (2003, p 42) was that the children's preference for one team or flag was juxtaposed with a strong negative reaction for the other. Their instant dislike of 'the other' demonstrated that even at this very young age these children were beginning to define themselves in relation to what they are not and were, therefore:

> [A]lready acquiring and assimilating an awareness and set of attitudes that underpin more explicit sectarian beliefs and behaviour among older children and adults. (Connolly and Healy, 2003, p 45)

When interviewing the older children, the researchers used unstructured interviews with same-sex friendship groups of three participants. The interviews were unstructured so the children could lead the sessions and by giving them the chance to bring up the conflict themselves it was anticipated that its relevance and significance in their own lives would become apparent.

During the sessions with the seven- to eight-year-olds it was clear that the children had become aware of the segregation of their community and the real (as opposed to symbolic) differences this separation generated. Yet the researchers found that it was through merging the real with the symbolic that young people had access to a language with which to make sense of their world (Connolly and Healy, 2003, p 47):

> *Int*: "Who are they?"
> *Mandy*: "Catholics. Bad people, throw bricks at all our homes [...]"
> *Int*: "So why do they throw bricks in at your houses?"
> *Mandy*: "Cos they're bad and because we don't support Celtic."

It is important to note that the children identify themselves not as 'I' but collectively as 'we', encompassing their family and community. It has been argued that the family is a site for the creation and transmission of ideas on violence (McKie and Jamieson, 2003). Stories and myths can also shape families and often, when they are afforded an epic status (Byng-Hall, 1990), they can inform the actions of future generations, particularly when the stories centre on a salient element of life, in this case the conflict. Thus history is often seen as an enlightening force but it can also be a confining or determining one. For example, young people can feel obligated to their families because they have been brought up with stories of their own parents' or grandparents' involvement in the conflict. These attitudes are not simply a reflection of those expressed by and with their family. Children are also actively constructing their own knowledge and understanding by using symbols that are available to them.

Connolly and Healy (2003, p 51) found that by the age of 10 and 11 children tended to have had direct personal experience of 'stone throwing and sporadic violence' with the 'other side' and were beginning to attach status to the knowing of IRA members. They could also place the conflict and the paramilitary organisations in a wider political and historical context. Many had learnt to do this either from direct personal experience or from listening to family stories. While it was found that attitudes also became more positive at this age due to wider cultural influences, such attitudes extended only to individuals known to them. However, these were coupled with "blanket rejections of the community from which those individuals came from" (Connolly and Healy, 2003, p 54).

This research clearly demonstrates the importance of cultural images for young children living in Belfast as signifiers of the segregated communities they live in. For the youngest children such images represented the notion of belonging to one group and not the other. As the children aged, the symbols could be used as a means to explain the apparent differences between communities. For all the age groups the ability to recognise 'the other' could mean safety or affirmation of their own culture. These findings have been supported by other research, for example McGrellis (2004). The importance of cultural images is subsumed in the oldest group of children by the importance of history. The historical context of 'the troubles' informs the language used by the oldest children, that is, they become aware of the meaning behind the cultural images. This knowledge of history, or rather the importance attached to it, has been highlighted since as an instigator for involvement in paramilitary activity (McGrellis, 2004).

Connolly and Healy's work highlights the importance of space and boundaries in both the creation and perpetuation of sectarianism. The Northern Ireland Housing Executive (1999, p 22) confirmed that almost 100% of tenants in Belfast live in segregated areas (see McGrellis, 2004, p 3). It is, therefore, of little surprise that children come to understand what they are in relation to what they are not. Families form a porous entity and orbit around which views and experiences are shaped. These views draw on and reinterpret histories and familial memories. Disappointingly, Connolly and Healy (2003) concluded that even when positive attitudes developed these were not enough to overcome the divisive, sectarian geography of Belfast.

Concluding comments

When it comes to the subject of violence in the domain of, and relationships within, families, the metaphor of boundaries enhances the potential to explore families as dynamic and interweaving, while imbued with social and cultural understandings. As discussed in the introductory chapter there is much greater recognition of families as 'porous', that is, the manner in which families reflect, (re)interpret, and are influenced by the wider world.

Here we have explored the role of families and kinship in creating and reinforcing collective identities and memories that are factors in sectarian and ethnic violence. Notions and images of 'the family' often conjure thoughts of privacy, security, warmth and intimacy but, for a notable number of people, 'the family' forms a context to experiences that create and recreate ideas and experiences of fear, intimidation and violence. Considering the contribution of sociology to the study of memory, violence and identity, Ray (2000, p 155) comments that "the view of modern societies as 'pacified' may obscure the routine sources of violence within 'stable' social relations". By placing both pacified and stable in quotation marks, Ray is drawing attention to the need in any sociological analysis of social relations to contest meanings attributed to these terms.

In recent decades there has been a growth in the reporting of inter-communal and neighbourhood violence that would seem to place families, friends, and neighbours in confrontation with each other. While inter-communal violence is not a new phenomenon (for example the partition of India after the Second World War and ongoing sectarian violence in South East Asia), conflicts in the former Yugoslavia brought the issue geographically closer to home and to the attention of numerous contemporary social commentators in Europe and North America. What processes are evident, as some families and neighbours who have lived side by side for many years become violent and confrontational with each other? Often the basis to these conflicts and movements of people would appear to be shifting levels of commitment and adherence to interpretations of histories, religious and social networks; to the boundaries associated with 'belonging to' or being 'excluded from' a community and collective sense of identity. So what role might families play in the (re)creation of ideas and activities in inter-communal violence and segregation?

The conceptual frame and metaphor of boundaries is a useful one as it promotes the study of families, relationships and violence through offering several dimensions that assist analysis. First, the idea of 'the family' is an entity. Families may be viewed as both internally coherent and externally unique. In these ways, families may be deemed to be part of an ethnic or community group as they demonstrate to wider familial and other networks that they manifest coherence in identity and practices that is appropriate to being part of that group, community or neighbourhood. Second, the physical demarcation of families is most obviously demonstrated through the home, street and neighbourhood. Across these locations and entities the physical demarcation of ethnic and other groups may become obvious and may also mark out territories considered critical to familial and community identity. Lastly, the notion of a frontier zone as also a boundary offers the potential to define our family ('us') and those outside the family or group identity ('them'). Ethnic, religious and nationalist conflicts can and do originate in and around challenges to the boundary of the family (us) and those considered different (them). The boundaries of religion/ethnicity are ones that can easily be transgressed through neighbourliness, shared norms, space and socioeconomic circumstances, but can quickly become fixed as political circumstances change.

In Bosnia, Bringa (1995) found that even though villagers defined themselves in terms of ethno-religious groups, socioeconomic factors were more significant for inclusion than nationality. In this case, boundaries were physical, localised and also contemporary. For the people their village was the entity to which they all belonged and it was this boundary that united and separated them from the state.

Therefore when the conflict began, the state had to work to redefine collective memories and boundaries of inclusion and exclusion to turn villagers against one another, creating different boundaries between groups and families. In their research, Connolly and Healy (2003) suggested that it was through the family that children first gained experience of the symbolic differences between the communities in which they lived. Yet, when they became older, the family was no longer the only source through which the boundaries were perpetuated. Once they left the boundary of the home to play, children became aware of the physical demarcations (for example the segregated housing separated by a barren piece of land) and therefore the real separations between 'them' and 'us'. In both studies the physical boundaries are relevant to the inclusion and exclusion of members. Yet it is also the symbolic boundaries created by history, culture and time that perpetuate collective identities and memories. Connolly and Healy (2003) noted that young people are not simply reflecting the attitudes that they have heard within their own family units. They are also actively constructing their own knowledge from the world around them.

As well as a need for further theoretical work, policy implications will also arise from such research. Studies on the segregation of Northern Ireland (McGrellis, 2004, p 4) have indicated that it tends to be when young people start work or leave home that they first have sustained contact with people from religious or ethnic backgrounds different to their own; it is then that the boundaries are transgressed. As Connolly and Healy (2003) noted, children may be accepting of an individual who was of a different religion to them, but this did not sway their opinion of the community from where that individual came.

In social science work on ethnic cleansing, sectarianism and genocide, there has been somewhat limited consideration of the role of families and family practices, albeit with notable exceptions such as the work of Bauman (1989), Bringa (1995, 2002) and that of Connolly and Healy (2003). Studies of violence between families (as is the case with violence within families) need to look at family members and family practices but also outside towards local social worlds and cultural systems. The family is a porous entity. It is influenced by, and also influences, wider society. The transgression of physical and symbolic boundaries is required. Metaphorical, physical and legislative spaces that offer people opportunities to define their own identities, and to respect those of others, must be promoted. These spaces might allow for identities to form without recourse to, or the experience of, violence and fear.

Note

[1] In football, Rangers is classed as a Protestant team and Celtic a Catholic one.

References

Arendt, H. (2002) 'Reflections on violence', in C. Besteman (ed) *Violence: A reader*, Basingstoke: Palgrave Macmillan.

Bauman, Z. (1989) *Modernity and the holocaust*, Cambridge: Polity Press.

Bringa, T. (1995) *Being Muslim the Bosnian way: identity and community in a central Bosnian village*, Princeton, NJ: University of Princeton Press.

Bringa, T. (2002) 'Averted gaze: genocide in Bosnia-Herzegovina, 1992-1995', in A.L. Hinton (ed) (2002) *Annihilating difference: The anthropology of genocide*, Berkeley, CA: University of California Press.

Brundtland, G.H. (2002) *Preface: World report on violence and health*, Geneva: World Health Organization.

Byng-Hall, J. (1990) Interview by Paul Thompson, 'The power of family myths', in R. Samuel and P. Thompson (eds) *The myths we live by*, London: Routledge.

Carnegie Commission on Preventing Deadly Conflict (1997) *Preventing deadly conflict: Final report*, New York, NY: Carnegie Corporation.

Cohen, S. (2001) *States of denial – knowing about atrocities and suffering*, Cambridge: Polity Press.

Connolly, P. and Healy, J. (2003) 'The development of children's attitudes towards "the troubles" in Northern Ireland', in O. Hargie and D. Dickson (eds) *Researching the troubles: Social science perspectives on the Northern Ireland conflict*, Edinburgh: Mainstream Publishing.

Ehrenreich, B. and Hochschild, A.R. (eds) (2002) *Global woman: Nannies, maids and sex workers in the new economy*, London: Granta Books.

Hinton, A. (2002) *Annihilating difference: The anthropology of genocide*, Berkeley, CA: University of California Press.

Hoffman, E. (2004) *After such knowledge: A mediation on the aftermath of the Holocaust*, London: Secker and Warburg.

Hynes, H.P. (2004) 'On the battlefield of women's bodies: an overview of the harm of war to women', *Women's Studies International Forum*, vol 27, pp 431-45.

McGrellis, S. (2004) 'Pushing the boundaries in Northern Ireland: young people, violence and sectarianism, families and social capital', ESRC Research Group Working Paper, London: South Bank University.

McKie, L. and Hearn, J. (2004) 'Gender-neutrality and gender equality: comparing and contrasting policy responses to "domestic violence" in Finland and Scotland', *Scottish Affairs*, vol 48, summer, pp 85-107.

McKie, L. and Jamieson, L. (2003) 'Families, identities and violence: creating and violating collective memories', paper presented at the Annual Conference of the British Sociological Association, York, 2003.

Mead, G. (1932) *The philosophy of the present*, LaSalle, IL: Open Court Publishing.

Misztal, B.A. (2003) *Theories of social remembering*, Maidenhead: Oxford University Press.

Morgan, D. (1996) *Family connections: An introduction to family studies*, Cambridge: Polity Press.

Northern Ireland Housing Executive (NIHE) (1999) 'Community relations and community safety', Internal Report, Belfast: NIHE.

Ray, L. (2000) 'Memory, violence and identity', in J. Eldridge, J. MacInnes, S. Scott, C. Warhurst, and A. Witz (eds) *For sociology: Legacies and prospects*, York: Sociology Press.

Ribbens-McCarthy, J. and Edwards, R. (2002) 'The individual in public and private', in A. Carling, S. Duncan and R. Edwards (eds) *Analysing families: Morality and rationality in policy and practice*, London: Routledge.

Robson, C. (2002) *Real world research: A resource for social scientists and practitioner-researchers* (2nd edn), Oxford: Blackwell.

Samuel, R. (1999) 'Resurrectionism', in D. Bowell and J. Evans (eds) *Representing the nation: A reader*, London: Routledge.

Scottish Executive (2000) *National strategy to address domestic abuse in Scotland*, Edinburgh: The Stationery Office.

World Health Organization (2002) *World report on violence and health*, Geneva: World Health Organization.

Young, I.M. (1997) *Interesting voices: Dilemmas of gender, political philosophy, and policy*, Princeton, NJ: Princeton University Press.

Part Four: Relationships and friendships

The challenges thrown up in previous chapters about families in society and the boundaries that may be constructed and confronted are taken even further in this final part. As the title of this book suggests, families should not necessarily be seen as the only or central arena for personal or intimate relationships. The boundaries between familial and friendship relationships may be changing. Some of the preceding chapters presaged such change, such as the importance of friendships to women in the fifties or to those affected by dementia. These themes are developed further in the next four chapters which give a more central place conceptually and empirically to 'non-family' living.

The first chapter, by Jamieson, focuses on practices of intimacy, moving the book from an analysis of families to relationships more widely. She notes that there are contradictory claims about the meaning and significance of intimacy and that there has been attention to boundaries in the conceptualisation of intimacy as well as in how it is practised. Typically, two main boundaries have been identified: boundaries between the familial and non-familial, although these are becoming increasingly blurred; and exclusionary boundaries between intimates (traditionally typified as couples) and the wider community, although again this boundary may be contested. Jamieson contends that not all practices of intimacy require exclusionary boundaries and that boundaries have been overemphasised in the conceptualisation of intimacy. However, she does not suggest doing away with the concept for analytical purposes, especially since there is considerable evidence that boundary work in relationships is often about power and hierarchies.

The second chapter concentrates on solo living as a way of understanding families, relationships and households. Wasoff, Jamieson and Smith provide quite detailed empirical analysis of who is living alone in the UK – the 'stocks' – and who is moving in and out of solo living – the 'flows'. The evidence suggests increasing levels of solo living at all stages of the lifecourse, indicative perhaps of a redrawing of the boundary between family and household and a reshaping of the boundaries of different lifecourse stages. However, the evidence also suggests that transitions between solo living and living with others is commonplace, so that the boundaries between solo living and family living are frequently crossed. More research is needed to understand the ways in which people on their own are connected to families, friends and wider social relationships although preliminary evidence suggests considerable connectedness, challenging assumptions about the isolation of those living on their own.

The third chapter, by Allan, provides a detailed analysis of the boundaries of friendships. This contribution starts by showing how patterns of partnership, family and household constitution have changed, making kin relationships more contestable. However, Allan argues that for most people the boundaries between family and friendship remain relatively well defined and continue to be important, although perhaps different emphases will emerge. He suggests that friendships are different from family relationships especially since the solidarities are different. Friendships, he contends, have boundaries that are fluid and more easily broken. So rather than conceptualising the boundary between family and friends as becoming intrinsically blurred, he suggests instead that the forms of solidarity associated with 'blood' ties may now be found in other relationships.

Roseneil, in the last chapter in this part, challenges this view. She argues that it is the way in which the sociologies of families and relationships have continued to centre the family in their theorising that has led to limited understandings of the diversity of personal life in contemporary society. This chapter pushes the boundaries of existing ways of thinking about personal relationships by focusing on those at the 'cutting edge' of social change, namely those living 'beyond the heteronorm'. Her research demonstrates the extent of friendship, ways in which family and partner are not necessarily central to people's lives and how a sense of permanence and obligation pertains to personal relationships. Boundaries are blurred between friendships and sexual relationships and the binary between homo- and heterosexual is itself being fractured at cultural and individual levels.

The concept of boundaries may help us to unpack family and relationship practices if it is used flexibly. Breaking boundaries and constructing new ways of conducting our personal and family lives may be the emergent normative, as well as analytical, framework. What is clear is that we need new frameworks and conceptual tools to understand and capture the experience of personal life in a way that does not make normative assumptions about how people go about sustaining relationships.

ELEVEN

Boundaries of intimacy

Lynn Jamieson

Introduction

This chapter reviews how the concepts of boundaries and boundary work are deployed in theorising intimacy, in order to assess how these concepts further our understanding of intimacy and social change. In everyday current usage, intimacy is often presumed to involve practices of close association, familiarity and privileged knowledge, strong positive emotional attachments, such as love, and a very particular form of 'closeness' and being 'special' to another person, associated with high levels of trust. Recent discussions of intimacy emphasise one particular practice of generating 'closeness' above all others, self-disclosure. Intimacy of the inner self, 'disclosing intimacy' or 'self expressing intimacy' has become celebrated in popular culture as the key to a 'good relationship' although some academic work has suggested that this type of intimacy may be more of an ideological construct than an everyday lived reality. The practices attended to in such a conceptualisation of intimacy suggest an absence or lowering of boundaries among intimates in comparison to the presence or heightening of boundaries between intimates and those outside their intimate relationships. In accounts of personal life, intimates are described as if encapsulated together by a protective boundary that stops distractions that would otherwise interfere with their intimacy or by an exclusionary boundary that keeps non-intimates out.

Although often not explicitly named as such, reference to boundaries and boundary work has been a longstanding aspect of theorising the place of personal life in social change. For social theorists of the emergence of 'modernity', the reconfiguration of 'public' and 'private' as separate spheres and renewed emphasis on individualism, and the conceptualising of individuals as having unique inner selves, were necessary precursors to the association of intimacy with private personal relationships. For some, private intimacy was also the product of another facet of modernity: the development of divisions of labour, specialisation and bureaucracy, resulting in interaction organised around the functions people perform or positions they occupy rather than 'whole persons'. Hence it is argued that individuals need intimacy to re-establish themselves in "holistic, multifaceted interactions that contrast with the segmental, single-faceted interactions of the relatively many role-relations" (Davis, 1973, p xxii).

The historical emergence of material and ideological divisions between 'public' and 'private' did not create gender neutral circumstances in which men and women pursued intimate relationships as equals. Feminist work continues to discuss how socially produced boundaries between genders are implicated in gender differences in types and degrees of intimacy. Some feminist theory draws on psychoanalysis to claim that a greater capacity for intimacy among women is a psychological consequence of the conventional divisions of labour in parenting and the distinctiveness of mother–daughter and mother–son relationships. Feminist theorists also offer accounts that give greater explanatory weight to material factors such as inequalities in social, economic and political opportunities constraining women to specialise in caring work and intimacy. Feminists have also analysed gendered cultural discourses about men's and women's differential emotional and romantic needs that get folded into their conceptions of the self.

Such theorising suggests that intimacy is impinged on or contingent on a number of other boundaries including gender boundaries and the construction of privacy and that intimacy itself requires boundary work. The notion of 'boundary work' is associated with the anthropologist, Fredrick Barth (1969). Barth observed that the creation and maintenance of social boundaries is an effortful activity involving cognition and coordinated social action. In other words, boundaries are created in ideas, thought, talk and writing, discourse that creates consequential difference and division. Boundaries must also be produced by more material forms of coordinated interaction, such as moderating flows of exchange and modifying movements of people across space and time. Many studies that explicitly discuss boundaries and boundary work are not primarily concerned with intimacy but with the creation of social divisions involving hierarchies and dominance such as gender, class and ethnicity. A number of theorists argue that intimacy requires the flattening of hierarchy among intimates and the creation of protective and exclusionary differences and divisions between intimates and non-intimates. For example, among the classical social theorists of the 19th century, Georg Simmel offered a detailed account of intimacy that emphasised the enactment of privacy and exclusivity to protect against and exclude non-intimates as well as intimates treating each other as 'whole persons' (see Simmel, 1950). Simmel noted that the intimate dyad, by definition, only lasts as long as both parties participate in what each shows or gives *only to the other*. It is their private, exclusive, exchange which generates trust and affect. In the 20th century, Erving Goffman discussed intimate relationships in terms of the everyday boundaries that people draw between the relative privacy of their 'back stage' and the performance they give in public (see Goffman, 1963). Intimates are people who not only go 'back stage' into the private domain but with whom tact and discretion, which he associates with role performance, is significantly less important. In the remainder of this chapter, aspects of these themes are traced to contemporary debates. The notion that intimacy relies on and is intensified by keeping 'others' at a distance has been a recurrent theme in theorising personal life. In the following section this is illustrated by a review of 20th-century 'sociology of the family' and its contemporary reworking. The subsequent sections review debate over the antithesis or sympathy between intimacy and civic engagement, first dealing with civic engagement as democratic citizens and then community participation. Finally, the chapter turns to a more general discussion of what the research literature suggests concerning if and when intimacy requires boundaries and boundary work.

Intensifying intimacy by keeping others distant

In the discipline of sociology from the 1950s through to the 1970s, personal relationships were typically discussed under the heading of the *sociology of the family*, which was preoccupied with what Talcott Parsons (1959) called 'the relatively isolated nuclear family', a household firmly centred on a heterosexual couple, solely occupied by the couple and their growing-up children. The couple were theorised as keeping emotional distance from everybody outside of their couple and parenting relationships. In Parson's view of social change, the marriage relationship and parent–child relationships became more emotionally intense when more distance was created between these relationships and all others, through geographical and social mobility and active boundary work on the part of the couple. He characterised this as a historical shift from a time when the family household was more immersed in a wider kin network and less clearly separated off (Parsons and Bales, 1956; Parsons, 1959).

In the sociology of this period, wider family or kin relationships, friendships and neighbouring relationships were typically studied in relation to this type of nuclear family household, which was referred to in both academic discussion and popular usage as 'the family'. In this approach, friends and neighbours were primarily seen as useful occasional supplements to 'the family', people called on when family resources, meaning those of the parenting couple, were stretched. Family relationships, meaning heterosexual couple and parent–children relationships, were unequivocally seen as the primary relationships in people's lives. In the hierarchy of significant relationships, wider kin were next, providing important sorts of support to families. Friends were positioned as rising in significance when kin and/or close family were absent, for example, in the case of the widowed who live geographically distant from kin.

Friendship was really only acknowledged as routinely of particular significance at one particular stage of the lifecourse, that of youth, the transition from childhood to adulthood. In the dominant theoretical paradigm of the period, functionalism, the main work of socialising children and stabilising adult personalities was performed by mothers within the emotionally intense interior of family households but somehow children have also to learn to move on from this environment. 'Peer relationships', as young people's forms of association and friendship were often called, were theorised as the relationships in which children learn to stand up for themselves, to compete, to form alliances and independence from their family. The fact that children's friendships were and typically still are gender segregated was seen as part of functional socialisation into appropriate gender roles. Girls learn femininity best with other girls; boys learn masculinity best with boys (Parsons, 1962). Youth cultures were blossoming all around analysts like Talcott Parsons and the most visible were heterosexually charged and mixed gender. 'Peer relationships' of youth were theorised as enabling young people to detach from their family of origin for long enough to recreate the conventions, form heterosexual relationships, marry and create their own new family of procreation, hopefully in that order. Youth cultures and peer groups enabled young people to position themselves ready to find a partner. Peers and friends, then, were reduced to institutions that give young people the mutual support to move their emotional focus temporarily outside the family, by providing a lifecourse-specific halfway house between 'family of origin' and 'family of procreation', while also reinforcing masculinity, femininity and heterosexuality.

With hindsight some of this theorising was recognised as expressing particular values rather than describing or advancing understanding of the ways in which lives were lived. The notion that family households turn in on themselves and become inviolable, emotionally intense, child-centred domains was not simply a theme in Parsons' work but became part of the orthodox historical account of the emergence of the conventional family. However, this was not an accurate description of how many families lived in the early 20th century (Jamieson, 1987). The historical development of a characterisation of the family as a 'haven in a heartless world', a private domain separated off from the wider social world by protective boundaries, relies on a conception of divisions between 'public' and 'private' that has been comprehensively deconstructed by feminist work as a construction that helps mask patriarchal arrangements (Millet, 1971; Mitchell, 1971). Parsons assumed that intimacy requires a boundary between home and work that was necessarily simultaneously a gender boundary between women at home and men at work. Many of the characteristics that Parsons described as functional for society were subsequently redescribed as key mechanisms for sustaining gender inequalities and the subordination of women. By the 21st century, many European family households consisting of parents and children are also dual earner households. Few now advocate a return to old gender division as an ideal. However, a persistent finding of research on parenting couples concerns the different parts played by men and women in sustaining intimacy in parent–child and couple relationships. Some research on domestic divisions of labour has demonstrated how gender inequalities are recreated while avoiding the discursive production of gender boundaries. In other words, it is no longer acceptable to acknowledge that women do the cooking and cleaning because they are women. It is perhaps not surprising that, despite this mental manoeuvre, for some couples the persistent facts of unequal divisions of labour sits uneasily with ideals of intimacy. Arlie Hochschild has repeatedly claimed that the central crisis of heterosexual couple relationships is a 'stalled revolution' with women doing more providing work without a matched contribution of men to caring work (Hochschild, 2003).

David Morgan (1991, 1992, 1996) has analysed how change in family and marriage across the 20th century came to be characterised as a shift 'from institution to relationship' (Burgess and Locke, 1945), with an implied shift from traditional and public obligations to private pleasures and values. But as Morgan notes, the privatised intimacy that 'relationship' implied in fact coincided with the emergence of 'psy' experts (see also Rose, 1996). Indeed, he argues that those with a vested interest in claims to treat marital and relationship problems also had an interest in characterising social change in terms of a shift to 'relationships'. One of the most influential academic accounts of marriage in the 1960s was Peter Berger and Hans Kellner's (1964) analysis of how marriage partners, which would now be written to include co-resident couples or couples living apart together (Holmes, 2004), created a stable sense of themselves and their world through dialogue. Berger and Kellner described how dialogic efforts screened off parts of the social world as 'not like us' and crystallised the individual's sense of self as part of the 'us' of the couple. Although not couched in the language later used by Anthony Giddens (1992), Berger and Kellner were describing something very close to Giddens' subsequent account of couples jointly constructing personal narratives of the self through a dialogue of self-disclosure. In Britain, David Morgan (1976) provided an overview of theoretical approaches to the family that drew on feminist critiques. He criticised Berger and Kellner for an idealised portrayal of marriage that failed to acknowledge the infrequency of men and women having equal voice or choice in the dialogue (Morgan, 1982).

Sociological theorising and research has moved a very long way since the 1960s. Few now speak about 'the family' as if there were one universally recognised type of family. Sociologists try to find out what 'family' means to people, male and female, at different ages, stages and circumstances and focus on 'family practices' (Morgan, 2002), how people 'do family'. This has not always involved explicitly considering whether and how people create discursive or interactional boundaries around 'family' in comparision to other relationships. However, it is clear that for many people boundaries are fairly flexible. Recent research suggests that the boundary between 'familial' and 'non-familial' relationships is increasingly blurred as the constellations that people designated as 'familial' become increasingly diverse. Long-term partnerships outside marriage, among both heterosexual and same-sex partners, are increasingly recognised as family relationships despite countercurrents (Dunne, 1997; Weeks et al, 2001; Roseneil and Budgeon, 2004). It is not generally assumed, a priori, that people have a finite capacity for intimacy and there is necessarily a zero sum equation between types of relationship. Some researchers suggest that friendships are the most significant relationships for a growing number of individuals outside of conventional couple relationships at all lifecourse stages. Some authors suggest that more open and less exclusive friendships may supplant couple relationships (Roseneil and Budgeon, 2004). The trends of increasing numbers of people living alone are sometimes interpreted in this light but, as Chapter Twelve in this volume indicates, many solo livers are not seeking alternative lifestyles. Theorising of gender differences is also much more sophisticated than in the 1960s. Much more is now known about family households as sites of violence, abuse and domination, situations in which abusers and dominators do boundary work to contain and control their intimates. Children, as well as adults, are given a voice in research and this has shown that their understandings of family boundaries and of intimacy may not coincide with those of their parents. It is no longer presumed that those who do share a family household necessarily have the same view and experiences of family life. Diversity is charted not just of types of household but of family practices and experiences across and within households. The starting point of research is more likely to be the whole constellation of intimate relationships.

These advances in research illustrate the complexity of 'doing intimacy' and of the potential parts played by boundary work. Nevertheless, the notion that intimacy is cherished by keeping others at a distance has remained a recurrent theme in both theoretical discussions and the research literature attempting to document how people live their lives. The notion that exclusivity is a necessary aspect of intimacy is retained in Anthony Giddens' *The transformation of intimacy* (1992), which has been a particular influential text among researchers of intimate relationships. This offered an optimistic analysis of the role of intimacy in social change. Giddens (1992) argued that a qualitative shift in intimacy began to occur in the late 20th century. In this period, the faster pace of social change and heightened awareness of risk and uncertainty, meant that conventional ways of doing things, including 'being a family', gender identities and sexual identities, were increasingly open to reworking, as people became more self-conscious of being makers of their own narratives of the self. In this climate, Giddens argued, people increasingly sought 'self-disclosing intimacy' to anchor themselves in one or more particularly intense personal relationship. He argued that people seek to anchor themselves in a 'pure relationship' in which mutual trust is built through disclosing intimacy.

In describing the mechanisms by which people constructed self-disclosing intimacy, Giddens suggested that exclusionary boundaries have to be drawn around intimate relationships. Although sexual exclusivity is not a necessary condition of the 'pure relationship' he envisaged some form of boundary work in order to secure trust. He referred to the psychoanalytic suggestion that dyadic sexual relationships in adulthood are a site for recreating the "feeling of exclusivity that an infant enjoys with its mother" (1992, p 138). He identified trust as a key element of intimacy that requires exclusionary practices; trust "is not a quality capable of indefinite expansion ... the disclosure of what is kept from other people is one of the main psychological markers likely to call forth trust and to be sought after in return" (Giddens, 1992, pp 138-9).

Authentic intimacy and public democracy or illusory intimacy and empty democracy?

Giddens' account in *The transformation of intimacy* does not share the suspicion of other analysts that devoting energies to exclusionary intimate relationships will detract from the wider social fabric. While acknowledging that exclusionary boundary work is necessary to create the trust and sense of being special he associates with disclosing intimacy, Giddens assumes that a personal life so constructed can coincide with civic engagement. Giddens is not the first author to claim compatibility between growing intimacy and civic engagement. The 18th-century philosophers of the Scottish Enlightenment saw intimate friendship as a 'modern' pattern made possible by the separation of personal relationships from commercial activities allowing friendship to become a matter of sympathy and affection devoid of calculation of interest (Silver, 1997). For thinkers like Adam Smith, however, the possibility of more intimate friendship did not herald growing indifference to non-intimates but rather coincided with the blossoming of an altruistic civil society. "No benevolent man ever lost the fruits of his benevolence. If he does not gather them from the persons from whom he ought to have gathered them, he seldom fails to gather them, and with a ten-fold increase, from other people" (Adam Smith, 1759, p 225, quoted in Silver, 1997).

A more pessimistic rendering of the associated changes in intimacy and civic engagement is more typical of current theorising. Just as Parsons' work suggested putting more emotional energy into 'the family' required withdrawal from wider kin, so many analysts suggest a tension between private intimacy and public or civic engagement. The more sophisticated versions of this concern also acknowledge that the division of public and private is an ideological construction, discursively produced. For example, Lauren Berlant offers a recent version of the argument that transformative civic engagement is undermined by the illusory promise of self-fulfillment offered by 'ideologies and institutions of intimacy' (Berlant, 1997; Berlant and Warner, 2000, p 317):

> Ideologies and institutions of intimacy are increasingly offered as the vision of a good life for the destabilised and struggling citizenry of the United States, the only (fantasy) zone in which a future might be thought and willed, the only (imaginary) place where good citizens might be produced away from the confusing and unsettling distractions and contradictions of capitalism and politics.

For Berlant, the ideological division between private intimacy and wider politics is partially effective in directing creative energies into non-subversive conventions of a frequently doomed to fail normal intimacy.

This sense of opposition is sometimes expressed as between exclusionary intimacy and inclusive community, as is discussed further in the next section. There seems to be support for this thesis in the suggestion that intense binding ties can be less integrative of the wider social fabric than weaker ties that bridge across boundaries between social groups (Granovetter, 1973; Putnam, 2000)

In contrast to fears of a retreat behind the protective boundaries of intimate life, other authors diagnose the problem of 'postmodernity' as the loss of any boundaries between personal life and the wider social world. There are long-running versions of the view that competitive individualism and rampant consumerism of capitalism washes over and corrupts all in its path including intimacy and personal life. This argument recognises the division between public and private as largely illusory and suggests that without any real protective boundaries around intimacy it is difficult to construct a meaningful personal life that could provide a nurturing ground for social transformation. Richard Sennett (1998, 2004) and Zygmunt Bauman (2003) have provided recent versions of this type of account. In their work, one way of reading the problem is the impossibility of creating the type of boundaries around intimate relationships that were imagined by family sociologists of the mid-20th century.

'Public community' versus 'private intimacy'

In 1995, Graham Crow and Graham Allan suggested that "intimacy implies a degree of intensity and uniqueness which it would not be possible to sustain with all members of a community, because intimacy and community imply different principles" (1995, p 10). The weight of evidence concerning how people 'do intimacy' in conducting their families, friendships and neighbouring relationships, however, indicates no such contradiction. Just as not all forms of 'individualism' are incompatible with commitment to collective action (Lichterman, 1996; Delanty, 2003, p 121) so not all forms of intimacy are incompatible with either 'community' or civic engagement.

Contemporary studies of particular places find some people who have a sense of community and for whom being a local is an important self-defining characteristic, involving a sense of a common cause with other locals, although most people do not live in circumstances that they would define in these terms. However, a village dweller who knows most of the residents in the locality, identifies it as a community and himself or herself as a local, does not inevitably have a pattern of intimate relationships that is constructed on different principles from that of an urban dweller who thinks neither in terms of community or being 'local' (Fischer, 1982, p 260). If asked to map their personal relationships in terms of their 'importance' or 'closeness', most rural and urban dwellers alike would identify an inner circle of friends and kin. The balance between friends and kin may vary across the urban/rural divide and also the number of people who are located within an outer envelope rather than an inner circle (see also Pahl and Spencer, 2004). However, the village 'local' is very unlikely to place all others designated as 'locals' in his or her inner circle. The practice of creating a boundary between those with whom one is particularly intimate and 'the rest' is widespread and not incompatible with community or civic engagement. Numerous studies have demonstrated the coexistence of willingness to help others in the locality and practices of intimacy that are reserved for an inner circle. For example, this is shown to be typical of Hightown on the Isle of Wight, England (Crow et al, 2002). Graham Crow returns to the issue of the relationship between community and intimacy with less certainty of their incompatibility in his book *Social solidarities* (2001). Here Crow notes: "The connection between 'intimacy' and 'community' is a problematic one in that the two are not always compatible. Situations in which they come into conflict test the loyalties of individuals by requiring them to identify one or other as priority" (2001, p 122). He goes on to suggest that people's first loyalties are not necessarily to their family but to a much narrower constituent of intimates, often the occupants of their family household, in other words, their inner circle of intimates.

Intimacy, social change and boundary practices?

The discussion thus far indicates the extent to which assumptions about boundaries and boundary work infuse much theorising and debate about social change and personal life. Assumptions about the need for boundaries around 'the family' dominated 'family sociology' in the mid-20th century. The notion that intimacy requires keeping 'others' at a distance has carried on into contemporary debate about our capacities for intimacy and the implications of changes in personal life for social cohesion, democratic citizenship and community participation. Current theoretical positions are not always well supported by research evidence. The pessimistic accounts of social change that suggest that people are increasingly unable to sustain intimate relationships because of their failure to create protective barriers against selfish individualism seem to have relatively little grounding in empirical work. While clearly there are episodes of discontent and upheaval in many people's intimate lives, the evidence does not typically suggest a turning away from intimate relationships. Most people sustain a personal social network of more or less intimate relationships and derive a great deal of pleasure from them. A case has also been made by reference to research for challenging the view that intimacy is incompatible with 'community'.

Existing research indicates that not all the basic activities that women and men use to create intimate relationships necessarily require protective or exclusionary boundaries in order to be successful. While boundaries often play a part in creating a sense of being the 'special one', the ideal of couple relationships for many, not all practices of intimacy create boundaries. Some caring activities and ways of spending time together need not be exclusive, dyadic or 'family only' projects. Across the range of parent–child, couple, other family relationships, and friendship relationships, there are many different ways of 'doing intimacy' documented in the research literature. Some of the ways in which relationships become different and special are forms of institutionalisation that sidestep the need for more conscious boundary creation or active boundary maintenance. For example, much of what distinguishes intimate relationships from other relationships concerns shared history, common property and shared projects.

Parent–child relationships, particularly mother-child relationships, are often thought of as intensely intimate family relationships but it is not obvious that this relationship typically relies on boundary work to protect its intimacy. Mothers and fathers may work to keep their children 'close' and actively seek to spend time with and to 'know' their children. However, a number of studies have shown that parental attempts at 'knowing' are sometimes experienced by children as monitoring and control rather than intimacy (Brannen et al, 1994; Solomon et al, 2002). For some children, their home life is separated off from their friendship relationships by boundary work that includes never or rarely bringing friends home. For example, children with drug- or alcohol-abusing parents sometimes adopt strategies that prevent the possibility of their friends being exposed to domestic chaos or strange behaviour by their parents (Bancroft et al, 2004). However, in Britain the majority of older school age children are friend focused and regularly bring children to their parental home across class backgrounds (Jamieson and McKendrick, 2005). In many children's lives, at least in middle childhood, it is practical acts of being cared for and expressions of interest, concern and love that reassure children that a parent cares about them. Low-key, everyday reassurance of a parent or parents 'being there'allows these relationship to be both a key intimate relationships and a taken for granted background support, while they focus on the dramas of friendship relationships (Borland et al, 1998).

Research on couples offers a mixed picture in terms of the place of boundary work. Some couples clearly operate protective and exclusionary practices to sustain intimacy and privilege their couple relationship above all others. But some research also suggests that boundary work is not the mainstay of couple relationships and some researchers suggest a shift away from coupledom as the focal point of intimacy. Gender differences and divisions continue to have implications for intimacy among heterosexual couples although the situation has changed radically since the mid-20th century. Intimacy, domesticity and femininity are not as routinely discursively produced as coterminous boundaries. Men and women both talk of seeking intimacy and equality although they invest differently in the work of sustaining relationships and households.

Research suggests that, at least up until late middle age, most adults are still seeking lifelong relationships. The meaning of marriage has changed in ways that have closed the moral distance between marriage and cohabitation without marriage (Jamieson et al, 2002). Commitment does not mean an obligation to stay together for life. For example, commitment, as seen by younger respondents in Jane Lewis's (1999, 2001) two generational study, rather than an *obligation* to stay with a partner through 'thick and thin' refers to the *presumption* that this will happen because love will last, the valued qualities of the other person will last and the relationship will remain good enough for a life together. In this sense, everyday ideals for life partnerships, married or otherwise, have moved closer to what Giddens (1991, 1992) describes as 'the pure relationship'. However, what subsequently sustains the relationship is a mixed repertoire of practices of intimacy and processes that subsequently institutionalise the relationship. Boundary work is only a part of this picture.

Although disclosing intimacy with its requirement for exclusivity may not be the bedrock of most couple relationships, this does not necessarily preclude the presence of some boundary practices as a routine part of couple relationships. The ideal of monogamy, for example, may provide some with reason for keeping others at a distance. A range of studies suggests that relatively exclusive and sexually monogamous couple relationships remain the dominant ideal sought by most people as their key source of intimacy in adult life. While significant numbers of people who subscribe to the ideal are not fully monogamous, monogamy is the dominant practice among heterosexual and lesbian couples. For example, Green (1997) found that serial monogamy was the dominant pattern of relationships in a London-based politically radical, lesbian feminist community. This was despite a degree of political suspicion of marriage-like couple relationships as potentially recreating the perceived deficiencies of heterosexual unions and undermining autonomy and freedom for political activism. Gay men may be less likely to practise sexual monogamy but use other forms of boundary work to protect their long-term relationships.

Non-monogamous couples may be particularly likely to use exclusionary rules to try and sustain a sense of having a unique and 'special' relationship because other conventional boundaries are absent (Jamieson, 2004). Some non-monogamous couples are very clear about which relationship is the primary relationship and have rules designed to ensure that other sexual relationships cannot interfere with its privileged time and space. For example, secondary relationships must only be conducted a certain distance from home or only in certain time intervals. Other couples require that 'other relationships' are brought home for scrutiny and to be made to confront the physical reality of an ongoing domestic partnership. The exceptional few who have two partners rather than a primary and secondary relationship may nevertheless still use practices of protecting and scheduling in 'special time' to create 'special relationships' with more than one partner.

Across the range of ways in which intimacy can be understood and practised, arguably self-disclosing intimacy is the most exclusive form of intimacy in terms of demanding privileged dyadic time. Although as Giddens claims, this form of intimacy may not be incompatible with civic engagement, time is finite even if capacity for engagement with others is not. The notion that it is important to know deeply another person and to constantly refresh that knowledge may demand a more exclusive devotion of time than other forms of doing intimacy. Trying to sustain multiple relationships on this basis, whether with children as a parent or with partners as an adult, may leave little time, particularly if negotiated around paid employment. Ironically, then, perhaps this understanding and practice of intimacy is the most suitable candidate for the claim that a shift to intimacy is to the detriment of 'community'. But then research also indicates that relatively few relationships are exclusively founded on self-disclosing intimacy.

Theorists are better equipped to describe social change if they pay attention to the details of the ways in which people 'do intimacy' and address lives as they are lived. However, research has rarely focused explicitly on the role of boundaries and boundary work in personal life. Assessing the value of particular theoretical positions would be greatly assisted if understandings of the place of personal relationships in social change included knowledge of the extent to which living personal lives and 'doing intimacy' involves protective or exclusionary boundaries. It is possible to draw lessons from existing research about the significance of a number of boundaries for intimacy and personal life. The discussion has touched on the boundary between familial and non-familial intimate relationships, the relationship between gender boundaries and intimacy and the significance of boundaries between personal life and 'community' or civil society. It has not been possible to explore any of these themes thoroughly not only because of the constraints of space but also because of the limits of existing research. There is a case for a much more explicit research focus on these themes and for a more direct exploration of the significance of boundary work within and between types of intimate relationships.

References

Bancroft, A., Wilson, S., Cunningham-Burley, C., Backett-Milburn, K. and Masters, H. (2004) 'Resilience and transition: the experiences of older children of drug- and alcohol-misusing parents', York: Joseph Rowntree Foundation.

Barth, F. (1969) *Ethnic groups and boundaries*, Boston, MA: Little Brown & Co.

Barth, F. (2000) 'Boundaries and connections', in A. Cohen (ed) *Signifying identities: Anthropological perspectives on boundaries and contested values*, London: Routledge.

Bauman, Z. (2003) *Liquid love: On the frailty of human bonds*, Cambridge: Polity Press.

Berger, P. and Kellner, H. (1964) 'Marriage and the construction of reality', in M. Anderson (ed) *The Sociology of the family* (2nd edn), Harmondsworth: Penguin.

Berlant, L. (1997) *The queen of America goes to Washington City: Essays on sex and citizenship*, Durham and London: Duke University Press.

Berlant, L. and Warner M. (2000) 'Sex in public', in L. Berlant (ed) *Intimacy*, Chicago, IL: University of Chicago Press.

Borland, M., Laybourn, A., Hill, M. and Brown, J. (1998) *Middle childhood: The perspective of children and parents*, London: Jessica Kingsley.

Brannen, J., Dodd, K., Oakley, A. and Storey, P. (1994) *Young people, health and family life*, Buckingham: Open University Press.

Burgess, E.W. and Locke, H.J. (1945) *The family: From institution to companionship*, New York, NY: American Book Company.

Crow, G. (2001) *Social solidarities*, Buckingham: Open University Press.

Crow, G. and Allan, G. (1995) 'Beyond "insiders" and "outsiders" in the sociology of community', paper delivered at the British Sociological Association Conference, University of Leicester, April.

Crow, G., Allan, G. and Summers, M. (2002) 'Neither busybodies nor nobodies: managing proximity and distance in neighbourly relations', *Sociology*, vol 36, pp 127-45.

Davis, M.S. (1973) *Intimate relations*, New York, NY: Free Press.

Delanty, G. (2003) *Community*, London: Routledge.

Dunne, G. (1997) *Lesbian lifestyles: Women's work and the politics of sexuality*, London: Macmillan.

Fischer, C. (1982) *To dwell among friends: Personal networks in town and city*, Chicago, IL: Chicago University Press.

Giddens, A. (1991) *Modernity and self-identity: Self and society in the late modern age*, Cambridge: Polity Press.

Giddens, A. (1992) *The transformation of intimacy: Sexuality, love and eroticism in modern societies*, Cambridge: Polity Press.

Goffman, E. (1963) *Behaviour in public places*, New York, NY: Free Press.

Granovetter, M. (1973) 'The strength of weak ties', *American Journal of Sociology*, vol 78, pp 1360-80.

Green, S. (1997) *Urban amazons: Lesbian feminism and beyond in the gender, sexuality and identity battles of London*, London: Macmillan.

Hochschild, A. (2003) *The commercialization of intimate life: Notes from home and work*, Berkeley, CA: University of California Press.

Holmes, M. (2004) 'An equal distance? Individualisation, gender and intimacy in distance relationships', *Sociological Review*, vol 48, pp 180-200.

Jamieson, L. (1987) 'Theories of family development and the experience of being brought up', *Sociology*, vol 21, 591-607.

Jamieson, L.(1998) *Intimacy: Personal relationships in modern societies*, Cambridge: Polity Press.

Jamieson, L. (1999) 'Intimacy transformed: a critical look at the pure relationship', *Sociology*, vol 33, pp 477-94.

Jamieson, L. (2004) 'Intimacy, negotiated non-monogamy and the limits of the couple', in J. Duncombe, K. Harrison, G. Allan and D. Marsden (eds) *The state of affairs*, Mahwah, NJ: Lawrence Erlbaum Associates.

Jamieson, L. and McKendrick, J. (2005) 'Teenagers' relationships with peers and parent', in J.F. Ermisch and R.E. Wright (eds) *Changing Scotland: Assessing the impact of devolution*, Bristol: The Policy Press.

Jamieson, L., Anderson, M., McCrone, D., Bechhofer, F., Stewart, R. and Li, Y. (2002) 'Cohabitation and commitment: partnership plans of young men and women', *Sociological Review*, vol 50, no 3, pp 354-75.

Lewis, J. (2001) *The end of marriage*, Cheltenham: Edward Elgar.

Lewis, J. (with Datta, J. and Sarre, S.) (1999) *Individualism and commitment in marriage and cohabitation*, Research Series no 8/99, London: Lord Chancellor's Department.

Lichterman, P. (1996) *The search for political community: American activists reinventing commitment*, Cambridge: Cambridge University Press.

Millet, K. (1971) *Sexual politics*, London: Rupert Hart Davis Ltd.

Mitchell, J. (1971) *Woman's estate*, Harmondsworth: Penguin.

Morgan, D. (1976) *Social theory and the family*, London: Routledge.

Morgan, D. (1982) 'Berger and Kellner's construction of marriage', Occasional Paper no 7, Manchester: University of Manchester, Department of Sociology.

Morgan, D. (1991) 'Ideologies of marriage and family life', in D. Clark (ed) *Marriage, domestic life and social change: Writings for Jacqueline Burgoyne (1944-88)*, London: Routledge.

Morgan, D. (1992) 'Marriage and society', in J. Lewis, D. Clark and D. Morgan (eds) *Whom God hath joined together: The work of marriage guidance*, London: Tavistock and Routledge.

Morgan, D. (1996) *Family connections: An introduction to family studies*, Cambridge: Polity Press.

Morgan, D. (2002) 'Sociological perspectives on the family', in A. Carling, S. Duncan and R. Edwards (eds) *Analysing families*, London: Routledge.

Pahl, R. and Spencer, L. (2004) 'Personal communities: not simply families of "fate" or "choice"', *Current Sociology*, vol 52 no 2, pp 199-221.

Parsons, T. (1959) 'The social structure of the family', in R.N. Anshen, (ed) *The family, its functions and destiny*, New York, NY: Harper.

Parsons, T. (1962) 'Youth in the context of American society', *Daedalus*, 91, reprinted in T. Parsons (ed) (1970) *Social structure and personality*, New York: Collier Macmillan.

Parsons, T. and Bales, R.F. (1956) *Family socialization and the interaction process*, London: Routledge and Kegan Paul.

Putnam, R. (2000) *Bowling alone: The collapse and revival of American community*, New York, NY: Simon and Schuster.

Rose, N. (1996) *Inventing ourselves: Psychology, power and personhood*, Cambridge: Cambridge University Press.

Roseneil, S. and Budgeon, S. (2004) 'Cultures of intimacy and care beyond the family: personal life and social change in the early twenty-first century', *Current Sociology*, vol 52, no 2, pp 135-59.

Sennett, R. (1998) *The corrosion of character: The personal consequences of work in the new capitalism*, London: Norton.

Sennett, R. (2004) *Respect: The formation of character in an age of inequality*, Harmondsworth: Penguin Books.

Silver, A. (1997) '"Two different sorts of commerce", or, friendship and strangership in civil society', in J. Weintraub and K. Kumar (eds) *Public and private in thought and practice: Perspectives on the grand dichotomy*, Chicago, IL: University of Chicago Press.

Simmel, G. (translated K. Wolff) (1950) *The sociology of Georg Simmel*, Glencoe: Free Press.

Smith, A. (1759) *The theory of moral sentiments*, reprinted 1976, Oxford: Clarendon.

Solomon, Y., Warin, J., Lewis, C. and Langford, W. (2002) 'Intimate talk between parents and their teenage children: democratic openness or covert control?', *Sociology*, vol 30, pp 965-83.

Weeks, J., Heapy, B. and Donovan, C. (2001) *Same sex intimacies*, London: Routledge.

TWELVE

Solo living, individual and family boundaries: findings from secondary analysis[1]

Fran Wasoff and Lynn Jamieson with Adam Smith

Introduction

There is a growing proportion of adults living alone, at ages that have conventionally been associated with coupledom, marriage and childrearing, as well as among older people and, given differential mortality, particularly older women. To what extent does the increase in people living alone mean a redrawing of boundaries around 'family' and 'household'? Those who live in one person households are not in 'family households' but to what extent have they stepped outside of families? If people now move in and out of situations in which they live alone across their adult life, has this reshaped the boundaries between youth and adulthood? If men and women display very different patterns of moving in and out of solo living, what are the implications of this for gender boundaries?

Solo living has been portrayed as removed from conventional family life in both optimistic and pessimistic terms. In Britain, a popular image of the single woman living alone was created in the novel *Bridget Jones's Diary*.[2] Bridget's diary reveals her preoccupations with her weight, diet, appearance and, above all, her desperation for a boyfriend. This portrayal is somewhat more sympathetic than some stereotypes offered in popular media. Portrayals of 'laddish culture' among young and not so young men and ladettes, their female equivalent, suggest that people are too selfish, self-obsessed or otherwise preoccupied with consumption, fun and personal project to sustain relationships with others (for example, as in the novel, *Morvern Callar*[3]). These portrayals suggest that solo livers are atomistic and, wittingly or unwittingly, place boundaries of selfishness between themselves and others. These negative stereotypes seem to fit with academic accounts that are very pessimistic about the future of personal life (Bellah et al, 1985; Beck, 1992; Bauman, 1995; Putnam, 2000). But in this realm of speculation, it is equally plausible to fit trends in solo living to more optimistic accounts of personal life (Skolnick, 1991; Giddens, 1992). Then, living alone is not about selfishly cutting others off but creating a base from which equal and intimate relationships with others can be sustained. Following the optimistic account of social change offered by Anthony Giddens (1992, 1998), women would be placed at the vanguard in this interpretation of solo living, seeking to develop more equal and deeper relationships and working to redraw boundaries by demanding more democracy and intimacy in their personal relationships with men. In contrast, it is consistent with some of the more pessimistic interpretations of social change, to characterise the abilities of both men and women solo livers to meaningfully connect with others as equally sapped.

Research evidence

With some exceptions, (Gordon, 1994; Hall et al, 1999; Heath and Cleaver, 2003; Chandler et al, 2004), there is scant research evidence to help us judge these claims concerning the significance of a growing number of people living alone. This chapter focuses on secondary analysis of household data in national longitudinal and cross-sectional datasets to create a detailed baseline picture of those living alone. In some sections of the analysis we have focused on subsets of respondents living alone or who have lived alone previously who are aged between 30 and 74. It was a theoretical decision, for the purpose of some of the analysis, to screen out younger adulthood and older old age. The age of 30 can be regarded as a boundary beyond which living alone carries more significance than in the twenties. Taking the age of 30 as our starting point to represent earlier (as distinct from early) adulthood, reflects the fact that living alone after the 30th birthday is more likely to be experienced as unusual, or as a possible alternative to marriage or cohabitation, rather than a prelude to it. This is the youngest age at which being partnered is the statistical norm; by age 30, two thirds of women and half of men are married (and some more are cohabiting) (ONS, 2004).

The cross-sectional surveys we analysed are the General Household Survey (for Britain) and the Scottish Household Survey (for Scotland), for recent years (from 1999) (ONS, 2004; Scottish Executive, 2004), yielding an album of recent annual snapshots of one person households and their circumstances. These include such topics as housing and consumer durables, social class, employment, income, education, health and social services and social security, and also, in the case of the Scottish Household Survey, disability and care, household expenditure, safety and social networks and smaller area geographic comparison such as rural/urban variation in the density of one person households.

The longitudinal dataset discussed here is the British Household Panel Survey (BHPS), with 10 waves since 1991, but a boosted Scottish sample allowing for standalone Scottish analyses only from 1999 (Berthoud and Gershuny, 2000). This is a large, multipurpose, rich dataset that has traced cohorts for 12 years. The BHPS has information on such subjects as personal relationships, ethnicity, health and care, crime, social and political attitudes, labour market behaviour, expectations and attitudes, income and wealth, expenditure, pensions, housing and education. The BHPS was used to produce an analysis of routes in and out of solo living and its permanence. The annual view that is possible in the BHPS complements other studies of this group using the Longitudinal Study that examined movements in and out of solo living at 10-year intervals (Hall et al, 1999; Chandler et al, 2004).

The analysis here provides a starting point from which to assess the stereotypes of solo livers as individuals within their self-constructed boundaries separating themselves from others or as otherwise outside of the boundary of the family versus the image of solo livers as pioneers doing positive boundary reconstruction. Such a starting point cannot be a full answer. In particular, what is lacking is any substantial body of recent qualitative data offering insight into the meaning of relationships and the significance of solo living across the lifecourse for those who are living alone.

An analysis of these data does, nevertheless, provide some evidence with which to judge the bigger questions. The existing quantitative data sources provide some detail of who lives alone, of their routes into and, sometimes, out of living alone and some insights into their pattern of connectedness with others. It is possible, for example, to ask questions of existing datasets that help to establish whether living alone is a growing 'lifestyle choice' and that may offer some clues about its meaning. Comparative cross-sectional analysis of the age and marital status of those living alone versus those who live with others, indicates how solo living is now spread across adult life, rather than being predominantly a feature of older age and widowhood. Moreover, its relative association with divorce and separation as opposed to never living with a partner may offer some clues about whether solo living should be characterised as voluntarily remaining or accidentally slipping outside of family household boundaries. Analysis of solo living by age across time establishes whether solo living is growing more rapidly at younger ages. Analysis by gender can quickly establish whether young women could reasonably be depicted as in the 'vanguard' or whether solo living is entered into equally by young men and women. Longitudinal household data that allow mapping of routes into or out of solo living enables further scrutiny of the extent to which living alone is an artifact of high rates of breakdown of relationships and strengthens evidence about the extent to which a growing proportion of those living alone have never lived with a partner. Variations that are not predicted by either model, such as regional differences, provide further puzzles to be unpacked.

Incidence of solo living in the UK, Britain and Scotland

UK-wide and within the nations of the UK, nationally representative data sources give us information about one person households and how their numbers vary geographically. According to the 2001 census for England and Wales one-person households comprise more than 30% of all private households (6.5 million) (ONS, 2003) compared to 26% in 1991 and 11% in 1961. Solo living is not only a feature of later life; over half of one person households consists of a person below retirement age. Viewed in relation to individuals, the UK is about average for the European Union in the proportion of its population living on their own: 13%. Nevertheless, the proportion who live alone increases with age, rising to 37% of people over the age of 65 (ONS, 2003).

Scotland has a higher proportion of one person households than England and Wales: 33% of all households, according to the 2001 census – 15% of households consisting of a person above retirement age and 18% below retirement age (GROS, 2004).

Secondary analysis of the General Household Survey for 2001 of individuals aged 30 to 74 living alone adds further evidence of geographic variation in the scale of individuals living alone across the nations of Britain. It is higher in Scotland (18% of individuals) and lower in Wales (13%) than the overall proportion in Britain (15%). For women, the difference across the nations is even greater: 18% of women lived alone in Scotland in 2001, compared to 13% of women in Britain as a whole, an excess rate of nearly 50% (Table 12.1).

Table 12.1: Solo living in Great Britain, 2001

	Percentage of people living alone as % of all individuals aged 30-74		
	All	**Men**	**Women**
GB total	*15*	*17*	*13*
Scotland	18	18	18
England	15	16	13
Wales	13	14	12

Source: Derived by secondary analysis from the General Household Survey 2001

Table 12.2: Trends in solo living in Great Britain: one person households as a % of all households, 1971-2002

	1971	1975	1981	1985	1991	1995	2001*	2002*
One adult aged 16-59	5	6	7	8	10	12	15	16
One adult aged 60+	12	15	15	16	16	15	15	15
Total % of one person households	17	21	22	24	26	27	30	31

Note: * weighted.
Source: ONS (2004, Table 3.2)

There is also a substantial difference in the incidence of solo living between some cities and elsewhere. In the cities of Aberdeen, Edinburgh and Glasgow, 38%, 38% and 41% of all households, respectively, consisted of one person, a much higher figure than in the rest of the country. This higher incidence is due to a higher proportion of all households consisting of one person below retirement age: 24%, 23% and 25% of all households, respectively in Aberdeen, Edinburgh and Glasgow.

While other studies using census data gave snapshots at 10-year intervals (Hall et al, 1999; Chandler et al, 2004), more frequent trend data on solo living in Great Britain is available from the General Household Survey, which allows us to trace a pattern of growth at more frequent intervals over the late 20th century. Between 1971 and 2002, the total proportion of one person households almost doubled from 17% to 31%. The growth in one person households for people of working age has been even more marked; the proportion of such households with someone aged 16 to 59 more than tripled from 5% to 16%. Over the last five years, the pattern has stabilised for both those above and below retirement age at 31%, or nearly one in three, of all households (Table 12.2) (ONS, 2004).

Viewed in relation to individuals rather than households, the proportion of people living alone has more than doubled since 1971 (Table 12.3), from 6% to 13% of the population living in private

Table 12.3: Trends in solo living in Great Britain: people living alone as a % of all people aged 16+, 1971-2002

	1971	1975	1981	1985	1991	1995	2001*	2002*
One adult aged 16-59	2	2	3	3	4	5	7	7
One adult aged 60+	4	5	6	6	7	6	7	6
Total % of one person households	6	7	9	9	11	11	14	13

Note: * weighted.
Source: ONS (2004, Table 3.2)

households in 2002, with the growth rate even greater for the working-age population.

Demographic projections suggest these trends will continue, for both older and younger age cohorts. Shaw and Haskey (1999) estimate there will be a growth of about 10% in the number of women living without partners between the late 1990s and 2011.

Flows in and out of solo living

In order to focus attention on the stages of the adult lifecourse where solo living is less frequent, and to examine the dynamics of solo living by age and gender, we use BHPS data between 1991 and 2001. This allows us to begin to build up a picture of solo living not only in terms of 'stocks' at anytime (that is, those who live alone at that time), but also in terms of 'flows'. While the BHPS is a longitudinal survey that traces a cohort over time, not all respondents are included in every sweep for survey design and operational reasons (Taylor, 2004).[4] In addition, some respondents will fall within the chosen age range for only some of the sweeps where they were interviewed. For our purposes here, we look only at those respondents who were both included in the survey and within the target age group over the entire 11 sweeps.[4] This group, which consists of those who lived alone throughout (always solo), who had lived alone for only part of the period and those who had never lived alone over the period (never solo), consists of over two thirds, 69%, of the entire cohort who met the inclusion criteria for any one sweep. We then focus for further analysis on those individuals who were in the target age group (30-74) for the entire period who had lived alone for at least one sweep.

There are 3,340 men, 4,055 women, a total of 7,395 people in the relevant age group for all 11 sweeps. Of these, 23% were alone (ever solo) for at least one sweep. The gender balance of this group

Table 12.4: Proportion of people aged 30-74 in all sweeps who ever lived solo, by gender as % of their age cohort, UK, 1991-2001[6]

	Men	%	Women	%	Total	%
Ever solo	774	23	960	24	1,734	23
Never solo	2,566	77	3,095	76	5,661	77
Total cohort	3,340	100	4,055	100	7,395	100

Source: Derived by secondary analysis from BHPS 1991-2001

is the same as those who had never lived alone during the period; 45% men: 55% women (Table 12.4).

Compared to the snapshot frequency of individuals in the population currently living alone, a 'stock' of 13% in 2002, we can see that the proportion of the population aged 30-74 who have lived alone at some point over the previous 11 years, the 'flow', was considerably larger, 23% of individuals, with proportions for men and women similar. Only 7% of the cohort had remained solo throughout the period. This suggests that transitions between solo living and living with others is commonplace and that the boundaries between solo living and family living are frequently crossed. Frequent crossings between solo living and family households seems to suggests that at least proportions of those living alone cannot be confirmed as determined solo livers who are actively creating boundaries between themselves and others.

Solo living by age and gender

Patterns of solo living in Britain vary by both age and gender and the likelihood of living alone varies across the lifecourse in a gender-specific pattern. Data from the 2002 General Household Survey (ONS, 2004, Table 3.4), as in Table 12.5, show that the likelihood of living alone increases with age. While women as a group are slightly more likely to live on their own than men (18% as opposed to 15% of those aged 16 or more), for those above retirement age, women are about twice as likely as men to be living alone. For those aged 25 to 44, the pattern is reversed, with men twice as likely as women to be living on their own. This raises some doubt about the thesis that young women living on their own are in the vanguard of social change, at least as far as propensity for solo living is concerned. Further evidence is required before further speculating about whether young men's greater propensity to live alone reflects a chosen path outside couple and family boundaries.

Table 12.5: Men and women living alone by age as a % of all people aged 16+, Great Britain, 2002

	Men	Women	Total
16-24	5	5	5
25-44	16	8	12
45-64	15	15	15
65-74	18	34	27
75+	29	60	48
All aged 16+	15	18	17

Source: ONS (2004, Table 3.4)

Solo living, marital history and childlessness

Those living on their own are diverse in terms of their partnership histories and include people who have not had a partner, whose partner lives elsewhere (living apart together, or 'LATs' (Levin, 2004)) or whose partnership has ended through separation, divorce or death. This is illustrated by looking at their current marital status (Table 12.6a). In the most recent year of the General Household Survey examined, the two largest groups are people who never married and those who are divorced or separated. The remainder, about one quarter, are widowed. However, this pattern is gender and age related.

For those above working age, almost two thirds of women are widows, whereas older men are equally likely to be single, divorced or separated or widowers. For those of working age, most men have never been married, whereas most women had previously been married and are currently either divorced or separated or widowed.

It cannot be assumed that those who are 'single, never married' will have been living solo all of their lives. Some may have lived with a partner outside marriage for a period. However, the extent of differences between men and women is unlikely to be modified if measurement of cohabitation were possible as well as marriage. In other words, it is likely that the higher proportion of men classified as 'single, never married' than women reflects a gender difference in propensity to partner and not simply to marry. If men living alone have been less likely to ever have partnered than women living alone and if never partnering means actively choosing a 'single's lifestyle' outside the 'family boundary' then men are more likely to choose this route than women.

The higher proportions of separation and divorce and widowhood among working-age women than men reflect their higher rates of

Table 12.6a: Marital status by gender and age of people living alone aged 30-74, Great Britain, 2001 (%)

	Men aged 30-59	Women aged 30-59	Men aged 60-74	Women aged 60-74	All solo
Single, never married	57.6	38.7	31.7	9.2	38
Divorced or separated	40.2	45.6	34.9	26.4	37.4
Widowed	1.8	15.3	33.	63.9	24.2

Source: Derived by secondary analysis from the General Household Survey 2001

Table 12.6b: Women expecting no children, by ageband, Great Britain (%)

	Children expected by women in total – expecting *none*					
	1998		2000		2001	
Ageband	Solo	Not solo	Solo	Not solo	Solo	Not solo
30-39	46.1	10.6	39.9	11.3	46.8	12.2
40-49	47	8.7	49.2	15.4	49.3	15

Source: Derived by secondary analysis from the General Household Survey 2001

exposure to marriage. The higher incidence of widowhood among women, even those below the age of 59, also reflects the different mortality rates of men and women exacerbated by the somewhat higher incidence of women marrying older men than of men marrying older women. Overall, the distribution of those living alone by marital status, age and gender is consistent with a view of men as more likely than women to remain outside the family boundary or on the margins of the family. However, until the further checking of the family connectedness of men and women reported later, it remains possible that neither household boundaries nor marital status are indicative of family boundaries and that never partnered men and women are, in practice, well integrated into personal and familial lives.

In the General Household Survey, women have been asked about their expectations of future children. This question is not asked of men. A much higher proportion of women over 30 living alone expect never to have children compared with their peers living in family households. Table 12.6b shows the proportion of women expecting to have no children. This is, of course, a difference partly created by the nature of the comparison. By definition, those in one person households are not living with children, but between the ages of 30-59 many of those not living alone will be living with

Table 12.7a: Housing tenure of solo person households by age group and gender, Great Britain, 2001 (%)

Housing tenure	Male 30-59	Male 60-74	Female 30-59	Female 60-74	Total
Owned outright	14.1	45.5	24.5	54.9	30.8
Buying with mortgage	45.3	10.7	41.8	7.9	30.5
Social rented	25.5	38.3	24.9	33.3	29.1
Private rented	15.0	5.6	8.8	4.0	9.6
Total	100.0	100.0	100.0	100.0	100.0

Source: Derived by secondary analysis from the General Household Survey 2001

Table 12.7b: Housing tenure of multi-person households by age group and gender, Great Britain, 2001 (%)

Housing tenure	Male 30-59	Male 60-74	Female 30-59	Female 60-74	Total
Owned outright	16.3	62.2	17.6	64.3	26.6
Buying with mortgage	64.5	19.3	61.2	15.4	53.3
Social rented	11.9	15.1	14.5	17.0	13.8
Private rented	7.4	3.4	6.6	3.3	6.2
Total	100.0	100.0	100.0	100.0	100.0

Source: Derived by secondary analysis from the General Household Survey 2001

children. Nevertheless the proportion of solo livers in the 30-39 age group expecting to remain childless is striking given that this is now an age at which many women have their first child. It is not possible to know whether this reflects resignation or a wish to remain childless and whether, therefore, to interpret this as a decision made by a large minority of solo living women not to create a family of procreation but rather to stay outside this particular family boundary.

Solo living, housing circumstances and economic status

Housing is an important dimension of socioeconomic circumstances as well as being an indicator of wider socioeconomic factors. Home ownership rates are indicative of the extent to which household members pool resources over time and use economies of scale within a household to acquire not only somewhere to live but also an opportunity for asset accumulation. General Household Survey data for 2001 comparing housing tenure of solo person and multiperson households (Tables 12.7a and 12.7b) show that solo living is associated with higher levels of renting, both social renting and private renting, and lower levels of home ownership, particularly where people are buying their homes with mortgages. People living

Table 12.7c: Economic status: 'permanently sick or disabled'

		Male 30-59	Male 60-74	Female 30-59	Female 60-74	Total
Scottish Household Survey 2001						
Solo	N	193	59	154	29	435
	%	22.2	13.2	20.0	3.1	14.4
Multi	N	137	60	162	17	376
	%	5.9	6.5	4.8	1.9	5.0
General Household Survey 2001						
Solo	N	268,187	118,659	199,304	19,894	606,044
	%	14.5	16.4	18.4	1.8	12.7
Multi	N	517,185	239,794	541,577	74382	1,372,938
	%	5.0	8.2	4.9	2.7	5.1%

alone are less than half as likely as those living with others to be homeowners with mortgages, across all age and gender groups. This suggests that many people living on their own are not able to pool resources with others that would make access to home ownership possible. Older men and women living on their own are also less likely to own their home outright than those currently living with others, although the gap is smaller for older women. This is most likely due to the high likelihood of being a widow and therefore to have lived in a shared household in the past. However, people living on their own are more than twice as likely to be living in rented housing, whether it is in the social rented sector or the private rented sector. Men of working age who live on their own are more than twice as likely to be in private rented housing than those who live with others.

It is possible to do some detailed comparison of the economic status of those who live alone and with others from both the Scottish Household Survey and the General Household survey. Both surveys show that, among people of working age, levels of economic inactivity are higher among those living alone. Men aged 30-59 were about twice as likely to be unemployed than their peers who live in family households. The difference was not quite as marked among women. Among both solo-living men and women, the proportion who were permanently unable to work was significantly higher than among the 'multi' population (see Table 12.7c).

Solo living and social capital

People who live alone have been portrayed negatively in terms of poorer connectedness to others, with weaker links to family, friends and community networks, higher levels of social exclusion and lower

Table 12.8: Solo and multi-person household links to family, friends and community (%)

	Solo %	Multi %
Family		
In past fortnight – went to visit relatives	59	68
In past fortnight – went out with relatives	37	40
In past fortnight – had relatives round	52	59
In past fortnight – spoke to relatives on phone	80	87
Friends		
In past fortnight – went to visit friends	56	61
In past fortnight – went out with friends	54	50
In past fortnight – had friends round	50	50
In past fortnight – spoke to friends on phone	75	82
Community		
In past fortnight – spoke to neighbours	81	85
In past fortnight – none of these	1	1
Feel involved in local community	22	29
Agree could rely on friends/relatives in neighbourhood if needed help	89	93
Agree could rely on friends/relatives in neighbourhood to watch home if empty	91	95
Agree could turn to friends/relatives in neighbourhood for advice/support	85	89
No serious problems or disputes with neighbours in past 12 months	92	92

Source: Derived by secondary analysis from the Scottish Household Survey 2000-01

levels of social capital. In the most negative stereotypes, solo livers are caricatured as selfishly creating boundaries between themselves and others, although evidence for such claims is often lacking. The degree to which people have dense links across households and into the wider community, whether they live alone or with others, is important when deciding where meaningful boundaries lie in terms of households, families and relationships. Arising from its social inclusion agenda, there has been considerable interest by governments in both the concept and the measurement of social capital, the sum of social trust, norms and social networks that people have. The concept of social capital, and its two main forms, bonding and bridging (Putnam, 2000), and the role of families in fostering it, are all controversial (Edwards et al, 2003).

The Scottish Household Survey contains a number of questions on social capital issues, particularly bonding social capital in the form of social networks (Scottish Executive, 2003). Analysing these in relation to solo adult households, as compared to multiperson households for 2001, we found slight differences between people living alone (solos) and those who live with others (multis), with slightly lower proportions of solos reporting positive responses on most of the measures of social capital, with the exception of going out with friends, where solos were more likely than multis to go out with friends. However, more striking than their differences was the similarity in patterns of response between people living alone and with others (Table 12.8).

Solos as a group report they are slightly less involved with their families, and with their local communities than multis, and report slightly lower levels of agreement that they could rely on friends/ relatives in their neighbourhood if they needed help, advice or support or to watch their homes if empty. They were similar in the degree to which they said they had no serious problems or disputes with neighbours in the past 12 months, both over 90%. In contrast, a higher proportion of solos reported going out with friends in the past fortnight, suggesting a stronger importance of peer networks than for those who live with others.

Looking at variations within the solo population by age and gender and comparing these with people who do not live on their own, we find that while the overall pattern is sustained, there are some notable differences (Table 12.9). Solo women report consistently higher levels of social involvement with family and community than men in the same age category. The most pronounced differences concern going out with and having relatives round, 64% of solo women aged 60-74 reported having relatives around in the past fortnight, compared to 48% of older men and 54% of younger women aged 30-59. Further analysis by marital status suggests that solo living men aged 30-59 who have never married and those who have previously been partnered are very similar in terms of their profile of face-to-face connections with friends and kin. Both are less connected than their female equivalents. Research on kin relationships has frequently described women as taking on more of a role of 'kin keepers' than men. It seems that this difference persists among men and women living on their own and that women living alone were only very slightly less likely to be in regular touch with relatives beyond their household than living in family households. It appears that the majority of women living outside family households are not outside of family boundaries in terms of their routine face-to-face personal connections. Also, it is important not to exaggerate the disengagement of men, given that half of men had visited a relative in the last fortnight and over 70% had spoken to one on the telephone.

Table 12.9: Solo person household links to family, friends and community, by age group and gender (%)

	Male 30-59	Male 60-74	Female 30-59	Female 60-74	All solo
Family					
In past fortnight – went to visit relatives	57 *(66)*	50 *(59)*	67 *(72)*	58 *(64)*	59 *(68)*
In past fortnight – went out with relatives	30 *(36)*	27 *(33)*	44 *(42)*	41 *(38)*	37 *(39)*
In past fortnight – had relatives round	38 *(57)*	48 *(60)*	54 *(61)*	64 *(62)*	52 *(59)*
In past fortnight – spoke to relatives on phone	73 *(85)*	74 *(85)*	84 *(90)*	87 *(96)*	80 *(87)*
Friends					
In past fortnight – went to visit friends	62 *(63)*	43 *(51)*	59 *(66)*	53 *(48)*	56 *(61)*
In past fortnight – went out with friends	62 *(54)*	40 *(42)*	57 *(52)*	49 *(39)*	54 *(50)*
In past fortnight – had friends round	52 *(50)*	39 *(47)*	56 *(53)*	47 *(44)*	50 *(50)*
In past fortnight – spoke to friends on phone	72 *(81)*	62 *(78)*	82 *(84)*	78 *(78)*	75 *(82)*
Community					
In past fortnight – spoke to neighbours	75 *(82)*	83 *(88)*	79 *(86)*	87 *(86)*	81 *(85)*
In past fortnight – none of these	2 *(1)*	3 *(1)*	0 *(1)*	1 *(1)*	1 *(1)*
Feel involved in local community	18 *(26)*	20 *(28)*	20 *(31)*	28 *(30)*	22 *(29)*
Agree could rely on friends/relatives in neighbourhood if needed help	80 *(92)*	88 *(95)*	90 *(92)*	95 *(94)*	89 *(93)*
Agree could rely on friends/relatives in neighbourhood to watch home if empty	85 *(95)*	90 *(95)*	92 *(95)*	96 *(97)*	91 *(96)*
Agree could turn to friends/relatives in neighbourhood for advice/support	77 *(87)*	86 *(91)*	85 *(590)*	92 *(91)*	85 *(89)*
No serious problems or disputes with neighbours in past 12 months	90 *(91)*	96 *(96)*	89 *(90)*	96 *(95)*	92 *(92)*

Note: Corresponding figures for multis are in parentheses.
Source: Derived by secondary analysis from the Scottish Household Survey 2000-01

Table 12.10: Transitions to or from solo living of people aged 30-74 in all sweeps who ever lived solo by gender, UK, 1991-2001[6]

	Men	%	Women	%	Total	%
Transition in or out of solo living	596	77	610	64	1,206	70
Always solo	178	23	350	36	528	30
Total ever solo	774	100	960	100	1,734	100

Transitions in and out of solo living

Since solo living has become an increasingly common stage in the lifecourse for many people, it is important to understand how and how often it changes for individuals over time. Do people remain alone in the long term or are there frequent household transitions? If there is change in and out of solo living, for whom is it changing and in what way? Are movements in one direction more common than movements in the opposite direction? Chandler and colleagues (2004) found that movements out of solo living are relatively infrequent, particularly as people get older. Hall et al (1999, p 284), using the longitudinal study[5] to compare those living alone in 1991 and 1981, found that 88% of those living alone in 1991 had not been living alone in 1981, showing that, at 10-year intervals, movements into solo living are frequent. These movements in and out of solo living were usually associated with household transitions and geographic mobility. Our analysis of 11 waves of the BHPS allows us to examine the dynamics of solo living, the extent and nature of transitions between solo living and living in households with others and variations by gender.

We saw earlier (Table 12.4) that solo living affects about one quarter of the cohort in our study over an 11-year period. Further analysis of the scale of transition for the population who have ever lived alone between 1991 and 2001 shows that about 70% of those who lived alone at some point will have made a household transition. Thus transitions are about twice as common as remaining alone permanently. Such transitions are more common for men than women, affecting 77% of men and 64% of women (Table 12.10) who have ever lived on their own over the relevant period, and the likelihood of making a transition is age sensitive, being more common for people of working age than above working age.

Conclusions

One person households have become a significant demographic group, whether measured in terms of people or households.

However, the very diversity and dynamism of the population of people living alone makes it impossible to label those living alone with one stereotype. The increase in people living alone may mean a redrawing of boundaries around 'family' and 'household'. Although those who live in one person households are, by definition, not in 'family households', this does not mean most solo livers see themselves as outside family boundaries. In fact, most remain family connected, keeping regular contact with relatives. However, women continue to do rather more keeping connected to relatives than men. There is no clear evidence of women being at the vanguard of the restructuring of family and gender boundaries through solo living.

Longitudinal analysis has shown that transitions in and out of solo living are much more frequent than cross-sectional surveys have suggested. Among younger age groups in particular, some of those who have moved from family households to solo living will move back to living in family households. Young men make more transitions than young women. Transitions in and out of solo living are complex. Such transitions are, in effect, crossing a family household/non-family household boundary and this study shows that such movements are quite commonplace. The scale of movement between one person and multiperson households is sufficiently significant to suggest that the study of family transitions needs to enlarge its frame of reference to include solo living as a source and destination of transition.

It is not clear if the greater flux of moving in and out of living alone across their adult life has reshaped the boundaries between youth and adulthood. If 'living alone' in circumstances other than bereavement or abandonment could be taken to mean the freedoms and selfishness of youth, then this experience is no longer confined to young people. However, with the exception of younger men, for the majority of people living alone, their route into solo living has involved an exit from a family household. Young men remain never partnered in larger numbers than young women. However, further research would be required before concluding that, therefore, young men are more likely to create selfish boundaries around themselves and to turn their backs on families.

A wider range of socioeconomic circumstance is found among those living alone, as with those living in households with others, but the majority are not enjoying a more privileged lifestyle in comparison to those living with others. Comparison of the housing circumstances of those who live alone and those who live with others shows that access to home ownership is lower, suggesting at least on this measure, some of those living alone lack some of the benefits of pooling household resources. Among those of working age, rates of economic inactivity are higher including the proportion unable to work.

Further questions and issues for research are suggested by this work, for example, a qualitative research agenda on the experience of living alone at different ages and places and for men and women. Which of those who live on their own see it as a choice? Who characterises living alone in positive and who in negative terms? How much conscious boundary and bridging work does living alone involve? In what ways and how does it vary according to living circumstances? Questions also arise as to the nature and extent of caring, and resource and risk pooling within wider kin networks and across households. The family is one of three welfare 'pillars' in society, that creates social solidarity through the reciprocity of its members (Esping-Andersen et al, 2002). Families and households are welfare providers as sources of care, income and resource pooling and redistribution, socialisation and social security more generally. Where families and households fail to provide these, challenges and demands are created for the other 'pillars' of welfare in society: markets and governments. Thus the growth of solo living presents a host of family policy questions and challenges, in particular, where such policies rest on assumptions about economies of scale, provision of care and pooling risk and resources within households. This applies to a number of policy domains, such as community care, health, housing and planning, income support, pensions, social care and employment. The growth in solo living may well have unintended or 'second order' consequences for wider social and family policies and the welfare state.

Notes

[1] This chapter is based on an ESRC-funded project, Solo Living across the Adult Lifecourse, carried out in 2004 by the authors.

[2] Helen Fielding (1996) *Bridget Jones's Diary*, London: Picador.

[3] Alan Warner (2002) *Morvern Callar*, London: Vintage.

[4] The BHPS has been carried out since 1991 and for the three most recent sweeps, 1999, 2000, and 2001, has had a boosted Scottish sample that allows for a standalone Scottish analysis. Here we present an analysis at a UK level based on 11 sweeps between 1991 and

2001. At the time of writing the 12th sweep had recently become available but is not included in this analysis.

[5] Their study also used the first four waves of the BHPS.

[6] In order to maximise the duration of the longitudinal sweep, in this analysis we only included respondents who were in the relevant age group for all sweeps and excluded those who met the age criteria for only some. Thus the effective age range moves from ages 30-63 in 1991 to ages 41-74 in 2001.

References

Bauman, Z. (1995) *Life in fragments: Essays in postmodern morality*, Oxford: Blackwell.

Beck, U. (1992) *Risk society: Towards a new modernity*, London: Sage Publications.

Bellah, R.N., Madsen, R., Sullivan, W.M., Swidler, A. and Tipton, S.M. (1985) *Habits of the heart: Individualism and commitment in American life*, Berkeley, CA: University of California Press.

Berthoud, R. and Gershuny, J. (eds) (2000) *Seven years in the lives of British families*, Bristol: The Policy Press.

Chandler, J., Williams, J., Maconachie, M., Collett, T. and Dodgeon, B. (2004) 'Living alone: its place in household formation and change', *Sociological Research Online*, vol 9, no 3, www.socresonline.org.uk/9/3/chandler.html

Edwards, R., Franklin, J. and Holland, J. (2003) *Families and social capital: Exploring the issues*, Families and Social Capital ESRC Research Group Working Paper no 1, London: South Bank University.

Esping-Andersen, G., Gallie, D., Hemerijk, A. and Myles, J. (2002) *Why we need a new welfare state*, Oxford: Oxford University Press.

GROS (General Register Office for Scotland) (2004) SCROL Scottish Census Online, www.scrol.gov.uk/scrol/browser/profile.jsp?profile= Householdand&Area=&mainLevel=, accessed 3 September 2004.

Giddens, A. (1992) *The transformation of intimacy*, Cambridge: Polity Press.

Giddens, A. (1998) *The third way: The renewal of democracy*, Cambridge: Polity Press.

Gordon, T. (1994) *Single women*, London: Macmillan.

Hall, R., Ogden, P.E. and Hill, C. (1999) 'Living alone: evidence from England, Wales and France for the last two decades', in S. McRae (ed) *Changing Britain: Families and households in the 1990s*, Oxford: Oxford University Press.

Heath, S. and Cleaver, E. (2003) *Young, free and single: Twenty-somethings and household change*, London: Macmillan.

Levin, I. (2004) 'Living apart together: a new family form', *Current Sociology*, vol 52, no 2, pp 223-40.

ONS (Office for National Statistics) (2003) *Census 2001: ONS National Report for England and Wales*, www.statistics.gov.uk/cci/nugget.asp?id=350

ONS (2004) *Living in Britain: The 2002 General Household Survey*, London: The Stationery Office.

Putnam, R.D. (2000) *Bowling alone: The collapse and revival of American Community*, New York, NY: Simon and Schuster.

Scottish Executive (2003) *Scotland's people volume 7: Results from the 2001/2002 Scottish Household Survey Annual Report*, Edinburgh: Scottish Executive, www.scotland.gov.uk/library5/finance/spv7-00.asp

Scottish Executive (2004) *Scotland's people: Results from the 2003 Scottish Household Survey Annual Report*, Edinburgh: Scottish Executive, www.scotland.gov.uk/library5/housing/shsar03-00.asp

Shaw, C. and Haskey, J. (1999) 'New estimates and projections of the population cohabiting in England and Wales', *Population Trends*, vol 95, p 7.

Skolnick, A. (1991) *Embattled paradise: The American family in an age of uncertainty*, New York, NY: Basic Books.

Taylor, M. F. (ed) (2004) *The British Household Panel Survey user manual volume A: Introduction, technical report and appendices*, Essex: Institute for Social and Economic Research, iserwww.essex.ac.uk/ulsc/bhps/doc/pdf_versions/, accessed 11 November 2004.

THIRTEEN

Boundaries of friendship

Graham Allan

Introduction

As other chapters in this book have shown, patterns of partnership, family and household constitution have altered quite dramatically over the last generation. In particular, partnership behaviour has changed with lower levels of marriage, higher rates of divorce and a far greater incidence of cohabitation (Allan and Crow, 2001). One consequence of this is the decreasing overlap between sex, marriage and birth, a trinity that had previously been strongly linked (Lewis and Kiernan, 1996). Importantly too, there are now more individuals living alone out of choice (see Wasoff, Jamieson and Smith in this volume) or who are sharing households with non-related others (Heath and Cleaver, 2003). With the rising numbers of stepfamilies, there are also more people living in 'family households' in which the kin relationships involved are potentially more contestable than was previously common. Moreover the 'family/kinship' connection of unregistered partnerships – the majority of cohabitations – is clearly also more problematic and contentious than the familial networks of those who are married.

One feature of these changes that is frequently highlighted is the greater uncertainty that now exists in different aspects of family membership. Whereas previously there was relative stability in family membership, this is no longer the case to anything like the same degree. The issue here is not that family relationships were constant or unaltered over time. The 'content' of these relationships obviously changed as people aged and developed different interdependencies and patterns of exchange. Rather the issue is the greater unpredictability that there now is about partnerships and lifecourse patterns, and the implications this has for family and household constitution. Changing practices of partnership formation and dissolution have been especially important in raising questions about cultural understandings of 'family', 'commitment' and the moral significance of individual happiness or satisfaction in the construction of the lifecourse (Giddens, 1991; Beck and Beck-Gersheim, 1995). To draw on Simpson's (1998) striking transposition, whereas once the stable *nu*clear family model captured family experience quite securely, increasingly the *un*clear family challenges our understandings of family cohesion and family boundaries.

While the sorts of change discussed here have resulted in more complex ideas of family boundedness emerging, they and other social and economic changes have also had an impact on understandings of friendship and its significance in the social lives we construct. Thus the growth of non-familial households, of gay and lesbian partnerships and of cohabitation more generally has led to increased attention being paid to friendship and other non-familial ties as forms of relationship that in some ways mirror, overlap or possibly replace the solidarities commonly associated with family ties (see, for example, Roseneil's chapter in this volume). So too the continuing decline of locality as a core element of many people's identities, increasing levels of short- and long-term geographical mobility and the development of new communication technologies have contributed to a perception that the realm of friendship is becoming more central to notions of self and in the management of everyday life (Allan, 2001). In some regards, the popularity of ideas about 'social capital' among politicians and policymakers also reflects this increased cultural awareness of the part that friendship plays in the maintenance of individual and social welfare (Puttnam, 2000; Phillipson et al, 2004).

While this chapter will not address the larger social transformations implied here, it will examine the nature of kinship and friendship in contemporary life, how they are constructed and the types of solidarity they entail. Given the concerns of this book, it will focus especially on the boundaries between friend and family relationships, the degree to which they are interchangeable and the distinctions that are made between them. Examining the boundaries and overlap between friendships and family ties will allow a better understanding of the ways in which informal ties and personal networks are shaped and developed. The main argument will be that despite significant changes, for most people the boundaries between family and friendship remain relatively well defined, with kin and non-kin relationships largely being understood as occupying different realms in their lives.

Constructing families

In order to consider these issues, it is useful to start by examining the nature of kinship and the ways in which 'families' are constructed. There is, of course, enormous variation in the details of this. As Finch and Mason (1993) have argued, family relationships are not rule bound or entirely norm governed but are emergent constructions in which past interactions, events, behaviour and knowledge shape current expectations. Nonetheless, there are common themes in what might be termed the routine character of kinship, common understandings that provide a backdrop within which ideas of 'family' and of appropriate family relationships are grounded. Two are of particular relevance here. First, there is the idea that family and kinship are something to do with common 'blood' and shared genetic makeup, which of itself contributes a sense of 'diffuse, enduring solidarity', to draw on Schneider's (1968) renowned phrase. Second, and clearly linked to this, is the idea of family and kinship ties forming an effective network. The relationships, in other words, cannot be regarded as 'standing alone'; instead each is linked to others in the kinship network with consequences for how each is organised and managed. Both of these features of 'family' warrant fuller discussion.

In developing his cultural account of American kinship representing 'diffuse, enduring solidarity', Schneider (1968) emphasised the principles of both 'blood' and 'marriage'. In the context of this chapter these can be taken as two defining criteria of 'family'. However, while marriage continues to be very important within family and kinship notions, changes in the demography of partnership formation and dissolution are having an impact on this. In particular, while ties of 'blood' continue to be seen as 'given' by nature and consequently unalterable, the rise in divorce, the growth of cohabitation as a form of partnership, together with increased numbers of children born outside marriage, make marriage a less certain basis of kinship than it once was. Significant issues arise, for example, about the family/kinship basis of blood relatives' non-married partners; about whether (and when) a child's ex-spouse (or ex-partner) remains family/kin; and about family/kinship connections to stepparents and their kin (Finch and Mason, 1993; Simpson, 1998; Hawker et al, 2001). In contrast, advances in DNA testing have tended to make issues of 'blood' connection appear more scientific and certain. Moreover, the policy emphasis in Britain and elsewhere on the lifelong obligations of biological parenting irrespective of partnership status may well further cement the prominence of genetics and 'blood' within routine understandings of kinship as enduring, if not always diffuse, solidarity.

The key issue here is that cultural constructions of family and kinship build on ideas of commonality and unity, with the idea of 'blood connection' representing and expressing this sense of unity and shared heritage very clearly. Family, in other words, is, like community, a term of inclusion and exclusion in which boundaries are of consequence. It reflects ideas about an in-group and an out-group, private and public spheres, an 'us' and a 'them'. The boundaries around 'family' are, of course, not 'set' or 'fixed'. They inevitably alter over time. Moreover, how they are perceived and presented depends on context. On different occasions, 'my family' – or indeed, 'our family' – will signify different collectivities of others. But whoever is involved, the point is that 'family' is not to be understood simply as a set of individual relationships connecting diverse people. It reflects a sense of more or less bounded unity between people who have a kinship in common, who are a family. This is not to idealise family life. As implied above, different members will have different ideas of who is and who is not included; the rise in divorce, remarriage and stepfamilies ensures this. There will also be disagreements and tensions between some of those involved, at least some of the time. Nonetheless, 'family' encapsulates a shared heritage, a collectivity of relationships and an element of commonality.

This is closely linked to the second theme about family being emphasised here: the idea that kinship operates as an effective network of relationships. There are a number of dimensions to this, although the overall issue is the way in which individual relationships are tied into other relationships through mechanisms inherent to the network structure. For example, the network characteristics of kinship typically ensure that news, information and gossip about family members flow readily between members, keeping them abreast of circumstances and events in each other's lives. Mothers in particular often perform this sort of 'kin keeper' role, in the process helping to sustain a sense of 'family'. Equally, however, the network structure facilitates a more active involvement between the members. Again, kin keepers can be effective in organising and arranging occasions that bring family members together. For example, if a geographically more distant sibling is visiting their parents, arrangements are often made for other siblings to be there at the same time. Similarly, family celebrations – birthdays, Christmas and the like – are usually organised in a manner that facilitates collective interaction.

There is, of course, nothing remarkable in these network influences on family solidarity. It is simply the way families are. Yet sociologically they are an important element within the construction of family. Of themselves, they render family relationships distinct from most – although not all – other relationships that are not so embedded in tight-knit network structures. Not only do these network features allow for knowledge of different members to be shared and for control to be exercised, they also foster the sense of collectivity referred to earlier. They help sustain the boundaries around 'family' that mark these relationships off from other types of tie. Moreover, by encouraging a continuing involvement, the positioning of family relationships within comparatively tight-knit networks contributes to the construction of family as enduring and 'inalienable' or at least as normally involving a different level of solidarity than can routinely be expected among those who are not family and share no blood connection.

Friendship

Although friendship, like family and kinship, can be regarded as belonging to the realm of informal and personal relationships, the solidarities normally involved are distinct from those of family (although see Roseneil, this volume). Certainly, neither of the aforementioned points applies to friendships. There is no cultural perception of friendship as involving anything as natural or inalienable as 'blood', neither is there normally an established, tightly knit network in which the friendship is located. In these regards, friendships are typically more 'free floating' than kinship, although, of course, this does not mean that friendship ties are therefore structurally 'disembedded'. As Adams and Allan (1998) have argued, the patterning of particular friendships, and of friendships networks more generally, are influenced by the social and economic contexts in which they develop.

Here it is worth reflecting briefly on the different status of friendship and kinship labels. Kinship terms are essentially 'categorical' ones and not dependent on the nature of the relationship that exists. In other words, kinship terms do not, of themselves, describe a particular quality or content of relationships – brothers, for example, may be highly involved with one another or they may meet rarely; they may feel a strong sense of mutual commitment or they may feel quite distant from each other. By the same token, the term 'friend' (and other equivalent labels) are 'relational' ones (Allan, 1989). The terms are only appropriate when the relational content is of a sufficient quality. Consequently, while a brother or a cousin remains as such no matter what the nature of their personal relationship, friends are only friends to the extent that they perceive their relationship to be of a given character. If gradually or otherwise it ceases to be so, then the friendship itself is likely to be questioned. It may take some time for this to happen, but if the necessary solidarity between the individuals is undermined, then the friendship is eroded.

As indicated, friendships also take a number of forms. This is likely to be so within any individual's friendship network. Some friends will be more important than others; for instance, some will have been known for longer, some will be seen more often, some trusted more. But equally different individuals may organise their friendships differently. Thus, in an early work examining the part friendship played in different family and community studies, Allan (1979) argued that there were class differences in the ways in which sociability was normally patterned. In particular, for reasons to do with their material circumstances, working-class sociability was more contextually bounded than middle-class friendship. Middle-class individuals tended to develop their friendships by 'decontextualising' the relationships, often using visiting and entertaining in the home as a key way of doing this (Allan, 1998). Those from working-class backgrounds were more likely to define sociability in terms of more specific and restricted interactional settings, with attempts only rarely made to include people from these settings in other spheres of their lives. Two consequences followed from this. First, the term 'friend' sat uneasily with this pattern, with the term 'mate' being far more commonly used. Second, and more importantly here, being so dependent on particular interactional settings, these 'mateships' usually became inactive if one or other individual ceased, for whatever reason, to be involved in the activities of that setting.

While the processes involved are most evident with mateships organised in this way, changes in friendships are far more routine than common ideological models of friendship, with their emphasis on 'best friends', usually imply (Allan, 1989). Because all modes of friendships are 'relational' in the way discussed earlier, changes in their 'content' can undermine the basis of their solidarity. This occurs especially whenever people's social or economic circumstances alter significantly. As with mateships, in part this can result from their no longer being able to participate in the settings in which the friendships were routinely activated and 'serviced'. This often results in the management of these friendships becoming more problematic; what was once easy and taken for granted becomes more difficult to negotiate. Take, for example, friendships made at work. Even if they are enacted in other settings as well, interaction at work is still likely to provide ready-made opportunities for expressing continuing solidarity. If that ceases, then in effect the friendships need a more determined effort if they are to be sustained. While attempts may be made to do this, the friendships are liable to fade in importance as shared experiences become less common and servicing the relationships more difficult.

Friendships are also liable to alter when people's social position changes. Because friendship is a relationship of equality, in terms of both exchange and status, those who are friends tend to occupy broadly similar positions to one another. When this status equivalence alters, the friendships involved are often undermined. For example, it is regularly reported that marked shifts occur in people's friendship networks following divorce or widowhood. There is a tendency, in particular, for previous friendships with married others to become more difficult to manage, in large part because of problems of maintaining balance and reciprocity. The longer-run outcome is that these friendships gradually wane with new, now more congruent, friendships emerging with people who are also 'uncoupled'. Equally, when individuals gain promotion or otherwise change their occupational status, this is routinely accompanied by changes in the personnel of their friendship networks, with friends congruent with the new status tending to replace those who are not (Allan, 1989).

Changes in friendships over time are quite normal. There is nothing exceptional about this; it is a routine aspect of the organisation of friendship in contemporary society. While accounts of friendship often idealise the commitment that 'true' friends have for one another, the mundane reality is that friendship ties are typically not that enduring. Sometimes they end as a consequence of significant disagreement, but far more frequently they simply fade as people's circumstances alter and as interaction becomes more difficult to manage. Of course, some friendships survive even though they now no longer involve regular exchange. However, this is comparatively rare, and of itself is usually taken as a signifier of the special – and peculiar – solidarity these ties entail. They have stood the test of time; they are the 'real' or 'true' friendships. Interestingly this point is often emphasised through the symbolism of kinship: "She's like a sister to me". However, most friendships are simply not like this. They are more contingent as well as more mundane and, as a result, less liable to endure as circumstances alter.

Friends as family

As mentioned earlier, the broad demographic changes there have been over the last 30 years in lifecourse options and patterns, including aspects of sexual expression, partnership formation and household composition, have raised questions about the extent to which ties of friendship might be replacing ties of kinship. This is most evident in some of the literature on the 'family' life of those who identify as gay and lesbian. In particular, there have been debates about the extent to which 'families of choice' have replaced families of birth in people's solidarities, commitments and obligations (Weston, 1991; Weeks et al, 2001; Roseneil, this volume). In line with other ideas of individualisation in late modernity, the argument is that people now have more freedom and choice than they did to negotiate which family and kinship ties they wish to honour and which they do not. They are no longer embedded to the degree they once were in close-knit networks in which family connection dominated and the boundaries between family and non-family were strongly policed (Crow and Allan, 1994).

Social networks have become more dispersed and more fragmented. This has been captured well by Pescosolido and Rubin (2000) in their analysis of the character of affiliations in contemporary society. Essentially, their argument is that contemporary shifts in economic and social life, involving greater flexibility and impermanence, have led increasingly to the emergence of a 'spoke' model of social network formation in which individuals are linked to a range of "connected but distinct social circles with some circles only loosely bound" rather than being embedded in a more integrated, overlapping network structure (Pescosolido and Rubin, 2000, p 62). As a result, the social controls that family members can collectively operate over each other have been lessened. With the decline of 'solidaristic' kinship networks, a greater propensity has opened up for individuals to 'select' those family members with whom they feel most comfortable and to pay less heed to those with whom they feel little or no compatibility.

If in this way the honouring of family and kinship ties becomes more a matter of individual selection and choice, the possibility has also been opened up for others, unrelated in a standard kinship sense, to be regarded as family. Such a possibility has long been recognised in the way that some families create 'honorary' or 'fictive' kin: people who, through their involvement and commitment, are treated 'as if family' despite having no kinship connection as such (Firth et al, 1970). However, the idea of 'families of choice' represents more than this. Rather than treating an individual who demonstrates particular solidarity to members of a family group as (to some extent) a member of the family, 'families of choice' suggests that 'family' itself can be constructed around non-kinship connection. In other words, the argument is that the forms of solidarity and commitment that culturally were previously understood as premised on 'blood' and marriage are now liable to be found among others where there is no such kinship link. Conversely solidarity and commitment between those who are 'blood' or 'marriage' related is no longer as 'mandated' or 'compulsory' as it was.

Yet, while elements of these ideas resonate with aspects of people's experiences, there are few grounds for thinking that the boundary between friendship and family/kinship is becoming *intrinsically* blurred. For some individuals this does, of course, happen. For a variety of reasons – separation/divorce, lifestyle divergence, emotional rejection, religious conversion – they may become estranged from some or all segments of their family and instead feel a strong and enduring commitment to particular friends. But for most people the evidence suggests that the domains of family and friendship remain relatively distinct. This does not mean that friends and family do not mix. Indeed, with greater affluence over the last two generations and an increased focus on the material and symbolic construction of the 'home' as an element of personal identity, the propensity to keep kin and non-kin separate has if anything been reduced. Nonetheless, for most people the demarcation between 'family' and 'non-family' remains comparatively clear, as it does in law. These ties continue to involve different solidarities, different expectations and different consequences.

In particular, the sense of obligation there is to genealogically closer family remains distinct for most people from the obligations experienced towards their friends. Thus, although negotiable (Finch and Mason, 1993), the claims that parents, children and siblings can make of each other and the commitments that are honoured are of a different order than those that friends make. As with Parsonian arguments about the prioritisation of the nuclear family, this does not mean that friends never make such claims on each other (Harris, 1983). It simply means that the commitment to family members is normally given priority and, indeed, that different types of obligation are expressed. The support offered and accepted between friends is usually, although not always, more limited and short term, with the patterns of reciprocation being organised differently. There is, of course, a wide range in the commitment and solidarity that friends feel towards one another. Some especially strong friendships can provide high levels of emotional and other forms of support. Nonetheless, in comparison to family ties, friendship is normally marked by a higher degree of reciprocity. That is, most friendships are built on an evident equivalence of exchange in which both sides routinely try to sustain a balance. Becoming too indebted to a friend runs counter to the cultural conventions governing friendship.

In contrast, family relationships do not involve the same emphasis on equality, balance and reciprocity as friendships. As a result, the levels of support received from family generally differs from that usually given by friends. Certainly it seems to be family members who commonly provide longer-term support and practical aid when it is needed. For example, research on care provision for infirm elderly people has consistently emphasised that family members are at the forefront of informal care provision, with friends rarely playing a major part practically (see, for instance, Clarke, 1995; Qreshi and Walker, 1989). Moreover, it would seem that where non-kin are active in providing this form of support, it is often at a relatively low level. As the need for care increases, so family members are likely to become more responsible for its provision, with friends, in turn, tending to leave these matters to 'family' who culturally are seen as the 'rightful' carers. Equally, studies have shown how other family members are considerably more involved in providing support to parents with disabled children than friends are. Aside from difficulties in servicing friendships because of the demands such caring makes, it would seem parents are often reluctant to accept support from friends precisely because of the difficulty of finding ways to reciprocate.

From a different perspective, recent work examining people's personal networks have also indicated that family and friends tend to occupy different social spaces. In particular, studies drawing on Antonucci's (Antonucci and Akiyama, 1987, 1995) techniques for mapping what she refers to as 'social convoys' have illustrated the different significance people attach to family and friends. The technique involves asking people to place those they know on a diagram of concentric circles, with those they feel most close to placed nearer the centre of the rings. The utility of the technique is that it facilitates discussion of the comparative significance of different relationships. While there is wide variation in the mappings produced, there are also consistencies in the patterns that emerge. In particular, it is evident that people typically fill the innermost ring with family members – husbands or wives, partners, children, siblings and/or parents. The outer rings tend to be populated more with friends, colleagues and workmates. In the discussions that are reported there appears to be a strong moral sense that family 'should' be located centrally, even when the relationships seem on the surface not to be particularly active (see for example, Phillipson et al, 2000; Pahl and Spencer, 2004a, 2004b). If nothing else, the consistent placing of these family ties in the centre of people's mappings can be understood as representing the recognition of difference in their ordering of family and friendship ties.

Conclusion

There have undoubtedly been significant changes in the patterning of personal relationships over the last two generations. These are most evident in aspects of family and household composition where changes in marriage, cohabitation and divorce have had a high impact. But equally there have been shifts in non-family relationships too. In particular, the sorts of structural change associated with late modernity have generated altered patterns of embeddedness within personal networks. As discussed earlier, Pescosolido and Rubin's (2000) arguments that a 'spoke' model of network constellation has become dominant represents one way of understanding these changes in the structure of people's informal relationships. Certainly people's social identities now appear to be less circumscribed by family and kinship connection than they previously were with friendships and other non-kin ties seeming to be increasingly important in the lifestyles that people are constructing.

Yet while the boundaries between family and non-family may be less firmly marked than they once were, this does not mean that they no longer exist or are of little consequence for people's lives. While changing patterns of partnership formation and dissolution have made the issue of who counts as a family member more contestable and complex, the vast majority of the population continue to accept that the solidarity and commitment occurring between family members differs significantly from the solidarity and commitment normally found between friends. The expectations that members of families can legitimately have of one another and the demands that they can make would be considered far more questionable within friendship. Of course there may be times in people's lives when friends become particularly significant. Arguably, young adulthood, the phase prior to 'settling down' into a longer-term partnership but after leaving home, may be such a phase, especially if it involves living in shared housing (Heath and Cleaver, 2003). But for most people most of the time, there is a clear division in their expectations of friends and of family.

In other words, the boundaries between the domains of family and friend continue to be important within people's constructions of their personal networks. It may be that some aspects of 'family' become increasingly problematic and, in Simpson's (1998) term 'unclear', with higher levels of committed partnership breakdown and higher numbers of stepfamilies. In this context, it is possible that different emphases will emerge governing the boundaries of family and kinship. However, there is little evidence that for most people this will entail the acceptance of a fully 'social' model of family in which membership has no bearing on established principles of kinship. For most, family will continue to be about 'blood', even if the role of 'partnership/marriage' becomes more contingent. Thus, while the boundaries around the two spheres may be less pronounced than they were, the domains of family and friendship are likely to remain discrete within most people's understandings of their 'micro-social worlds' (Pahl and Spencer, 2004a).

References

Adams, R. and Allan, G. (1998) 'Contextualising friendship', in R. Adams and G. Allan (eds) *Placing friendship in context*, Cambridge: Cambridge University Press.

Allan, G. (1979) *A sociology of friendship and kinship*, London: Allen and Unwin.

Allan, G. (1989) *Friendship: Developing a sociological perspective*, Hemel Hempstead: Harvester Wheatsheaf.

Allan, G. (1998) 'Friendship and the private sphere', in R. Adams and G. Allan (eds) *Placing friendship in context*, Cambridge: Cambridge University Press.

Allan, G. (2001) 'Personal relationships in late modernity', *Personal Relationships*, vol 8, pp 325-39.

Allan, G. and Crow, G. (2001) *Families, households and society*, Basingstoke: Palgrave.

Antonucci, T. and Akiyama, H. (1987) 'Social networks in adult life: a preliminary examination of the convoy model', *Journal of Gerontology*, vol 4, pp 519-27.

Antonucci, T. and Akiyama, H. (1995) 'Convoys of social relations: family and friendship within a life span context', in R. Blieszner and V. Hilkevitch Bedford (eds) *Handbook of aging and the family*, Westport, CT: Greenward Press.

Beck, U. and Beck-Gersheim, E. (1995) *The normal chaos of love*, Cambridge: Polity Press.

Clarke, L. (1995) 'Family care and changing family structure', in I. Allen and E. Perkins (eds) *The future of family care for older people*, London: HMSO.

Crow, G. and Allan, G. (1994) *Community life*, Hemel Hempstead: Harvester Wheatsheaf.

Finch, J. and Mason, J. (1993) *Negotiating family responsibilities*, London: Routledge.

Firth, R., Hubert, J. and Forge, A. (1970) *Families and their relatives*, London: Routledge and Kegan Paul.

Giddens, A. (1991) *The transformation of intimacy*, Cambridge: Polity Press.

Harris, C.C. (1983) *The family in industrial society*, London: Allen and Unwin.

Hawker, S., Allan, G. and Crow, G. (2001) 'La multiplication des grands-parents', in C. Attius-Donfut and M. Segalen (eds) *Le siècle des grand-parents: Une géneration phare, ici et ailleurs*, Paris: Autrement.

Heath, S. and Cleaver, E. (2003) *Young, free, and single? Twenty-somethings and household change*, Basingstoke: Palgrave.

Lewis, J. and Kiernan, K. (1996) 'The boundaries between marriage, non-marriage, and parenthood', *Journal of Family History*, vol 67, pp 372-87.

Pahl, R. and Spencer, L. (2004a) 'Capturing personal communities', in C. Phillipson, G. Allan and D. Morgan (eds) *Social networks and social exclusion*, Aldershot: Aldgate.

Pahl, R. and Spencer, L. (2004b) 'Personal communities: not simply families of "fate" or "choice"', *Contemporary Sociology*, vol 52, pp 199-221.

Pescosolido, B. and Rubin, B. (2000) 'The web of group affiliations revisited: social life, postmodernism, and sociology', *American Sociological Review*, vol 65, pp 52-76.

Phillipson, C., Allan, G. and Morgan, D. (eds) (2004) *Social networks and social exclusion*, Aldershot: Aldgate.

Phillipson, C., Bernard, M., Ogg, J. and Phillips, J. (2000) *Family and community life of older people*, London: Routledge.

Puttnam, R. (2000) *Bowling alone: The collapse and revival of American community*, New York, NY: Simon and Schuster.

Qreshi, H. and Walker, A. (1989) *The caring relationship*, Basingstoke: Macmillan.

Schneider, D. (1968) *American kinship: A cultural account*, Englewood Cliffs, NJ: Prentice Hall.

Simpson, B. (1998) *Changing families*, London: Berg.

Weeks, J., Heaphy, B. and Donovan, C. (2001) *Same sex intimacies: Families of choice and other life experiments*, London: Routledge.

Weston, K. (1991) *Families we choose: Lesbians, gays and kinship*, Albany, NY: Columbia University Press.

FOURTEEN

Living and loving beyond the boundaries of the heteronorm: personal relationships in the 21st century

Sasha Roseneil

Introduction

In the west, at the start of the 21st century, more and more people are spending longer periods of their lives outside the conventional family unit.[1] Processes of individualisation are challenging the romantic, heterosexual couple and the modern family formation it has supported. The normative grip of the sexual and gender order that has underpinned the modern family is weakening. In this context, much that matters to people in their personal lives increasingly takes place beyond the boundaries of 'the family', between partners who are not living together 'as family', and within networks of friends.

This chapter pushes at the boundaries of existing ways of thinking in the sociologies of family and personal relationships. It develops a queer analytic for the study of personal relationships, which is grounded in an appreciation of the variety of ways in which people live outside the heteronorm. Its central argument is that if we are to understand the current state, and likely future, of personal relationships, sociologists should decentre the family and the heterosexual couple in our intellectual imaginaries. Far more of people's affective life has probably always taken place outside the boundaries of the family than sociology has recognised and social change is increasing the importance of extra-familial relationships.[2] The first section of the chapter provides a critique of sociology for the heteronormative frameworks within which it has studied personal relationships. The second section then proposes an extension of the framework for the analysis of contemporary transformations in the realm of intimacy, arguing for the importance of a queer analysis of social change, and suggests that there is a need for research focusing on those who are at the cutting edge of these processes of social change. The chapter ends with an overview of the findings of my research on the relationship practices of those who are living and loving beyond the heteronorm.

Thinking beyond the heteronormative family

As the global success of a plethora of television series such as 'Friends', 'Seinfeld', 'Ellen', and 'Will and Grace' attests, popular culture is proving rather better than sociology at proffering stories that explore the burgeoning diversity of personal lives. In each of these programmes it is the sociability of a group of friends, rather than a conventional family, that provides the love, care and support essential to everyday life in the city. The popularity of these programmes suggests that they speak in significant ways to the lives of their viewers. Yet, if we seek our understanding of relationships from the sociological literature, it seems as if love, intimacy and care are almost exclusively practised under the auspices of 'family'.

There *have* been significant shifts within specific subfields of the sociologies of family and gender. For example, they have sought to meet both the empirical challenge of changes in family and gender relations, and the theoretical challenge of anti-essentialist, postmodern, black and minority ethnic feminist and lesbian and gay emphases on difference and diversity. They have, most notably, moved on from an early focus on the study of 'family and community', which were "yoked together like Siamese twins" (Morgan, 1996, p 4), through the early phase of feminist intervention, which focused on unequal gender divisions of care and intimacy in the family,[3] to a predominant concern today with the analysis of family change – particularly through the study of divorce, re-partnering and cohabitation – and recognition of family diversity.[4]

Moreover, many family sociologists have engaged with the problem of the concept of 'family', in a time of increasing levels of family breakdown and re-formation. David Morgan (1996), for instance, suggests that we should use 'family' not as a noun, but as an adjective, and proposes a notion of 'family practices' to counter the reification of the concept. Others have sought to deal with social change and the challenges posed by lesbian and gay movements and theorists by pluralising the notion of 'family', so that they now always speak of 'families'. The approach currently dominant in

Anglo-American sociologies of gender and family emphasises the diversity of family forms and experiences and how the membership of families changes over time, as they break down and re-form. Certainly, in its more liberal-minded incarnations, this approach welcomes lesbian and gay 'families of choice' into the 'family tent' (Stacey, 2002, 2004).

This shift has been an important one. It acts as a counter to the explicitly anti-gay and anti-feminist political discourse of 'family values', which developed in the US and UK during the 1980s and 1990s.[5] However, these moves to pluralise notions of 'family', even when they embrace the study of lesbian and gay families, are insufficient to the task of understanding the full range of contemporary formations of personal life for two reasons. First, they leave unchanged the heteronormativity of the sociological imaginary; and, second, they are grounded in an inadequate analysis of contemporary social change. We need to move beyond the boundaries of conventional sociological thinking about family/families, to develop new ways of conceptualising the heterogeneity of contemporary intimate life.

Sociology continues to marginalise the study of love, intimacy and care beyond the 'family', even though it has expanded the scope covered by this term to include a wider range of 'families of choice'.[6] The discipline is undergirded by heteronormative assumptions; in other words by "institutions, structures of understanding and practical orientations that make heterosexuality seem not only coherent – that is, organised as a sexuality – but also privileged" (Berlant and Warner 2000, p 312). Researchers still produce analyses that are overwhelmingly focused on monogamous, dyadic, co-residential (and primarily hetero) sexual relationships, particularly those that have produced children, and on changes within these relationships. Jo Van Every's (1999) systematic survey of British sociological research and writing on families and households published in 1993 found "an overwhelming focus on the 'modern nuclear family' " consisting of married couples who lived together in households only with their children. She argues convincingly that "despite all the sociological talk about the difficulty of defining families and the plurality and diversity of family forms in contemporary (postmodern?) societies, sociologists were helping to construct a 'normal' family which looked remarkably similar to that which an earlier generation of sociologists felt confident to define" (1999, p 167). In other words, researchers remain constrained within the boundaries of the conventional family.

The 'non-standard intimacies' (Berlant and Warner, 2000) created by those living non-normative sexualities pose a particular challenge to a discipline that has studied personal life primarily through the study of families. Some lesbians and gay men refer to their emotional networks quite consciously – often with a knowing irony – as 'family'.[7] However, when writers such as Kath Weston (1991), Jeffrey Weeks et al (2001) and Judith Stacey (2004) adopt the term 'families of choice' to refer to lesbian and gay relationships and friendship networks, this may actually direct attention away from the extra-familial, radically counter-heteronormative nature of many of these relationships.

Considerable evidence from sociological and anthropological research suggests that friendship is particularly important to lesbians and gay men.[8] Networks of friends form the context within which lesbians and gay men lead their personal lives, offering emotional continuity, companionship, pleasure and practical assistance. Sometimes rejected, problematised and excluded by their families of origin, lesbians and gay men build and maintain lives outside the framework of the heterosexual nuclear family, grounding their emotional security and daily lives in their friendship groups. Weeks et al (2001) and Roseneil (2000a) draw attention to the blurring of the boundaries and movement between friendship and sexual relationships that often characterises contemporary lesbian and gay intimacies. Friends become lovers, lovers become friends and many have multiple sexual partners of varying degrees of commitment (and none). Indeed, an individual's 'significant other' may not be someone with whom she or he has a sexual relationship. Non-heteronormative intimacies – significant, life-defining relationships between friends, non-monogamous lovers, ex-lovers, partners who do not live together, partners who do not have sex together, those who do not easily fit the 'friend'/'lover' binary classification system – and the networks of relationships within which these intimacies are sustained (or not) have the following significance: they decentre the primary significance that is commonly granted to sexual partnerships and they mount a challenge to the privileging of conjugal relationships in research on intimacy. These practices, relationships and networks largely fail to be registered in a sociological literature that retains an image that, without ever explicitly acknowledging it, sees the heterosexual couple as the heart of the social formation, as that which pumps the lifeblood of social reproduction.

Sociology's tendency to fuse the study of (hetero)sex and intimacy means that the discipline fails to accord real attention to non-sexual intimacies or to sexual relationships outside the conjugal couple model.

In fact, little has changed since Beth Hess pointed out in 1979 that there is "no large corpus called the 'sociology of friendship'"[9] to provide an alternative archive for the study of intimacy and care beyond the family. But it is not just the heteronormativity of the discipline that has rendered friendship largely invisible. Equally important is the fact that the sociological tradition, from the founding fathers onwards – Tonnies's distinction between Gemeinschaft and Gesellschaft, Marx's work on alienation, Durkheim on forms of social solidarity, Weber on bureaucratisation, the Chicago school on urbanisation – has assumed that the development of modernity renders social relationships increasingly impersonal and affective bonding is seen as increasingly marginal. The result is that the discipline has never granted as much importance to the study of informal, private and sociable relationships as it has to matters of public, economic and political organisation.[10]

Friendship lies in the realm of the pleasurable, emotional and affective, areas that have been relatively neglected by serious-minded, order-seeking sociologists concerned with issues of structure, regulation and institutionalisation. There have been exceptions, as in the ethnographic work of Whyte (1943) on 'street corner society', as in the work of Simmel (1950), of Litwak and Szelenyi (1969) on 'primary groups' of kin and friends, and in the 1950s and 1960s, in the British tradition of community studies (eg Young and Willmott, 1957 and Willmott and Young, 1967). More recently there has been a small number of studies of friendship,[11] and there is a growing field of research on new forms of sociability facilitated by new technologies,[12] but there is no subfield of the discipline devoted to the study of friendship comparable to the well-established sociology of family and kinship. It is time for this to change, time for more research that focuses on friendship, 'non-conventional' forms of sexual/love relationships, the boundaries and the interconnections between the two.

Queer social change and the analysis of contemporary personal life

A substantial body of literature takes as its starting point the belief that we are living through a period of profound social change in the organisation of contemporary personal life. For example, in the context of a wider argument about the undoing of patriarchalism, Manuel Castells (1997) suggests that the patriarchal family is under intense challenge and that lesbian, gay and feminist movements around the world are key to understanding this challenge. Anthony Giddens' (1992) argument about the 'transformation of intimacy' and Ulrich Beck and Elisabeth Beck-Gernsheim's (1995, 2002) work on the changing meanings and practices of love and family relationships suggest that, in the contemporary world processes of individualisation, detraditionalisation and increased self-reflexivity are opening up new possibilities and expectations in heterosexual relationships.[13]

With a (rather cursory) nod in the direction of feminist scholarship and activism, such work recognises the significance of the shifts in gender relations mainly due to the changed consciousness and identities that women have developed in the wake of the women's liberation movement. Giddens considers that the transformation of intimacy currently in train is of "great, and generalizable, importance" (1992, p 2). He charts changes in the nature of marriage such as the emergence of the "pure relationship" characterised by "confluent love", a relationship of sexual and emotional equality between men and women. He links this with the development of "plastic sexuality" freed from "the needs of reproduction" (1992, p 2). He identifies lesbians and gay men as 'pioneers' in the pure relationship and plastic sexuality and hence at the forefront of processes of individualisation and detraditionalisation.[14] Beck and Beck-Gernsheim argue that "the ethic of individual self-fulfilment and achievement is the most powerful current in modern society" (2002, p 22). They believe that the desire to be "a deciding, shaping human being who aspires to be the author of his/her life" is giving rise to unprecedented changes in the shape of family life. Family membership shifts from being a given to a matter of choice. As social ties become reflexive and individualisation increasingly characterises relations among members of the same family, we are moving into a world of the 'post-familial family' (Beck-Gernsheim, 1998).

While this body of work perhaps overstates the degree of change and underplays the continuance of gender inequalities and class differences in intimate life (for instance, Jamieson, 1998), it maps the theoretical terrain from which investigations of the future of personal life must proceed However, this body of literature does not exhaust the resources for theoretical analysis of contemporary social change on which those seeking to understand cultures of intimacy and care should draw. It is important that we consider also how the wider sexual organisation of the social is undergoing transformation. I have argued elsewhere (Roseneil, 2000b, 2002) that we are currently witnessing a significant destabilisation of the homosexual/heterosexual binary that has characterised the modern sexual order. I have proposed that there are a number of 'queer tendencies'[15] at work in the contemporary world that are contributing to this fracturing of the binary. For example, there is a trend towards the 'normalisation' of the homosexual (Bech, 1999) in most western nations, as there are progressive moves towards the equalisation of legal and social conditions for lesbians and gay men.[16] The passing in the UK of the Civil Partnerships Act in 2004 is one of the most obvious examples of this, granting as it does a legal status close to marriage for lesbian and gay couples who choose to register their partnership. This brings some lesbians and gay men institutionally much closer to the heteronorm, and marks a significant shift in public understandings of the notion of a conjugal couple. Homosexual and heterosexual ways of life thus become less marked as different by law, social policy and in public culture.[17]

Most significantly, for my argument here, there is a tendency towards the decentring of heterorelations, both socially and at the level of the individual. The heterosexual couple, and particularly the married, co-resident heterosexual couple with children, no longer occupies the centre-ground of western societies and cannot be taken for granted as the basic unit in society. This is a result of the dramatic rise in divorce rates over the past 30 years, the increase in the number of births outside marriage (and to a lesser extent outside any lasting heterosexual relationship – births to mothers who are 'single by choice'), the rise in the proportion of children being brought up by a lone parent, the growing proportion of households that are composed of one person and the climbing proportion of women who are not having children. Individuals are being released from traditional heterosexual scripts and the patterns of heterorelationality that accompany them. In 2003, only 22% of households in the UK comprised a heterosexual couple with dependent children (National Statistics, 2005) and broadly similar patterns are observable across Europe, North America and Australia.[18]

Postmodern living arrangements are diverse, fluid and unresolved, constantly chosen and rechosen and heterorelations are no longer as hegemonic as once they were. We are experiencing the 'queering of the family' (Stacey, 1996), as meanings of family undergo radical challenge and more and more kinship groups have to come to terms with the diverse sexual practices and living arrangements chosen by their own family members. At the start of the 21st century there can be few families that do not include at least some members who diverge from traditional, normative heterorelational practice, whether as divorcees, unmarried mothers and fathers, lesbians, gay men or bisexuals. As I shall show later in the chapter, at the level of individual experience, as heterorelations are decentred, friendship networks become more important in people's everyday lives and the degree of significance and emotional investment placed in romantic coupling comes to be re-evaluated.

This queering of the social calls into question the normativity and naturalness of both heterosexuality and heterorelationality. It increasingly means that ways of life that might previously have been regarded as distinctively 'homosexual' are becoming more widespread.[19] Giddens' rather throwaway remark that lesbians and gay men are forging new paths for heterosexuals as well as for themselves is picked up by Jeffrey Weeks, Catherine Donovan and Brian Heaphy who suggest that "one of the most remarkable features of domestic change over recent years is ... the emergence of common patterns in both homosexual and heterosexual ways of life as a result of these long-term shifts in relationship patterns" (Weeks et al, 1999, p 85). They see both homosexuals and heterosexuals increasingly yearning for a 'pure relationship', experiencing love as contingent and confluent and seeking to live their sexual relationships in terms of a friendship ethic (Weeks et al, 2001).

What this suggests is that there is a need for more research exploring the personal relationships of those who are in the avant garde of these processes of social change. The 'Care, friendship and non-conventional partnership project' set out to do just that.

Living and loving beyond the heteronorm

The 'Care, friendship and non-conventional partnership project'[20] investigated how the most 'individualised' in our society – people who do not live with a partner – construct their networks of intimacy, friendship, care and support. The project explored who matters to people who are living outside conventional families, what they value about their personal relationships, how they care for those who matter to them and how they care for themselves. We carried out in-depth interviews with 53 people aged between 25 and 60 in three locations: a former mining town that is relatively conventional in terms of gender and family relations; a small town in which alternative, middle-class, 'downshifted' lifestyles and sexual non-conformity are common; and a multi-ethnic inner-city area characterised by a range of gender and family practices, a higher-than-average proportion of women in the labour force and a large number of single person and non-couple households. We talked to men and women with and without children, of a diversity of ages, ethnic origins, occupations and sexual orientations and with varying relationship status and living arrangements. This gave us detailed insight into the texture of people's emotional lives.

Across a range of lifestyles and sexualities, we found evidence of three interesting and interrelated relationship practices:

(1) a prioritising of friendship;
(2) a decentring of sexual/love relationships within individuals' life narratives;
(3) experimenting beyond heteronormative conjugality.

Friendship occupied a central place in the personal lives of our interviewees. Whether they were in a heterosexual couple relationship or not, the people we interviewed were turning to friends for emotional support. Jools, a heterosexual woman of 28 from the former mining town, spoke for many people when she said: "I think a friendship is for life, but I don't think a partner is ... I'd marry my friends. They'd last longer". There was a high degree of reliance on friends, as opposed to biological kin and sexual partners, particularly for the provision of care and support in everyday life and friendship operated as a key value and a site of ethical practice for many. Far from being isolated, solitary individuals who flit from one unfulfilling relationship to another, most of the people we interviewed were enmeshed in complex networks of intimacy and care and had strong commitments and connections to others. In contrast to the mythology of the singleton in desperate search for a marriage partner – exemplified by Bridget Jones – very few showed any yearning to be part of a conventional couple or family. A great many, both of those with partners and of those without, were consciously placing less emphasis on the importance of the couple relationship. Instead, they were centring their lives on their friends. Of those with partners, almost all had *chosen* not to live together. Very few saw cohabitation as the inevitable and desirable next stage of their relationship and were thus implicitly challenging the heteronormative expectation that a sexual relationship moves in a predetermined direction towards cohabitation and 'settling down'.

Many of the interviewees had experienced the ending of a marriage or a long-term cohabiting relationship and the pain and disruption this had caused had made them question the wisdom of putting all their emotional eggs in one basket. Only one of the interviewees saw her partner as the most important person in her life, to the exclusion of others. She was a recent migrant to Britain whose family lived overseas. For everyone else, the people who mattered were either friends or a combination of friends, partner, children and family. This was not a temporary phase and people did not return to conventional couple relationships as soon as an opportunity arose. Re-interviewing people 18 months later, we found a remarkably consistent prioritisation of friendship.

Friends were an important part of everyday life in good times and bad. Most of the people we spoke to put considerable effort into building and maintaining friendships in the place where they lived. A good number had moved house, or had persuaded friends to move house, with the aim of creating local friendship networks that could offer reciprocal childcare and help in times of illness, as well as pleasurable sociability. It was friends, far more than biological kin, who offered support to those who suffered from emotional distress or mental health problems and who were there to pick up the pieces when love relationships ended. Many of the people we interviewed were opening up their homes to people who were not part of their conventionally defined family. It was not just the 20-somethings who spent much of their leisure time hanging out with friends at each other's homes or having people round to dinner, for parties and barbecues. Friends were invited to stay during periods of homelessness, when out of work or when they were depressed or lonely.

What this research suggests is that social researchers are failing to see the extent to which, often as a matter of preference, people are substituting the ties of friendship for those of blood, particularly in terms of everyday care and emotional support. They are failing to register the ways in which the relationships at the heart of many people's intimate lives cannot be understood in terms of 'the family'.[21]

Imagining relationships beyond 'the family': an agenda for future research

Casting a queer lens on intimacy and care challenges the boundaries of existing ways of thinking about personal relationships. It demands that sociologists study those – of a range of sexualities – who are not part of conventional families or couples. As more and more people are spending significant parts of their lives outside these forms of relationships, this offers us a perspective on those who are living at the forefront of social change. In the context of individualisation and the destabilisation of the homosexual/heterosexual binary, practices of intimacy and care can no longer – if indeed they ever could – be understood solely through a focus on families. The concept of a family, which suggests clear boundaries – family members inside, others outside – is less and less useful for understanding how people live their personal relationships and whom it is who matters to them. Instead, an exploration of *networks and flows of intimacy and care*, the extent and pattern of such networks, the viscosity and velocity of such flows and the implications of their absence is likely to prove much more fruitful for future research than attempts to interpret contemporary personal lives through redefinitions of the concept of 'family'.[22] The sociological gaze must focus on intimacies and practices of care wherever they take place – in domestic spaces, public spaces, work spaces, virtual spaces – between friends, sexual partners, family, neighbours, work colleagues, civil acquaintances. This will bring to light these practices, that have rarely been studied by sociologists of the family. A new sociology of personal relationships is needed that can register a fuller range of practices of intimacy and care, one which is unbound from heteronormative assumptions.

Notes

[1] This chapter draws on Roseneil (2004) and Roseneil and Budgeon (2004).

[2] Anthropology has been much better as a discipline at recognising the importance of non-familial relationships, both wider kin relations and friendship.

[3] For example, Graham (1987), Duncombe and Marsden (1993) and Finch (1989).

[4] For example, Silva (1996), Stacey (1996), Smart and Neale (1999) and Silva and Smart (1999).

[5] For example, Roseneil and Mann (1996), Stacey (1996), Weeks (1995) and Jaggar and Wright (1999).

[6] Ingraham (1996) argues that feminist sociology and the sociology of gender, and their studies of marriage, family and sexual violence, in particular, depend on a heterosexual imaginary and argues for a shift from the study of gender to the study of heterogender.

[7] Weston (1991), Nardi (1992, 1999), Preston with Lowenthal (1996) and Weeks et al (2001). Weeks et al (2001) discuss the differences between their interviewees in relation to the adoption of the term 'family' to describe their intimate relationships and acknowledge that many reject the term.

[8] For example, Altman (1982), Weston (1991), Nardi (1992, 1999), Weeks (1995), Preston with Lowenthal (1996), Roseneil (2000a) and Weeks et al (2001).

[9] Quoted in Jerrome (1984, p 699).

[10] This argument is made by one of the few sociologists to make the study of friendship their central field of research interest: Graham Allan (1979, 1989) and Adams and Allan (1998).

[11] Hess (1972, 1979), Booth and Hess (1974), Fischer et al (1977), Fischer (1982a, 1982b), Allan (1979), Jerrome (1984), O'Connor (1992), Hey (1997), the contributors to Adams and Allan (1998), Nardi (1999) and Pahl (2000), Willmott (1986, 1987).

[12] For example, Rheingold (1993), Shields (1996), and Wakeford (1998).

[13] The research of Finch (1989) and Finch and Mason (1993) on family obligations suggests that family ties are now understood less in terms of obligations constituted by fixed ties of blood and more in terms of negotiated commitments, which are less clearly differentiated from other relationships.

[14] In this acknowledgement of non-heterosexual identities and

practices Giddens' work differs from that of Beck and Beck-Gernsheim, whose discussion fails to acknowledge its exclusive concern with heterosexuality.

[15] The word 'tendencies' is used deliberately to suggest the still provisional nature of these shifts and with the existence of countervailing tendencies in mind. The use of the term is indebted to Sedgwick (1994).

[16] Adam (2002). On US exceptionalism, see Adam (2003).

[17] For a critique of the limitations of the Civil Partnership Act from a queer perspective, see Roseneil (2004).

[18] I acknowledge that the majority of births outside marriage are to cohabiting couples and, in general, I acknowledge the increase in the prevalence (Ermisch and Francesconi, 2000; Lewis, 2001) and the social acceptability of cohabitation among heterosexual couples (Barlow et al, 2001). This does not, however, diminish the argument about the significance of the social decentring of, first, the married heterosexual couple, and second, the heterosexual couple, per se.

[19] Bech (1997, 1999) makes a similar argument, but pushes it further arguing that in continental northwestern Europe, we are seeing "the disappearance of the homosexual".

[20] This project was led by Sasha Roseneil, with Shelley Budgeon and Jacqui Gabb as research fellows. For a more detailed discussion of the methodology and findings, see Roseneil and Budgeon (2004). For other work on intimacy and care beyond the conventional family, see contributions to Budgeon and Roseneil (2004).

[21] This research can therefore, be read as diverging from the argument advanced by Allan (this volume) that "the boundaries between family and friendship remain relatively well defined, with kin and non-kin relationships largely being understood as occupying different realms in people's lives". However, it must be remembered that the population

being studied in this research, while of growing social significance, is not representative of the population as a whole.

[22] See Urry (2000) for a powerful exposition of the value of metaphors of mobility and flow for the understanding of the contemporary social world.

References

Adam, B. (2002) 'Families without heterosexuality: challenges of same-sex partnership recognition', paper presented to the ESRC Research Group for the Study of Care, Values and the Future of Welfare International Seminar 4, January 2002, www.leeds.ac.uk/cava

Adam, B. (2003) 'DOMA and American exceptionalism', *Journal of History of Sexuality*, vol 12, no 2, pp 259-76.

Adams, R.G. and Allan, G. (eds) (1998) *Placing friendship in context*, Cambridge: Cambridge University Press.

Allan, G. (1977) *A sociology of friendship and kinship*, London: George, Allen & Unwin.

Allan, G. (1989) *Friendship: Developing a sociological perspective*, Hemel Hempstead: Harvester Wheatsheaf.

Altman, D. (1982) *The homosexualization of America*, New York, NY: St. Martin's Press.

Barlow, A., Duncan, S., James, G. and Park, A. (2001) 'Just a piece of paper? Marriage and cohabitation in Britain', in A. Park, J. Curtice, K. Thomson, L. Jarvis and C. Bromley (eds) *British social attitudes: The 18th report*, London: Sage Publications.

Bech, H. (1997) 'Real deconstructions: the disappearance of the modern homosexual and the queer', paper presented at the 14th World Congress of Sociology, Montreal, 26 July-1 August.

Bech, H. (1999) 'After the closet', *Sexualities*, vol 2, no 3, pp 343-9.

Beck, U. and Beck-Gernsheim, E. (1995) *The normal chaos of love*, Cambridge: Polity Press.

Beck, U. and Beck-Gernsheim, E. (2002) *Individualization*, London: Sage Publications

Beck-Gernsheim, E. (1998) On the way to a post-familial family: from a community of needs to elective affinities, *Theory, Culture and Society*, vol 15, nos 3-4, pp 53-70.

Berlant, L. and Warner, M. (2000) 'Sex in public', in L. Berlant (ed) *Intimacy*, Chicago, IL: Chicago University Press.

Booth, A. and Hess, E. (1974) 'Cross sexual friendships', *Journal of Marriage and the Family*, vol 36, pp 38-47.

Budgeon, S. and Roseneil, S. (2004) 'Beyond the conventional family: intimacy, care and community in the 21st century', *Current Sociology*, vol 52, no 2, pp 123-280.

Castells, M. (1997) *The power of identity*, Oxford: Blackwell.

Duncombe, J. and Marsden, D. (1993) 'Love and intimacy: the gender division of emotion and emotion work', *Sociology*, vol 27, pp 221-41.

Ermisch, J. and Francesoni, M. (2000) 'Cohabitation in Great Britain: not for long, but here to stay', *Journal of the Royal Statistical Society, Series A*, vol 163, no 2, pp 153-71.

Finch, J. (1989) *Family obligations and social change*, Cambridge: Polity Press.

Finch, J. and Mason, J. (1993) *Negotiating family responsibilities*, London: Routledge.

Fischer, C. (1982a) 'What do we mean by "friend"? An inductive study', *Social Networks*, vol 3, pp 287-306.

Fischer, C. (1982b) *To dwell among friends*, Berkeley, CA: University of California Press.

Fischer, C., Jackson, R.M., Stueve, C.A., Gerson, K. and McCallister Jones, L. with Baldassare, M. (1977) *Networks and places*, New York, NY: Free Press.

Giddens, A. (1992) *The transformation of intimacy: Sexuality, love and eroticism in modern societies*, Cambridge: Polity Press.

Graham, H. (1987) 'Women's poverty and caring', in C. Glendinning and J. Millar (eds) *Women and poverty in Britain*, Brighton: Wheatsheaf.

Hess, B. (1972) 'Friendship', in M.W. Riley, M. Johnson and A. Foner (eds) *Aging and society*, vol 3, New York, NY: Russell.

Hess, B. (1979) 'Sex roles, friendship and the life course', *Research on Ageing*, vol 1, pp 494-515.

Hey, V. (1997) *The company she keeps: An ethnography of girls' friendships*, Buckingham: Open University Press.

Ingraham, C. (1996) 'The heterosexual imaginary: feminist sociology and theories of gender', in S. Seidman (ed) *Queer theory/sociology*, Oxford: Blackwell.

Jaggar, G. and Wright, C. (eds) (1999) *Changing family values*, London: Routledge.

Jamieson, L. (1998) *Intimacy: Personal relationships in modern societies*, Cambridge: Polity Press.

Jerrome, D. (1984) 'Good company: the sociological implications of friendship', *Sociological Review*, vol 32, no 4, pp 606-715.

Lewis, J. (2001) *The end of marriage? Individualism and intimate relations*, Cheltenham: Edward Elgar.

Litwak, E. and Szelenyi, I. (1969) 'Primary group structures and their functions: kin, neighbours and friends', *American Sociological Review*, vol 34, pp 465-81.

Morgan, D.H.J. (1996) *Family connections*, Cambridge: Polity Press.

Nardi, P. (1992) 'That's what friends are for: friends as family in the gay and lesbian community', in K. Plummer (ed) *Modern homosexualities: Fragments of lesbian and gay experience*, London: Routledge.

Nardi, P. (1999) *Gay men's friendships: Invincible communities*, Chicago, IL: Chicago University Press.

National Statistics (2005) *Social trends no 35* (C. Summerfield and B. Gill (eds)), Basingstoke: Palgrave Macmillan.

O'Connor, P. (1992) *Friendships between women: A critical review*, Hemel Hempstead: Harvester Wheatsheaf.

Pahl, R. (2000) *On friendship*, Cambridge: Polity Press.

Preston, J. with Lowenthal, M. (1996) *Friends and lovers: Gay men write about the families they create*, New York, NY: Plume.

Rheingold, H. (1993) *The virtual community: Homesteading on the electronic frontier*, Menlo Park, CA: Addison-Wesley.

Roseneil, S. (2000a) *Common women, uncommon practices: The queer feminisms of greenham*, London: Cassell.

Roseneil, S. (2000b) 'Queer frameworks and queer tendencies: towards an understanding of postmodern transformations of sexuality', *Sociological Research Online*, vol 5, no 3, www.socresonline.org.uk/5/3/roseneil.html

Roseneil, S. (2002) 'The heterosexual/homosexual binary: past, present and future', in D. Richardson and S. Seidman (eds) *The lesbian and gay studies handbook*, London: Sage Publications, pp 27-44.

Roseneil, S. (2004) 'Why we should care about friends: an argument for the queering of the care imaginary in social policy', *Social Policy and Society*, vol 3, no 4, pp 409-19.

Roseneil, S. and Budgeon, S. (2004) 'Cultures of intimacy and care beyond the family: personal life and social change in the early twenty-first century', *Current Sociology*, vol 52, no 2, pp 135-60.

Roseneil, S. and Mann, K. (1996) 'Backlash, moral panics and the lone mother', in E. Silva (ed) *Good enough mothering? Feminist perspectives on lone motherhood*, London: Routledge.

Sedgwick, E. Kosofsky (1994) *Tendencies*, New York: Routledge.

Shields, R. (ed) (1996) *Cultures of internet: Virtual spaces, real histories, living bodies*, London: Sage Publications.

Simmel, G. (1950) *The sociology of Georg Simmel* (trans and ed K. H.Wolff and R. Bendix), New York, NY: Free Press.

Silva, E.B. (1996) (eds) *Good enough mothering? Feminist perspectives on mothering*, London: Routledge.

Silva, E. and Smart, C. (eds) (1999) *The new family*, London: Sage Publications.

Smart, C. and Neale, B. (1999) *Family fragments*, Cambridge: Polity Press.

Stacey, J. (1996) *In the name of the family: Rethinking family values in the postmodern age*, Boston, MA: Beacon Press.

Stacey, J. (2002) 'Fellow families? Genres of gay male intimacy and kinship in a global metropolis', CAVA International seminar paper at www.leeds.ac.uk/cava/papers/intseminar3stacey.htm.

Stacey, J. (2004) 'Cruising to familyland: gay hypergarny and rainbow kinship', *Current Sociology*, vol 52, no 2, pp 181-99.

Urry, J. (2000) *Sociology beyond societies: Mobilities for the twenty-first century*, London: Routledge.

Van Every, J. (1999) 'From modern nuclear family households to postmodern diversity? The sociological construction of "families"', in G. Jagger and C. Wright (eds) *Changing family values*, London: Routledge.

Wakeford, N. (1998) 'Urban culture for virtual bodies: comments on lesbian identity and community in San Francisco Bay Area cyberspace', in R. Ainley (ed) *New frontiers of space, bodies and gender*, London: Routledge.

Weeks, J. (1995) *Invented moralities: Sexual values in an age of uncertainty*, Cambridge: Polity Press.

Weeks, J., Donovan, C. and Heaphy, B. (1999) 'Everyday experiments: narratives of non-heterosexual relationships', in E. Silva and C. Smart (eds) *The 'new' family?*, London: Sage Publications.

Weeks, J., Heaphy, B. and Donovan, C. (2001) *Same sex intimacies: Families of choice and other life experiments*, London: Routledge.

Weston, K. (1991) *Families we choose: Lesbians, gay men and kinship*, New York, NY: Columbia University Press.

Whyte, W.H. (1943) *Street corner society*, Chicago, IL: Chicago University Press.

Willmott, P. (1986) *Social networks, informal care and public policy*, London: Policy Studies Institute.

Willmott, P. (1987) *Friendship networks and social support*, London: Policy Studies Institute.

Willmott, P. and Young, M. (1967) *Family and class in a London suburb*, London: Nel Mentor.
Young, M. and Willmott, P. (1957) *Family and kinship in East London*, London: Routledge and Kegan Paul.

Conclusion

FIFTEEN

Perspectives on social policies and families

Fran Wasoff and Sarah Cunningham-Burley

Introduction

The Centre for Research on Families and Relationships (CRFR) is committed to building links between academic research, policy and practice. The ideas behind this book emerged from ongoing discussions about furthering links across organisations and agencies concerned with policy and practice, research, and the exploration of families more generally. Given the range of research on families and relationships that we at CRFR and other colleagues are engaged in we were keen to disseminate work as widely as possible. The theme of boundaries offers one way to capture the fluidity of 'families and relationships' and the concept of boundary work to embed such conceptualisations within the practical realities of 'doing family and relationships', family practices and practices of intimacy and friendship. In compiling this book we have focused on concepts and findings we hope will be of interest to policymakers, researchers and those studying the diverse and shifting nature of family life.

Boundaries as a conceptual device

Boundaries are certainly not new ways to understand families and relationships. Indeed, as the chapters by Hill (Chapter Five) and by Sweeting and Seaman (Chapter Six) note, the concept is used within family systems theory and within family therapy: boundaries are seen as essential to good family functioning. However, these authors also warn that boundaries are concepts imposed by adults (whether academics or family practitioners) and their traditional use marginalises the agency of children in challenging boundaries and constructing their own meaningful bridges across domains. These limits pose challenges to the sociologies of families and relationships of both a methodological and conceptual nature.

Other chapters, too, draw on traditional notions of boundaries, for example Allan (Chapter Thirteen) describes how, for the most part, the boundaries between familial relationships and friendships remain quite clear, while admitting there is greater flexibility in these boundaries in contemporary society. Jamieson (Chapter Eleven) also highlights how family theory has worked with the notion of exclusionary boundaries in its conceptualisation of families and also of intimacy. On the one hand, she challenges such theorising, suggesting that practices of intimacy do not necessarily demarcate intimate relationships from communal activity. On the other hand, she makes us aware that exclusionary practices within familial and other personal relationships persist, sometimes harbouring violence and creating hierarchies. McKie and Lombard (Chapter Ten) take this argument further in their discussion of violence and families in which they explore the family/community boundary within situations of communal violence.

In other contributions, the boundary between home and paid work or training and home and school are explored, with attention paid to the experience of those operating at these interfaces. Cunningham-Burley, Backett-Milburn and Kemmer (Chapter Two) explore how the construction of a clear boundary between home life and work life is used by mothers in paid employment as a way of maintaining a balance between caring and providing. However, such strategies are risky and fragile and the everyday needs from work or home cross these boundaries, resulting in breaches that require restabilisation. Scott and Innes (Chapter Three) further explore this theme through an analysis of the shifting boundaries of care between the family and the state, as mothers take up training for employment. They suggest that policy in the UK oversimplifies boundaries and fails to recognise the blurred category of mother and worker. Women on low incomes in particular are located at the intersection of class, gender and state boundaries. The relationship between family and home and wider social institutions is elaborated in the chapter by Shucksmith, McKee and Willmot (Chapter Four) as they explore how the intrusion of school into home life through unbalanced 'partnerships' alters boundaries within the family as well as boundaries between the state (in the form of schools) and home. The interface between education and home has become more permeable, although they argue this tends to unidirectional; parents and children are very differently resourced to deal with the new participation agenda.

The boundary metaphor can also help to conceptualise families and relationships across different times (historical and biographical) and spaces (household, place, community). Backett-Milburn, Airey and McKie (Chapter Eight) focus on the interplay between changing social and cultural trends relating to work and care, biographical time and the experience of ageing to suggest that the boundaries of caring and providing influence well-being. In this way they begin to challenge conventional boundaries around ageing through a focus on personal agency. Other chapters in this volume also focus, through in-depth qualitative research, on the everyday practices of boundary maintenance and deconstruction. Bancroft, Wilson, Cunningham-Burley, Masters and Backett-Milburn's contribution (Chapter Seven) shows how parental substance misuse transgresses established boundaries but that children's responses to this situation redefine them. The concept of boundary can relate to knowledge and risk as well as roles and responsibilities.

The disruption to established roles and responsibilities caused by illness is a theme taken up by Weaks, Wilkinson and Davidson (Chapter Nine) in their exploration of case studies of couples where one is affected by dementia. New practices of intimacy and family may have to be established. This may result in changed boundaries between couples and between the couple and their friendship networks. Challenges to the bounding of household and family are also made in the contribution by Wasoff, Jamieson and Smith (Chapter Twelve) where the phenomenon of solo living suggests that family and personal relationships are increasingly less likely to be physically related to household. Their analyses also suggest fluidity over time as people move in and out of different household arrangements. Those living beyond the family, and outside of the still dominant heterosexual couple formation, challenge such normative structures. As Roseneil (Chapter Fourteen) argues, they are breaching boundaries and binaries and constructing new ways of living. Focusing empirical attention on those shaping and experiencing different living arrangements and relationship practices means that the boundaries of conventional sociological thinking can be broken. Roseneil identifies the blurring of boundaries as a feature of the lives of those living beyond the heteronorm.

Boundaries can be seen as a useful conceptual device for understanding a range of interfaces from roles and gendered relationships within families and relationships to the relationship between families, family members and wider social institutions.

They can also be deeply challenging concepts, requiring reflexivity in theorising to disturb the normative assumptions on which they may be based. Boundaries are also flexible devices, as they are often breached or permeated through the practices of everyday life as well as state actions. The notion of boundaries as frontiers, extending or challenging what is taken for granted also suggests their adroitness as a drive for action and change.

Boundaries and boundary work in a policy context

Boundaries can blur, move and expand or contract around what they enclose or divide. They can be created, reconfigured, crossed, disturbed contested and disputed, or remain static. Boundaries can be permeable or not, and boundary movements can be welcomed or resisted. Applying the theme of boundaries to the policy area, we can read many of the recent social and family policies in terms of boundary definition and boundary shifting work.

Many policy analysts have addressed the transformation of family policy that has taken place under the Labour government in the UK since 1997 (Wasoff and Dey, 2000; Millar and Ridge, 2001a; Dex and Smith, 2002; Wasoff and Hill, 2002; Millar, 2003; Williams, 2004, 2005). Some of the dominant themes have been critical appraisals of the growing prominence of family issues on policy agendas, how much they have recognised the scale and character of family transformation, the extent to which family policies actually support families in myriad forms and needs, the governance of family policies and the changing relationship or boundary between families and the state.

We can see the emphasis on 'joined-up' policymaking in terms of a blurring of the boundaries across policy areas. There are numerous examples of recent partnership working at policy and practice levels and also through the establishment of different types of institutions that embrace diverse disciplines. Policy boundaries are created and reconfigured. The Scottish Parliament and the Welsh Assembly created new boundaries or demarcations within central government between reserved and devolved policy areas, adding further complexity to the policymaking environment (Wasoff and Hill, 2002). In relation to key areas of family policy, this is particularly evident in relation to work–life balance, social inclusion and early years' policies. Family policy itself crosses boundaries – for example between government departments and between state and voluntary sector.

The shifting boundary of responsibility for care between families and the state has been a strong theme of childcare policies since 1997, where the state has assumed a much greater role for the care and support of children and the boundary between state and family, or the market or voluntary sector and family, as providers of childcare has not only moved but has also become more permeable than it was under the previous Conservative government, which tended to the view that childcare was a family responsibility in which the state had little legitimate role.

The Labour Party Manifesto (2005, p 75) sums up the government's broad aim:

> Government does not bring up children, but it must support parents in their key role. We will help parents balance work and family, expand paid leave, deliver the biggest ever expansion in childcare and end child poverty in a generation.

Universal nursery education provision for three- and four-year-olds has substantially expanded; the National Childcare Strategy has substantially expanded the scale of childcare provision for the under-fives. However, as previous chapters have suggested, such expansion does not necessarily meet the needs of parents, especially mothers in paid employment. There has also been an expansion of after school and school holiday provision for older school-age children that has also pushed out the boundary of care between family and state within the education system, although this is not universally affordable or accessible.

While the expansion of universal services has been partly driven by work–life balance policy agendas, the expansion of targeted childcare services, such as those delivered through Sure Start, are driven by the child poverty and social inclusion policy agendas, of which encouraging paid work as a route out of poverty is an underlying theme. There is a tension between targeting the most vulnerable and developing non-stigmatised universal services: the boundary between state and state-supported provision for childcare and informal care by family or friends may be flexible, but care is still predominantly a gendered, family responsibility.

Complementing the expansion in provision has been an increase in financial support for families, particularly for lower income families, another area in which family/state boundaries have seen substantial movements and where the state has assumed greater responsibility for the adequacy of income for families where parents are in paid employment. Most significant has been the Working Families' Tax Credit, later the Working Tax Credit (WTC), which guarantees a minimum income for families with children where at least one partner is in full-time work. The WTC and the Child Tax Credit have both been much more widely targeted than the in-work benefits they replaced. The Inland Revenue, which administers these tax credit schemes, estimate that 90% of families where a parent is in paid work are eligible for tax credits (www.taxcredits.inlandrevenue.gov.uk/Qualify/WhatAreTaxCredits.aspx). The generosity of the universal benefit, Child Benefit, has also been modestly enhanced and a universal Child Trust Fund was introduced in 2003. Adam and Brewer (2004, pp 12-14) observe that spending by government via tax credits and social security benefits on child-contingent support increased from £13.41 in 1975 to £32.57 in 2003 per child per week, mainly between 1999 and 2003.

Child support policies tell a different boundary story, one of resistance to government attempts to reconfigure the boundaries between family, labour market and state in the package of support for children whose parents live apart (Ridge, 2005). Both parents with care, mainly mothers, but particularly non-resident parents, mainly fathers, have strenuously resisted efforts to shift the burden of support for children and their carers away from the state and towards non-resident biological parents. Closely linked to the child support reforms have been New Labour's welfare-to-work policies (Millar and Ridge, 2001b), such as the New Deal for Lone Parents, which also attempted to shift the balance or move the boundary of the income package for lone parents away from 'benefit dependency' towards 'making work pay' through a raft of social security benefit and taxation reforms; these issues were taken up in the first section of this volume.

Elsewhere in the lifecourse, family policy has been less active and there has been far less movement of the boundary between family and state in relation to the provision or financial support of care, with the significant exception of Scotland, where the policy of free personal care for the elderly introduced in 2002 signalled the state assuming more responsibility (and families correspondingly less) for the cost of care of dependent adults over 65.

To take another children's policy example, we can see the emergence of fuzzier boundaries between those governing and those who are governed. Some of the new approaches to governance, and New Labour's modernisation and social inclusion agendas, emphasise partnership and participation, as shown in relation to education and home. These suggest a blurring of the governance relationship between the state and families. Partnerships between service providers and service users and the greater focus on consultation regarding new policy initiatives both point to a blurring of the boundary between government and the governed. These changing governance framings will impact on everyday experience in expected and unexpected ways. In the early years policy area, for example, policy development has set high store in consultation with users and in developing governing structures that include parent users of services. However, issues raised in this volume suggest that the participation agenda between schools and parents is not necessarily empowering for parents but can be read as the encroaching of state education into family life.

The permeability of the boundary between the private world of families and the public world of the state has increased in the area of policies around domestic abuse. From the mid-1970s the feminist refuge movement challenged that boundary and prompted the Select Committee on Violence in Marriage to focus parliamentary attention on what had hitherto been seen as a 'private matter between spouses'. Although many grassroots and local activities and a number of policy and legal responses emerged in the 1980s and 1990s, it has been from 1997 in particular that this issue has assumed increasing visibility on the public policy agenda with initiatives and policies springing from various parts of government. There are now over 300 refuges in Britain, although many still run on a shoestring with demand outstripping supply. In England and Wales, domestic violence policies have been developed by the police, probation service, the social and health services, and housing services and legal protection for victims, both married and unmarried, has been enhanced in the 1996 Family Law Act, recognising the ineffectiveness of previous remedies such as injunctions. Boundary blurring across policy domains has also developed over the last 10 years, with the emergence of interagency initiatives and partnerships at both local and national levels (Hague, 1999; Harwin et al, 1999). A different, and more comprehensive and joined-up policy route has developed in Scotland, via the Scottish Partnership on Domestic Abuse in 1998, followed by the National Strategy to Address Domestic Abuse (Scottish Executive, 2003), which is organised around the themes of prevention, protection and provision. Here too we can see similar challenges to established boundaries between family and state and across policy areas. While primary prevention and seriously eroding the underlying causes of domestic violence seems to remain a distant goal and, as Gill Hague remarks (1999, p 144) "domestic violence policy remains ambivalent", it looks as if government no longer considers this issue as a private matter between partners in which the state has no legitimate role.

Further instances of boundary shifting in family policies can be seen around work–life balance policies that have changed the relationship between families and the labour market. Such policies recognise that the 'male breadwinner model' of the family no longer characterises family life due to changes in both men's and women's employment patterns. Parental leave and flexible work times policies have made the boundary between work and family a more elastic and variable one, such as the changes embodied in the flexible working legislation (2002 Employment Act) since 2003 in which parents of children aged under six (or parents of a disabled child up to the age of 18) can ask their employer for a more flexible working pattern, for example, different work hours, different times of work, to work from home and so on.

Social and demographic change, particularly the rise in solo living as outlined in the final section of this volume, has meant that the boundary between family and other living arrangements has been reconfigured and policy has had to embrace the growing diversity in family formation and the prevalence of family transitions. Nowhere is this more obvious than in relation to family law that has redrawn its own boundaries substantially over the last 20 years. Legislation such as the 1996 Family Law Act, the 2004 Civil Partnership Act and the Family Law (Scotland) Bill, in its committee stage at the time of writing, has expanded the range of kinship relationships embraced by family law. We have seen important changes to the rights and responsibilities of unmarried fathers towards their children, of same-sex couples who can now enter into a registered partnership with similarities to marriage, of stepparents, unmarried cohabiting couples and the financial protection they might seek when relationships become violent or break down.

Whether the scale of change we have seen since 1997 will be sustained over the life of the third Labour government, whether the full gamut of changes in family life will ultimately find expression in policy and whether the government ultimately realises its work–life balance, social inclusion and child poverty reduction objectives remains to be seen. However, it is difficult to see how the redrawing of the position and nature of the boundaries over many social and family policies that has reconfigured the relationship between families and the state can easily be reversed. However, other boundaries seem rather impervious to change, for example the persistence of highly gendered relationships of care. The challenge for individuals, their families and communities is to resist those boundaries that constrain or restrict quality of life and well-being and to create flexible, permeable boundaries that reflect changing needs and wishes regarding personal life, work and leisure across the lifecourse. The need for flexibility should be reflected in policymaking, whether through laws that take into account the importance of a range of personal relationships beyond the family or through the provision of housing that reflects different trends in household formation. However, the need for flexibility, often a strategy for getting by in everyday life, needs to be reflected in the everyday relationships between the public sphere (for example, employers) and the private sphere (for example, mothers who care and earn or provide). Rather than shoring up boundaries that perhaps reassert power relationships, flexibility should enable boundaries such as those between work and home to be crossed without being compromised.

References

Adam, S. and Brewer, M. (2004) *Supporting families: The financial costs and benefits of children since 1975*, Bristol: The Policy Press.

Dex, S. and Smith, C. (eds) (2002) *The nature and pattern of family-friendly employment policies in Britain*, Bristol: The Policy Press.

Hague, G. (1999) 'Domestic violence policy in the 1990s', in S. Watson and L. Doyal (eds) *Engendering social policy*, Buckingham: Open University Press.

Harwin, N., Hague, G. and Malos, E. (1999) *The multi-agency approach to domestic violence: New opportunities, old challenges?*, London: Whiting and Birch.

Labour Party (2005) *Britain forward not back: The Labour Party manifesto 2005*, London: The Labour Party.

Millar J. (2003) 'Social policy and family policy', in P. Alcock, A. Erskine and M. May (eds) *The student's companion to social policy*, (2nd edn) Oxford: Blackwell.

Millar, J. and Ridge, T. (2001a) 'Parents, children, families and New Labour: developing family policy?', in M. Powell (ed) *Evaluating New Labour's welfare reforms*, Bristol: The Policy Press.

Millar, J. and Ridge, T. (2001b) *Families, poverty, work and care: A review of literature on lone parents and low-income couple families*, Department for Work and Pensions Research Report no 153, Leeds: Corporate Document Services.

Ridge, T. (2005) 'Supporting children? The impact of child support policies on children's well-being in the UK and Australia', *Journal of Social Policy*, vol 34 no 1, pp 121-42.

Scottish Executive (2003) *Abuse: Preventing domestic abuse: A national strategy*, Edinburgh: Scottish Executive, www.scotland.gov.uk/library5/social/pdaa-00.asp

Wasoff, F. and Dey, I. (2000) *Family policy*, London: Routledge.

Wasoff, F. and Hill, M. (2002) 'Family policy in Scotland', *Social Policy and Society*, vol 1, no 3, pp 171-82.

Williams, F. (2004) *Rethinking families*, London: Calouste Gulbenkian Foundation.

Williams, F. (2005) 'New Labour's family policy' in M. Powell, L. Bauld and K. Clarke (eds) *Social policy review*, vol 17, Bristol: The Policy Press.

Index

Note: Contributors to this book are in **bold**

A

Aberdeen
  study 60-1
active joint parenting 98
adult-child division 84
ageing process 133-4
Airey, Laura ix 127, 131-47, 263
alcohol misuse *see* children managing parental substance abuse
Allan, Graham ix 186, 198, 227-40, 262
Alzheimer's disease 151-3
  see also families, relationships and dementia
ambivalence 114-17
authentic intimacy or illusory intimacy 196-8
  Bauman, Zygmunt 197-8
  Berlant, Lauren 197
  Giddens, Anthony 196
  Parsons, Talcott 196-7
  postmodernity 197
  Scottish Enlightenment 196
  Sennett, Richard 197-8
  Smith, Adam 196

B

back stage 191
Backett-Milburn, Kathryn ix-x 19, 23-8, 74, 111-25, 127, 131-47, 262-3
balancing work and family life *see* work-family balance
Bancroft, Angus x 74, 111-25, 263
Barth, Frederick 190-1
Bauman, Zygmunt 197-8
belonging 176
benefits 42
Berger, Peter 194
Berlant, Lauren 197
biomedical perspective 134
blood ties 229-30
Bosnia 128, 169, 171, 175-7, 181-2
  ethnic cleansing 171
bottom lines 82
boundaries
  challenging 12-15
  children 77-8
  as conceptual device 261-4
  firm 9-12
  permeable 32-6
boundaries and balances 27-36
  boundary construction 28-32
  permeable boundaries 32-6
  public-private boundary 27-8
  work-home boundary 27-8
boundaries and boundary practices 5-8
  boundary metaphor 5-7
  boundary studies 6
  definition 5-6
  family 7
  government policies and services 7-8
  public/private boundary 7-8
  women and work 8
boundaries and boundary work in policy context 264-9
  Child Benefit 266
  Child Tax Credit 266
  Child Trust Fund 266
  Civil Partnership Act 2004 268
  Employment Act 2002 268
  Family Law Act 1996 267-8
  Family Law (Scotland) Bill 268
  Inland Revenue 266
  Labour Party Manifesto 265
  National Childcare Strategy 265
  National Strategy to Address Domestic Abuse 267
  New Deal for Lone Parents 266
  nursery education 265
  Scottish Parliament 264
  Scottish Partnership on Domestic Abuse 1998 267
  Select Committee on Violence in Marriage 267
  Sure Start 265
  welfare-to-work policies 266
  Welsh Assembly 264
  Working Tax Credit (WTC) 266
boundaries and bridges *see* families and relationships
boundaries of friendship 227-40, 262
  commitment 228
  constructing families 229-31
  family households 227-8
  friends as family 234-7

friendship 231-4
gay partnerships 228
kinship 228
lesbian partnerships 228
non-familial households 228
non-kin relationships 228
nuclear family 228
partnership behaviour 227
social capital 228
unclear family 228
boundaries of intimacy 185, 189-206, 262
authentic intimacy or illusory intimacy 196-8
back stage 191
Barth, Frederick 190-1
boundary work 190-1
Goffman, Erving 191
individualism 189-90
intimacy 189-91
intimacy intensification 191-6
intimacy, social change and boundary practices 199-203
modernity 189-90
mother-daughter relationships 190
mother-son relationships 190
private sphere 189-90
public community versus private intimacy 198-9
public sphere 189-90
self-disclosure 189
Simmel, Georg 191
sociology of the family 191
whole persons 191
boundaries, memories and identities *see* violence and families
boundary
ambiguity 95
breaking 186-7
crossing 46-7
maintenance 30
metaphor 5-7
roles 131-2, 135
studies 6
work 190-1, 201
boundary construction 28-32
boundary maintenance 30
lone parents 29
managing well 30
part-time work 29-30
traffic between spheres 32
work and socialisation of children 31-2
work type 28-9
worker identity 31
working mother 30-1
bounded system 153
breaching of boundaries 32-6
Bridget Jones's Diary 207, 249
Bringa, Tone 128, 170, 175-7, 181-2
British Household Panel Survey (BHPS) 209, 212-13, 221

C

care 40-1
caring patterns 40-1
citizen as carer 41
citizen as worker 41
conceptualisation 40
diaries 43
family poverty 41
government policies 41
index 43-4
lone parents 41
low income families 40-1
marginalisation 48-9
nursery education 40
in relationships of people with dementia 161-2
UK childcare policy 40-1
see also gender, care, poverty and transitions
Care, friendship and non-conventional partnership project 248-50
caring 44-6
care index 44
invisibility of Families in societycare 45
patterns 40-1
provisioning 45-6
time and location issues 45
Centre for Research on Families and Relationships (CRFR) 4-5, 261
challenging boundaries 12-15
division of labour 14
divorce 12
families with adult dependent children 13
family responsibilities 14
fertility 12
geographical boundaries 15
government policies 13
grandparents as carers 14
lone parent families 13-14
non-resident families 13
same-sex couples 13
stepfamilies 13-14
women and labour market 12
change negotiation and boundary limits 47-8

childcare 47-8
changing families *see* challenging boundaries
child
abuse 87-8
poverty 81
protection 87-8
symptom 84
Child Benefit 266
Child Tax Credit 266
Child Trust Fund 266
childcare arrangements 32-5, 47-8
children
behaviour 86
preferences 32, 34
questionnaire 100
safety 86
socialisation 11-12, 31-2, 57
Children Act 1989 98-9
children, families and relationships 4, 73-129
children managing parental substance misuse 111-25
children's boundaries 77-94
family within/beyond household boundary 95-110
children managing parental substance misuse 74, 111-25, 263
discussion 122-3
family 111-12
parent-child boundary 111-12
parental substance misuse 111-12
risk and knowledge 118-20
roles and responsibilities 112-18
space and time 120-1
young carers 111
Children (Scotland) Act 1995 98-9
children's boundaries 73-4, 77-94, 261
boundary 77-8
children's choice and influence 77
family systems and boundaries 83-5
family therapy and boundaries 85-6
identity, family and trust 78-81
parent-child negotiations of boundary setting 81-3
professionals and boundary setting 86-8
psychodynamic theory 88
school 77
transitional space 88-9
chronic illness 159
citizen
as carer 41
as worker 41
citizenship 50
civic plurality 175
Civil Partnerships Act 2004 247, 268
co-parenting 98
collective memories 177
collective past 174-5
collusion 113
collusion and boundary maintenance 114-17
ambivalence 114-17
parentified child 114-17
commitment 201, 228
committed-dependent relationship 153
community 198-9
competing or complementary discourses 49-50
Connolly, P. 128, 170, 177-80, 182
consistency 82
constructing families 229-31
blood ties 229-30
kin keepers 230-1
Schneider, D. 229
construction 172
see also our home, my family
contested boundaries *see* families, public institutions and violence
continuity theory 157-8
control 83
of children 86
couples 200-2
crime 87, 122-3
critical incidents 68
Crow, Graham 198-9
Social solidarities 199
cultural images 177-80
Cunningham-Burley, Sarah x 3-19, 23-38, 74, 111-25, 261-70
custodial parenting 98

D

dangerous neighbourhoods 81-2
data cleaning 100, 107
Davidson, Shirley x 127-8, 149-67, 263
death and fighting 177
dementia 150-3
Alzheimer's disease 151
diagnosis 149-50
research into dementia and relationships 152-3
social constructionist perspective 150-3
Sterin, Gloria 151-2
stigmatisation 151-2
syndrome 150

see also families, relationships and dementia
Denmark
child poverty 42
disabled parents 88
discipline 103
disclosure 112
disengaged relationships 86
diversity 195
division of labour 10-12, 14
divorce 12
domestic labour 11-12
double shift 24
drugs *see* children managing parental substance abuse
dysfunctional families 86

E

education *see* families, education and 'participatory imperative'
Education Act 1870 57
ego psychology 78-9
Employment Act 2002 268
enmeshed relationships 86
Erikson, E.H. 78-9
ethnic cleansing 171
see also historical legacies
ethno-religious identity 173-7
European Social Fund 39, 43
exclusion 181
rhetoric of 176
expressivity 103
extended family 80
external boundaries 84-5
external interactions 85

F

falling to bits but keeping it together 138-43
health, illness and family 140-3
redrawing boundaries around ageing 139-40
families
with adult dependent children 13
changing 12-15
of choice 235, 243-4
as porous 180
as private domain 10
see also constructing families
families, education and 'participatory imperative' 20, 57-72, 262
citizenship 58
parent-teacher confrontation 60
parental involvement in education 58-60
partnership 58-9
public policy provision 57
schooling 61-5
socialisation of children 57
study 60-1
talking back 65-8
Total Schooling 58-9, 61-5
families, public institutions and violence 174-5
collective past 174-5
families and relationships 3-18
boundaries and boundary practices 3-8
Centre for Research on Families and Relationships (CRFR) 4-5
challenging boundaries 12-15
diversity 3-4
family 3-4
family reconfiguration 4
firm boundaries 9-12
interpreting families and relationships 8-9
policy 4-5
research 4-5
traditional values 3-4
families, relationships and dementia 127-8, 149-67, 263
boundary crossing 149-50
care in relationships of people with dementia 161-2
case studies 153-61
dementia 150-3
dementia diagnosis 149-50
families in society 4, 19-72
families, education and 'participatory imperative' 57-72
families and relationships 3-18
gender, care
poverty and transitions 39-55
work-family balance: mothers' views 23-38
family 3-4, 80, 111-12
boundaries 7
boundary 95
dynamics 85
dysfunction 84
history 173
home 11
honour 175
households 227-8
identities 85
poverty 41

practices 97, 194, 242-3
realignments 84
reconfiguration 4
responsibilities 14
rules 86-7
sociology 199
status 10
subsystems 83-4
systems 87
therapy 83, 86
values 243
see also heteronormative family and beyond
Family Law Act 1996 267-8
Family Law (Scotland) Bill 268
family structure research 96-104
living with dad 100-2
parenting across households 103-4
research studies 99
respondents' perceptions and researchers' categories 97-9
subjectivity and family structure 96-7
West of Scotland 11 to 16 Study 96, 99
Young People's Family Life 96, 99
family systems and boundaries 83-5
adult-child division 84
child symptom 84
control 83
external boundaries 84-5
external interactions 85
family dysfunction 84
family identities 85
family realignments 84
family subsystems 83-4
family systems theory 83-4
family therapy 83
internal boundary 83
particularistic alliances 84
renegotiation of family boundaries 84
self-presentation 85
family systems theory 83-4, 95
family therapy and boundaries 85-6
disengaged relationships 86
dysfunctional families 86
enmeshed relationships 86
family dynamics 85
nuclear families 85
parental conflicts 85
subsystems 85
family within/beyond household boundary 74, 95-110
boundary ambiguity 95
discussion 104-7
family boundary 95
family structure research 96-104
family systems theory 95
non-resident birth fathers 95
fathers
role 9
fertility 12
Finland
child poverty 42
firm boundaries 9-12
division of labour 10-12
domestic labour 11
families as private domain 10
family home 11
family status 10
man role 11-12
nuclear family 10-11
orthodoxy 9-12
same-sex couples 11
socialisation of children 11-12
ties and bonds 11
woman role 11-12
working mothers 12
flexibility 32-6
flows in/out solo living 212-13
foster carers 82
France
childcare policy 40
friends as family 234-7
families of choice 235
mapping social convoys 236-7
Parsons, Talcott 235-6
spoke model 234
friendship 194-5, 231-4
changes 233-4
see also boundaries of friendship
functionalism 192

G

gay
families 243-4
men 201, 248
partnerships 228
gender
of child 79
culture 51
differences 200-1
gender, care, poverty and transitions 20, 39-55, 262
care 40-1
gender, care and transitions: case study 41-50
gender culture 51
labour market policies 39

low income households 39
worker culture 51
gender, care and transitions: case study 41-50
boundary crossing 46-7
care diaries 43
care index 43
care marginalisation 48-9
caring 44-6
change negotiation and boundary limits 47-8
child poverty 42
competing or complementary discourses 49-50
locality 42-3
low income households 41-4
General Household Survey 2001 208-13, 215-17
geographical boundaries 15
Giddens, Anthony 201-2, 208, 245-6, 248
The transformation of intimacy 195-6
Goffman, Erving 191
government policies 4-5, 7-8, 13
benefits 42
care 40-1
minimum wage legislation 41
National Childcare Strategy 41
on paid work 23-4
tax credits 24, 41-2
grandparents as carers 14

H

health, illness and family 140-3
ambivalence 142
health, illness and well-being 4, 127-84
families, relationships and dementia 149-67
violence and families 169-84
women's health and well-being at mid-life 131-47
Healy, J. 128, 170, 177-80, 182
Hess, Beth 244-5
heteronormative family and beyond 242-5
families of choice 243-4
family practices 242-3
family values 243
gay families 243-4
Hess, Beth 244-5
lesbian families 243-4
Morgan, David 242
non-heteronormative intimacies 244
non-standard intimacies 243-4
Simmel, Georg 245
sociology of friendship 245
street corner society 245
Van Every, Jo 243
Hill, Malcolm x-xi 73-4, 77-94, 262
historical legacies, ethnic cleansing and global identities 175-7
belonging 176
Bosnia 175-7
Bringa, Tone 175-7
civic plurality 175
collective memories 177
death and fighting 177
ethno-religious identity 175-7
family honour 175
Muslims 175-7
private spaces 176
rhetoric of exclusion 176
rhetoric of inclusion 176
rhetoric of peacekeeping 177
Second World War 176-7
women and gender differences 175
Hochschild, Arlie
stalled revolution 193
home *see* our home, my family: construction and preservation
homosexual/heterosexual binary 246-7, 251
hurried child syndrome 64

I

identity, family and trust 78-81
child poverty 81
ego psychology 78-9
Erikson, E.H. 78-9
extended family 80
family 80
gender of child 79
identity of child 79
inferred personal and affectual boundaries 78
intermediate space 80
introjection 79
projection 79
psychodynamic theories 79
safety of place 81
strangers 81
transitional space 79
trust boundaries 80-1
we groups 79
Winnicott, D.W. 79
inclusion
rhetoric of 176

India 181
individualism 189-90
inferred personal and affectual boundaries 78
Inland Revenue 266
Innes, Sue xi 20, 39-55, 262
institutionalisation 200
inter-communal violence 169-74
intergenerational boundaries 88
intermediate space 80
internal boundary 83
International Monetary Fund (IMF) 10
interpreting families and relationships 8-9
  father role 9
  fuzzy boundaries 9
  mother role 9
  traditional family values 8-9
  women and work 9
  work-life balance 9
intimacy 189-91
  see also boundaries of intimacy
intimacy intensification 191-6
  Berger, Peter 194
  diversity 195
  family practices 194
  friendships 194-5
  functionalism 192
  Giddens, Anthony 195-6
  Hochschild, Arlie 193
  Kellner, Hans 194
  Morgan, David 193-5
  Parsons, Talcott 191-3
  peer relationships 192-3
  socialisation of children 192
  sociology of the family 191
  solo living 195
  violence and families 195
intimacy, social change and boundary practices 199-203
  boundary work 201
  commitment 201
  community 199
  couples 200-2
  family sociology 199
  gay men 201
  gender differences 200-1
  Giddens, Anthony 201-2
  institutionalisation 200
  lesbian couples 201
  monogamy 201
  non-monogamous couples 201-2
  obligation 201
  parent-child relationships 200
  presumption 201
  pure relationship 201
  secondary relationships 202
  self-disclosure 202
  substance abusing parents 200
introjection 79
invisibility of care 45

J

Jamieson, Lynn xi 185-6, 189-225, 262-3
Job Centre Plus 50
Joseph Rowntree Foundation 19, 124

K

Kellner, Hans 194
Kemmer, Debbie xi-xii 19, 23-38, 262
kin keepers 230-1
kinship 228
knowingness 134

L

Labour Force Survey 132
Labour Party Manifesto 265
legitimacy 112
lesbian 248
  couples 201
  families 243-4
  partnerships 228
life stages 143-4
lifestyle choices 134-5, 209-10
living alone *see* solo living
living with dad 100-2
  children's questionnaire 100
  data cleaning 100
  parental questionnaire 100
living and loving beyond heteronorm 228, 248-50
  Care, friendship and non-conventional partnership project 248-50
  see also personal relationships beyond the heteronorm
living-apart-together 98
Lombard, Nancy xii 128, 169-84, 262
lone mothers 25-7, 48
lone parent families 13-14, 25, 29, 98
  care 41
low income households 39-44

M

McKee, Lorna xii 20, 57-72, 262
McKendrick, John H. xii-xiii 3-18
McKie, Linda xiii 3-18, 127-8, 131-47, 169-84, 262-3
managing well 30
Mandela, Nelson 170
mapping social convoys 236-7
marginalisation of care 48-9
marital interaction
  dementia 153
Masters, Hugh xiii 74, 111-25, 263
medical model
  dementia 152
men
  role 11-12
mid-life *see* women's health and well-being at mid-life
minimum wage legislation 41
Misztal, Barbara *Theories of social remembering* 174
mobile phones 83
monogamy 201
Morgan, David 193-5, 242
Morvern Callar 207
mother gap 49
mother-daughter relationships 190
mother-son relationships 190
mothers
  good mother 36
  role 9
  see also working mothers
Muslims
  Bosnia 175-7

N

narratives 173
National Childcare Strategy 41, 265
National Strategy to Address Domestic Abuse 267
networks and flows of intimacy and care 251
New Deal for Lone Parents 266
New Deals for Lone Parents and Partners of the Unemployed 41
new motherhood 27
non-familial households 228
non-family living 185
non-heteronormative intimacies 244
non-kin relationships 228
non-monogamous couples 201-2
non-resident birth fathers 95
non-resident families 13
non-standard intimacies 243-4
Northern Ireland 128, 169, 177-80, 182
Northern Ireland Housing Executive 180
Norway
  child poverty 42
not being adult 113-14
nuclear family 10-11, 85, 172, 228
nursery education 24, 40, 265
nurturing 172

O

obligation 201
orthodoxy 9-12
  new 98
our home, my family: construction and preservation 171-4
  construction 172
  ethno-religious history 173-4
  family history 173
  inter-communal violence 171-4
  narratives 173
  nuclear family 172
  nurturing 172
  preservation 172-3

P

parent
  boundaries 81-3
  conflicts 85
  continuing to 'be there' 117-18
  involvement in education 58-60
  questionnaire 100
  rights 82-3
  substance misuse 111-12
parent-child
  boundary 111-12, 122-3
  relationships 200
parent-child negotiations of boundary setting 81-3
  bottom lines 82
  consistency 82
  dangerous neighbourhoods 81-2
  foster carers 82
  mobile phones 83
  parental boundaries 81-3
  parental rights 82-3
  pushing boundaries 82-3
parent-teacher confrontation 60
parentified child 114-17
parenting across households 103-4
  discipline 103

expressivity 103
Parsons, Talcott 191-3, 196-7, 235-6
part-time work 29-30
particularistic alliances 84
partnered mothers 25-7
partnership
behaviour 227
with parents 58-9, 68-70
patriachalism 245-6
peacekeeping
rhetoric of 177
peer relationships 192-3
permeable boundaries 32-6
breaching of boundaries 32-6
childcare arrangements 32-5
children's preferences 32, 34
flexibility 32-6
school holidays 34-5
work demands 32
work-family balance 32
personal relationships beyond the heteronorm 241-57, 263
heteronormative family and beyond 242-5
living and loving beyond heteronorm 248-50
queer social change and contemporary personal life 245-8
relationships beyond family 250-1
polysubstance use *see* children managing parental substance abuse
post-familial family 246
postmodern living 247-8
postmodernity 197
poverty *see* gender, care, poverty and transitions
preservation 172-3
see also our home, my family
presumption 201
primary caregiver perspective 152
private interests and public domain 177-80
Connolly, P. 177-80
cultural images 177-80
Healy, J. 177-80
Northern Ireland 177-80
Northern Ireland Housing Executive 180
space and boundaries 180
private spaces 176
private sphere 189-90
professionals and boundary setting 86-8
child abuse 87-8
child protection 87-8
children's behaviour 86
children's safety 86
control of children 86
crime 87
disabled parents 88
family rules 86-7
family systems 87
family therapy 86
intergenerational boundaries 88
young carers 88
projection 79
provisioning 45-6
psychodynamic theories 79, 88
public community versus private intimacy 198-9
Allan, Graham 198
community 198-9
Crow, Graham 198-9
public sphere 189-90
public-private boundary 7-8, 27-8
pure relationships 201, 248
pushing boundaries 82-3

Q

queer social change and contemporary personal life 245-8
Care, friendship and non-conventional partnership project 248
Civil Partnerships Act 2004 247
gay men 248
Giddens, Anthony 245-6, 248
homosexual/heterosexual binary 246-7
lesbians 248
patriachalism 245-6
post-familial family 246
postmodern living 247-8
pure relationships 248
queer tendencies 247
queer tendencies 247

R

reciprocity
dementia 152-3, 155-6
redrawing boundaries around ageing 139-40
relationships beyond family 250-1
homosexual/heterosexual binary 251
networks and flows of intimacy and care 251
queer lens 250-1
relationships and friendships 4, 185-257
boundaries of friendship 227-40

boundaries of intimacy 189-206
boundary breaking 186-7
non-family living 185
personal relationships beyond the heteronorm 241-57
solo living, individual and family boundaries 207-25
renegotiation of family boundaries 84
research 4-5
research into dementia and relationships
Alzheimer's disease 152-3
committed-dependent relationship 153
marital interaction 153
medical model 152
primary caregiver perspective 152
reciprocity 152-3
spouse perspective 152-3
respondents' perceptions and researchers' categories 97-9
active joint parenting 98
Children Act 1989 98-9
Children (Scotland) Act 1995 98-9
co-parenting 98
custodial parenting 98
family practices 97
living-apart-together 98
lone parent family 98
new orthodoxy 98
shared care 98
solo parenting 98
two parent family 98
risk and knowledge 118-20
risk to children 118-20
risk to parents 119-20
roles and responsibilities 112-28
collusion 113
collusion and boundary maintenance 114-17
disclosure 112
legitimacy 112
not being adult 113-14
parental substance misuse 112-13
parentified child 112-13
parents continuing to 'be there' 117-18
secrecy 112
stigma 112
young carers 112-13
Roseneil, Sasha xiii 186, 228, 241-57, 263
Rwanda
ethnic cleansing 171

S

safety of place 81
same-sex couples 11, 13
Schneider, D. 229
school holidays 34-5
schooling 61-5
Scotland
child poverty 42-3
domestic violence 170-1
Scott, Gill xiii-xiv 20, 39-55, 262
Scottish Enlightenment 196
Scottish Household Survey 208-9, 217-18
Scottish Parliament 264
Scottish Partnership on Domestic Abuse 1998 267
Seaman, Peter xiv 74, 95-110, 261
Second World War 176-7
secondary relationships 202
secrecy 112
Select Committee on Violence in Marriage 267
self-disclosure 189, 202
self-presentation 85
Sennett, Richard 197-8
shared care 98
Shucksmith, Janet xiv 20, 57-72, 262
Simmel, Georg 191, 245
Smith, Adam xiv 185-6, 196, 207-25, 263
social capital 228
social constructionist perspective
dementia 150-3
social policies and families 261-70
boundaries and boundary work in policy context 264-9
boundaries as conceptual device 261-4
Centre for Research on Families and Relationships (CRFR) 261
socialisation of children 192
sociology
of the family 191
of friendship 245
solo living, individual and family boundaries 185, 195, 207-25, 263
Bridget Jones's Diary 207
flows in/out solo living 212-13
Giddens, Anthony 208
Morvern Callar 207
research evidence 208-10
solo living by age and gender 213-14
solo living, housing circumstances and economic status 216-17

solo living, marital history and childlessness 214-16
solo living and social capital 217-20
solo living in UK, Britain and Scotland 210-21
transitions in and out of solo living 221
solo parenting 98
space
and boundaries 180
and time 120-1
spoke model of social network formation 234.237
spouse perspective
dementia 152-3
stepfamilies 13-14
Sterin, Gloria
Alzheimer's disease 151-2
stigma 112
stigmatisation
dementia 151-2
strangers 81
street corner society 245
subjectivity and family structure 96-7
US National Survey of Families and Households 96
substance abusing parents 200
subsystems 85
Sure Start 61, 265
Sweden
childcare policy 40
Sweeting, Helen xv 74, 95-110, 261

T

talking back 65-8
critical incidents 68
tax credits 24, 41-2
ties and bonds 11
time and location issues 45
Total Schooling 58-9, 61-5
hurried child syndrome 64
Sure Start 61
traditional values 3-4, 8-9
traffic between spheres 32
transitional space 79, 88-9
transitions in and out of solo living 221
trust boundaries 80-1
two parent family 98

U

UK
2001 Census 132-3, 210
child poverty 42
childcare policy 40-1
Civil Partnerships Act 2004 247
Conservative government and education 58
Department of Work and Pensions 41
General Household Survey 105
labour market policies 39
mother gap 49
New Labour and education 58, 68-70
work/care arrangements 51
unclear family 228
United Nations (UN) 10
US National Survey of Families and Households 96

V

Van Every, Jo 243
violence in and between families 170-1
Bosnia 171
inter-communal violence 170-1
Rwanda 171
Scotland 170-1
violence and families 128, 169-84, 195, 262
belonging 181
Bosnia 169, 181-2
Bringa, Tone 181-2
case studies 175-80
Connolly, P. 182
exclusion 181
families as porous 180
families, public institutions and violence 174-5
Healy, J. 182
India 181
inter-communal violence 169-70
Northern Ireland 169, 182
our home, my family: construction and preservation 171-4
Rwanda 169
violence in and between families 170-1

W

Wasoff, Fran xv 185-6, 207-25, 261-70
we groups 79
Weaks, Dot xv 127-8, 149-67, 263
welfare-to-work policies 266
well-being 133
Welsh Assembly 264
West of Scotland 11 to 16 Study 96, 99
whole persons 191

Wilkinson, Heather xv-xvi 127-8, 149-67, 263
Willmot, Helen xvi 20, 57-72, 262
Wilson, Sarah xvi 74, 111-25, 263
Winnicott, D.W. 79
women
and gender differences 175
good mother 36
and labour market 12
lives at mid-life 136-8
role 11-12
in their fifties 135-6
and work 8-9
work ethic 27
see also solo living
women's health and ageing at mid-life 133-5
ageing process 133-4
biomedical perspective 134
boundary roles 135
knowingness 134
lifestyle choices 134-5
well-being 133
women's health and well-being at mid-life 127, 131-47, 263
ageing process 131-2
boundary roles 131-2
falling to bits but keeping it together 138-43
study 135-8
women in their fifties 135-6
women's health and ageing at mid-life 133-5
women's lives at mid-life 136-8
work
demands 32
type 28-9
work-family balance: mothers' views 19-20, 23-38, 262
boundaries and balance 27-36
double shift 24
government policies on paid work 23-4
lone parent 25
nursery education 24
study 25-7
tax credits 24
work-home boundaries 23
working mothers 23-5
work-family balance 32
work-home boundaries 7-8, 23
work-life balance 9
worker
culture 51
identity 31
working mothers 12, 23-5, 30-1
good mother role 36
lone mothers 25-7
new motherhood 27
partnered mothers 25-7
study 25-7
work ethic 27
Working Tax Credit (WTC) 266
World Health Organisation (WHO) 10
Health behaviour in school-aged children 2001-2 106-7
World report on violence and health 170

Y

young carers 88, 111-13
see also children managing parental substance abuse
Young People's Family Life 96, 99, 103